AUG 3 1 2009

DATE DUE

On Becoming an Alchemist

On Becoming an

Alchemist

A Guide for the Modern Magician

Catherine MacCoun

Trumpeter
Boston & London
2008

Trumpeter Books
An imprint of Shambhala Publications, Inc.
Horticultural Hall
300 Massachusetts Avenue
Boston, Massachusetts 02115
www.shambhala.com

9 8 7 6 5 4 3 2 1

First Edition

Printed in the United States of America

♾ This edition is printed on acid-free paper that meets the American
National Standards Institute z39.48 Standard.

Distributed in the United States by Random House, Inc., and in Canada
by Random House of Canada Ltd

Interior design and composition: Greta D. Sibley & Associates

Library of Congress Cataloging-in-Publication Data
MacCoun, Catherine.
On becoming an alchemist: a guide for the modern magician / Catherine
MacCoun.—1st ed.
p.   cm.
ISBN 978-1-59030-369-6 (hardcover: alk. paper)
1. Magic. 2. Alchemy. 3. Self-help techniques. 4. Self-actualization
(Psychology) I. Title.
BF1621.M33 2008
133.4'3—DC22
2007033783

Contents

PART ONE

Principles

1

In Quest of
the Philosopher's Stone

IN 1365 or thereabouts, Nicholas Flamel, a young scrivener living in Paris, purchased a gilded book for two florins. In an age when books were luxury items, two florins was ridiculously cheap. It was like finding the Gutenberg Bible on the remainder table at Barnes and Noble. He suspected the book had been stolen, or perhaps hidden and then discovered by someone who had no idea of its value.

The volume was handwritten on some strange material that looked to Flamel like shavings of tree bark. It was divided into three sections of seven leaves each, and every seventh leaf was covered with hand-painted images. The first page named the author as "Abraham the Jew, Prince, Priest, Levite, Astrologer, and Philosopher" then went on to rain down curses on anyone who dared to read further, unless he be a priest or a scribe. Though probably not the kind of scribe this Abraham had in mind, Flamel figured he was covered by the exemption and went on reading.

He gathered that the book was a self-help manual for Hebrews who were having trouble paying their taxes to the Roman Empire. It claimed that base metals could be transmuted into silver and gold with the aid of a philosopher's stone and went on to explain how to make one. The text was as forthright as a cookbook, but for one point: it neglected to specify the main ingredient, referring to it vaguely as the *prima materia* (i.e., first matter). This was about as helpful as saying, "The main ingredient is the main ingredient."

There were, however, some beautiful illuminated figures illustrating the *prima materia*. One depicted a young man with winged feet whom Flamel took to be the god Hermes/Mercury. An old man with an hourglass on top of his head and a scythe in his hand was chasing after Mercury. Next came a picture of a flower with a blue stem and red and white petals, growing on a mountaintop, surrounded by dragons and griffins. After this came a picture of a rosebush growing near a hollow oak tree. From the base of the rose bush sprang an underground stream. Many people were digging, trying to find the stream, while one man was trying to weigh it. The pictorial narrative concluded with an image of soldiers killing babies and collecting their blood. This last picture was the only one that suggested anything like a procedure to Flamel. He figured it depicted Herod's "slaughter of the innocents." Flamel happened to know of a cemetery dedicated to the Holy Innocents, so he went there and buried some "hieroglyphics" he had copied from the book.

Apart from that, he was stumped. He spent many days pondering the pictures, but still could not work out how to get started. Seeing that he was becoming depressed, his young bride Peronelle (whom, he tells us, "I loved as much as myself") asked, "What's the matter, Nicholas?" He showed her the book. She was entranced by it and began to study it along with him. Although she, too, was unable to discover what was the matter, sharing the mystery with her brought him much consolation.

Flamel made painstaking copies of the puzzling illustrations and showed them to every scholar he could find. Most of them were clueless and scoffed at the notion of a philosopher's stone. But one, a physician named Anselm, claimed to know exactly what the symbols meant and went on to offer explicit instructions. He said, for example, that quicksilver (mercury) could only be fixed—that is, deprived of volatility—by decocting it in the blood of very young children.

Alas, Anselm's exegesis proved "more subtle than true." Flamel writes, "This explanation sent me astray through a labyrinth of innumerable false processes for one and twenty years, it being always understood that

4

I made no experiments with the blood of children, for that I accounted villainous."

After twenty-one years of being stuck at the very beginning, Flamel reckoned he'd better seek out the source of the text. Perhaps in Spain he could find a Jewish priest who would clue him in on the Cabbala. With his wife's blessing, he set off on the traditional pilgrimage to the church of St. James Compostela. Though he failed to find such a priest, he met a merchant on the return voyage who introduced him to a very learned converted Jew named Master Canches. Canches immediately recognized Flamel's copied illustrations and was keen to know where the original book might be found. Flamel offered to show it to him in exchange for an interpretation of the pictures. Canches agreed, and from him Flamel learned the identity of the *prima materia*. But before he could explain how to prepare it, Canches took sick. He died after seven days of profuse vomiting. Flamel buried him and returned home.

After three more years "pondering the words of the philosophers and proving various operations suggested by their study" he was at last able to prepare the basic ingredient. Once he accomplished that, the rest was so easy he "could scarcely miss." He need only follow the book's instructions word for word. On 17 January 1392, in the presence of his wife, he used the philosopher's stone to transmute half a pound of mercury into pure silver. On 25 April, he again applied the stone to half a pound of mercury and this time produced pure gold. After that, he and Peronelle went on to make gold three more times. Together they endowed fourteen hospitals and seven churches, built three chapels, and restored seven cemeteries.

Matter Matters

By now you have likely concluded that this story is an allegory, beginning as it does with the improbably low price of the book and culminating in the even more improbable transmutation of mercury into gold. You are figuring that everything in it probably stands for something else. If you can uncover the hidden meaning of the various components— the beloved wife, the clueless scholars, the pilgrimage, the cemetery, the blood of innocents, and so forth—you will be able to discern some sort of spiritual path leading to a result that is described metaphorically as "gold." You may also be aware that the psychologist Carl Jung made an intensive study of texts such as this one, finding in them many of the images that arose in the dreams of his patients. He concluded that these images were fixtures of the collective unconscious and that alchemy was an ancient form of depth psychology.

All of this is true, as far as it goes. Read as an allegory, the tale will reward years of study and meditation. It is full of symbols and descriptions of inner (that is, psychological or spiritual) processes. But is it *merely* an allegory? That is, are we meant to conclude that none of these events actually happened in the external world?

Nicholas Flamel was a real person who died in 1415 and was buried at the church of St. Jacques-la-Boucherie. When the church was demolished in 1717, the inscribed tablet on his grave was lost. It eventually resurfaced on the rue des Arias in the shop of a grocer who was using it as a chopping block for his herbs. According to the inscription on the tablet, one Nicholas Flamel, a scrivener, made numerous gifts to charity, including endowments to various churches and hospitals in Paris. In those days, a scrivener was roughly the equivalent of a typist— a low paid clerical worker. How did a scrivener manage to become a philanthropist?

To be sure, a great many charlatans and con artists have called themselves alchemists. In medieval Europe, pseudo-alchemists would demand quantities of gold, silver, and jewels from the rich and credulous, their only act of magic being to make these riches vanish along with themselves. It is likely that some alchemists used a knowledge of chemistry and metallurgy to produce alloys that merely resembled gold. In 1317, Pope John XXII issued a decree forbidding the practice, as did the Roman emperor Diocletian more than ten centuries earlier. Yet the ranks of alchemists have also boasted some of history's greatest scientific minds. Isaac Newton was an alchemist. So was Basil Valentine, the father of modern chemistry, and Roger Bacon, the English physician, astronomer, and mathematician. It was Bacon who first articulated the principle of empiricism: that the experience of our physical senses is the arbiter of scientific truth. Not only was he an alchemist, but it would appear from some of his writings that he himself had produced the philosopher's stone. Is it plausible that these self-declared empiricists would apply not only their scientific minds but their scientific *equipment* to an enterprise that was nothing but a metaphor? Would they risk their credibility on an endeavor that was nothing but a scam?

My aim is not to convince you that literal base metals have, in the past, been transmuted into literal gold. It cannot be proven to the satisfaction of modern historians, much less modern scientists. What does seem clear is that alchemy is not merely a metaphor. It is, as Jung described, an inner process. But the contemporary alchemists who still pursue their work in physical laboratories insist that it is not *just* an inner process. To eliminate the material aspects from consideration is, from their perspective, to miss the point altogether. One who produces the philosopher's stone must necessarily undergo a profound inward change, a drastic rearrangement of body, soul, and spirit. Yet the motive for that inward change is to produce outward change, that is, to rearrange the stuff of this world. The alchemist's aim is to work magic. The traditional *practical* goals of alchemical magic—to promote human health and material well-being—are to be taken literally.

Throughout history, religious people have tended to believe that the world was divided into spirit and matter, and that spirit was the good part. Heaven was pictured as "up there" and thus higher—in both a spatial and an evaluative sense—than "down here." Many spiritual practices reflect this. They attempt to make a person more spirit-like and less body-like. They help a person either to transcend or to live more harmoniously in a material world that is, for the most part, taken as a given. As Karl Marx observed when he called it "the opiate of the masses," spirituality that is dismissive of the material tends to support the earthly status quo.

To the alchemist, matter is in no way to be despised. Matter *matters*. Alchemists are not content merely to adapt to the world. They want to change it. To them, the test of spiritual truth is whether you can do something with it. They seek to understand the inner workings of the world in order to participate actively in its creation.

Many people conceive magical deeds as defying natural laws. The magician dons special robes, lights candles, recites incantations, and conducts peculiar rites. From an empirical point of view, there appears to be no causal connection between the magician's actions and the desired result, i.e., no reason why muttering some words over a crystal should cause his grandmother to send him a check or his home team to win the Super Bowl. If the desired result is achieved, it must be by means of the supernatural. Whatever that is.

The supernatural is not a concept for alchemists. Many of their procedures sound like the operations of cooks or chemists: boiling, cooling, dissolving, separating, drying, fermenting, etc. Whether applied literally, as in the case of laboratory alchemy, or more metaphorically, cooling as in "chilling out," they are things that regular people do, too. When these procedures work, it is for reasons that, to the alchemist, appear perfectly natural, perfectly logical.

Say you've just spilled red wine on a white silk shirt. You dab helplessly at the stain, certain the shirt is ruined. Then your hostess pours some white wine over the red wine. Abracadabra, the stain disappears. "Like magic," you might be tempted to say. You don't really mean that this feat defies the laws of nature. You assume there's some reason for it that a chemist could explain. What makes it seem magical is that the solution is at once so unexpected (getting rid of a wine stain by spilling more wine) and so effective. The magic lies not in defying the laws of nature, but in knowing them and applying them to such remarkable effect. This is what alchemical magic really is like. The alchemist can achieve extraordinary results from ordinary actions because he or she understands, better than the average person, how the world works.

At Findhorn, a windswept trailer park on the coast of Scotland, cabbages the size of beach balls were grown in soil that was little more than sand. The results were so improbable that Findhorn acquired the reputation of being a magical place, and its gardeners magical people. While it seems more unlikely than the wine trick, the garden's spectacular yield was not the result of anything supernatural. The Findhorn residents took the sort of actions that are familiar to any gardener: enriching the soil, staking, watering and so forth. What was unusual was the source of their information. They took instruction from the devas (nature spirits) who guided the growth of particular plant species. For instance, the Spinach Deva would tell them that the spinach plants wanted to be farther apart. The Tomato Deva would request that a windbreak be left in place until the plants had set fruit. The Pea Deva would counsel, "Don't worry about the slugs. They're not a threat to us." Unexceptional actions proved exceptionally effective because the gardeners were being taught to perceive the garden from the plants' point of view.

In ancient and medieval times, alchemy and physical science were the same discipline. The conflict that led to their eventual divorce had more to do with methods of investigation than results. To be affirmed as a fact by modern science, a phenomenon must be evident to any observer. Practically speaking, this means that it must be detectable by the physical senses, either directly or through the use of scientific instruments. Observations must also be repeatable. Experimental results are only considered valid if they reoccur consistently when others undertake the same experiment. Furthermore, observations must be free from observer bias. To reduce the possibility of wishful perception, scientists set out to *disprove* their own hypotheses.

These rules set an admirable standard of intellectual honesty and facilitate the debunking of prejudice, superstition, and dogma. Adopting them enabled the physical sciences to advance very rapidly. They tended, though, to marginalize alchemists, whose methods of knowing included meditation, dreams, visions, and conversations with non-corporeal beings. No matter how impressive the resulting cabbages, listening to the Cabbage Deva does not pass muster as a scientific method of inquiry.

The scientific method is very good at knowing some things, but it can be an impediment to knowing other things. Suppose, for instance, a gentleman is attracted to a certain lady and wishes to become better acquainted with her. Can he achieve this by measuring her, taking her temperature, and subjecting her to a CAT scan? Not only will these operations fail to tell him what he really wants to know, but they are likely to so annoy the object of his inquiry that she stops returning his calls. What he really wishes to know—the intimate secrets of her body and soul—can only be learned if he *ceases* to be objective. She will entrust her secrets to him only if he displays clear bias in her favor. And the more exclusive his knowledge of her—that is, the less it can be confirmed by any observer besides himself—the more precious it is to him.

The alchemist would argue that all natural phenomena have something in common with the lady. They unfold some of their secrets to objective, scientific inquiry while bestowing others only on the subjective observer. The soul of a thing—whether animal, vegetable, or mineral—reveals itself only in active relationship to another soul. And there is a knack to this. Some souls are better at knowing than are other souls. The range and accuracy of the soul as an instrument of perception can be developed and enhanced. The procedures for developing its faculties are no less demanding than the scientific method. Magic is the practical application of what the soul perceives. It is also a test of whether one has perceived correctly, for magic either works or it doesn't.

Alchemists want to understand the *whole* world in both its material and its non-material aspects. They are willing to forego scientific consensus (and thus risk being labeled as crackpots) in order to study phenomena and apply principles that they can perceive, whether or not others share their perceptions. This is not the same as being superstitious. Nor is it the same as being religious. If alchemists don't feel compelled to demonstrate what they believe to the readers of *Scientific American,* neither do they feel compelled to believe what they can't demonstrate *to themselves.* What for a religious person might be a creed is, to the alchemist, a working hypothesis. Confronted with a spiritual teaching or religious belief, an alchemist is less likely to ask, "Is it true?" than "Is it workable?" A workable idea is one you can act on with good result.

It is characteristic of alchemists to treat the pursuit of physical science as a spiritual discipline and to approach the spiritual with scientific rigor and practicality. For alchemists, the spiritual and the material are two different aspects of the same world. That insight into one is insight into the other is both an article of faith and a working hypothesis. Alchemists set out to demonstrate it *because* they believe it.

Magic the Hard Way

At first blush, magic sounds like an easy way of doing things. That's part of its appeal. If you could really turn lead into gold, you wouldn't have to get up and go to work in the morning. Yet when you read alchemists' accounts of their quest for the philosopher's stone, doing things "the easy way" seems insanely difficult. It took Nicholas Flamel most of his adult life to produce eight ounces of gold. Surely he could have managed the same result just by getting a better job.

If all you really want to do is pay your taxes to the Roman Empire, I would recommend you buy a book on personal finance. While alchemy can indeed help you to achieve that and other practical results, and the task of raising money is entirely worthy of alchemical attention, it's a bit like buying a cow when all you want is a glass of milk. For the alchemist, even a modest outward result can require tremendous inner effort, because changing what is inside is how the alchemist goes about changing what is outside.

All magicians operate on the assumption that inward events can influence outward events, that external phenomena can be altered by what goes on in the human mind. Contrary to popular belief, it is an assumption shared by most scientists. They have to go out of their way to eliminate mental factors from physical experiments. When testing a new drug, for example, they must control for the placebo effect, that is, the fact that a certain percentage of patients will get better if you give them a sugar pill and tell them it's medicine. The separation of material events from mental events is an artificial condition that occurs only in the science lab. It's not how things work in the real world.

If you're like most people, you occasionally deploy your mental powers in the hope of influencing what happens. Perhaps you have discovered that you can make some of your desires come true by visualizing or using affirmations or other forms of "positive thinking." And if you haven't discovered that, you most certainly will have discovered that you can make some of your worries come to pass by worrying. You might pray, send "light" or "good energy" or simply kind thoughts to people who seem to need your help. You wouldn't bother unless you believed that what goes on in your mind could potentially make a difference. By employing special techniques to concentrate and project thought, magicians can achieve some remarkable effects. You yourself will probably develop this ability in the course of becoming an alchemist. But the magic of thought projection alone is not alchemy.

In Tibetan alchemy, the philosopher's stone is a magical diamond. It is said to have the power to transmute poison into medicine. To be sure, the basic magic of mind control might enable an adept to drink poison without getting sick. Like lying on a bed of nails or walking over hot coals, the stunt entails concentrating so powerfully that one remains unaffected by what is harmful. The magician doesn't change and neither does the poison. But to render the harmful *beneficial* is a different sort of procedure altogether. It requires an intimate knowledge of the poison; a knowledge that cannot possibly be gained by remaining unaffected.

Between you and anything that you might wish to influence there is a relationship. If either party in a relationship changes, the relationship itself is changed. In turn, any change in the relationship changes *both* parties. So if you wish to change something, the first thing you must do is discover the true nature of your relationship to it. Then you will be able to see how to change it by changing yourself. This is the basic logic of alchemy.

Sounds simple, doesn't it? Alas, it is much easier said than done, for discovering the true nature of a relationship is not at all easy. Our perception is clouded by our hopes and fears, our opinions, preconceptions, likes, and dislikes. Often what obscures it most is our very desire to change an object in the first place. Let me give you a down-to-earth example.

Our would-be magician is a young woman called Annie. One night she goes out to a bar where a handsome guitarist named Carlos is performing. During a break between sets, they strike up a conversation and Carlos asks for Annie's phone number. Annie is thrilled. Over the next few days, she eagerly awaits a call that never comes. By day five, she is so frustrated that she decides to resort to magic.

How shall she go about it? Annie's first idea is to apply visualization. She lights a candle, closes her eyes, and concentrates on a mental picture of her desire: the phone ringing, Carlos's voice, her witty remarks, his laughter, his inviting her out on a date. Once she has perfected the mental picture, she attempts to send it his way, hoping that it will inspire him to act.

Will that work? Maybe. Maybe not. But even if it does work, it's not alchemy. Annie is attempting to change Carlos, but she hasn't changed anything about Annie.

Instead of focusing on Carlos himself, let's look at what's happening in the relationship between them. Outwardly, Annie is in a passive position, waiting for Carlos to take the initiative. Inwardly, though, Annie is the pursuer. Her body is sitting still, but her soul is chasing Carlos. As your grandmother probably told you, guys don't like to be chased. So when the visualization fails, Annie decides to attempt the time-honored magic of "playing hard to get." She turns off her cell phone so that if Carlos tries to call he will get her voice mail.

This maneuver isn't alchemy either. She has only succeeded in changing her outward behavior, not her inward state. She is still hoping to manipulate the object of her desire. The real problem here is that she hasn't discovered the true nature of her relationship to that object. She has only seen one aspect of it: the fact that, inwardly, she is the pursuer. But what, exactly, is she pursuing. Who is Carlos? What does he really mean to her?

Annie works at an office job that bores her. Her life, as she sees it, is conventional and uninspired. Carlos attracts her because he is a musician. She imagines he leads an arty, bohemian life and that being a part of it would make her own life a lot more interesting. What your grandmother probably *didn't* tell you is that when you become infatuated with someone you hardly know, what you have actually fallen in love with is an unrealized potential in yourself. You have a big crush on what you yourself secretly wish to become. In other words, Annie isn't having a relationship with the actual Carlos at all. The true nature of the relationship is the longing of the conventional Annie for the arty and bohemian Annie. Annie is chasing *herself*.

The "poison" here is Annie's frustrated longing for a different life. The alchemy begins with tasting that, swallowing it, experiencing its nature, and feeling its full effects. If our heroine is willing to do that, something in her will change. Perhaps she will quit her boring job. Perhaps she will begin to cultivate her own thwarted creativity, or go on an adventure, or seek out more interesting friends. I don't know exactly what she'll do, but if she has perceived the relationship accurately, Annie will change. She will become more like the person she imagines Carlos to be.

Will this cause him to telephone? Beats me. The question has lost its importance. Alchemical magic always begins with a specific desire, like wanting someone to phone. No desire is too silly, too trivial, or too self-ish to serve as your base matter. (That's why they call it base matter.) But if you're really doing alchemy, the outcome might bear no resemblance at all to what you thought you were going for. Alchemical procedures change the alchemist and, in the process, often change the very desire that gave rise to them.

Environmentally Responsible Magic

Imagine for a moment that it was impossible to dispose of garbage. Imagine you had to find a way to recycle every single thing you currently throw away. You would end up inventing alchemy. To transmute is to take a lowly thing and make it valuable, to take a harmful thing and make it helpful. You could say it's a form of sacred ecology.

Recycling occurs all the time in the natural world. Take for example the compost heap. It's made of things that don't look or smell very nice—manure, kitchen waste, rotted lawn clippings—and crawling with bugs and worms. You throw a handful of this muck into a hole, along with a bulb that looks and smells like a small onion. In spring, what emerges from that hole is a narcissus. How was all that dark, stinky stuff transformed into something fragrant and so white? Where did the perfume come from? The whiteness? Organic matter was recycled and biologists can explain how, yet there's no explaining away the sheer wonder of it, no accounting for how base matter got recycled into something so gorgeous. Alchemists would say that nature aspires to the sublime, attaining it by way of procedures that people can study and replicate. The logic of the compost pile can be applied to many human aspirations and endeavors, with equally sublime results. The magician is merely abetting the magical tendencies of nature itself.

While you probably see the point of recycling newspapers and kitchen scraps, you might not see what recycling has to do with less tangible phenomena such as negative thoughts, feelings, experiences, and life situations. Why would you bother to recycle seemingly worthless conditions such as hostility or disappointment, depression or addiction? Wouldn't it be better simply to get rid of them altogether?

Let's play "What if?" for a moment. We know that the physical things we flush or throw away don't disappear from the earth. We make our homes clean by sending rejected items and substances elsewhere, to become someone else's problem. What if the same were true of the thoughts and feelings we treat as junk? What if, just as our bodies live in a collective atmosphere that we breathe, our minds partake of a collective atmosphere that we "inhale" and "exhale" when we think? Like the air in our lungs, thoughts would only be temporarily private. What you breathed out would later be breathed in by others.

When you cough or sneeze, microbes that have been inside you are driven out into the common atmosphere where they are likely to infect someone else. If this were true of thoughts as well, becoming hostile or fearful or despondent would be like catching a virus. Rejecting these feelings would be like coughing or sneezing. There would also be such a thing a thought pollution. In rush hour traffic, you might feel headachy and vaguely nauseous when road rage emissions exceeded EPA standards. The popular media might be seen as smokestacks spewing sulfurous blasts of greed, anxiety, restlessness, and titillation. When political campaigns turned ugly, your mind might need to don a gas mask. Just as the physical atmosphere is refreshed by wind and rain and sweetened by all sorts of pleasing aromas, bright new ideas would clear away the stale air. Confident thoughts might smell like fresh-turned earth, loving thoughts like cookies baking.

In cold weather, you can actually see the shape of your out breath. It disperses so quickly that, after a moment, nothing you have breathed out could be traced back to you. This is generally true of thoughts as well. Most of them are diffuse even while we are thinking them and become more so after they leave us. But we can also exhale in a more deliberate way. You blow on a match to extinguish it. When building a fire in a fireplace, you might blow on a flame to encourage it to catch. You might blow on your eyeglasses to moisten the lenses before wiping them or blow on your fingertips to make nail polish dry faster. Depending on your intention, the air you exhale can either abet fire or extinguish it, add moisture or subtract it. If you understand that thoughts are like air, then you can achieve all sorts of useful effects by exhaling them on purpose. This is the basic idea behind thought magic. The technique is to form a clear intention then "blow" it in the right direction.

Wind can move air pollution elsewhere, but it can't change bad air into good air. For that, we need plants. Their respiration is the opposite of ours: they breathe in carbon dioxide and breathe out oxygen. What is waste for them is essential for us, and vice versa. Our garbage is their compost. Alchemists are to the thought environment what plants are to the physical environment. They can take in the "hazardous waste" of human experience and return it to the world as nourishment, refreshment, and beauty.

The body's immune system is set up to reject as foreign whatever does not resemble its own genetic material. But the body doesn't normally react that way to what we eat. It doesn't marshal antibodies to repel the foreign invasion of a Big Mac and fries. Instead, it transmutes this dubious material into energy and replacements for its own depleted cells. When you attain the philosopher's stone, your inner life becomes less like an immune system and more like a digestive system. What you instinctively wish to reject as foreign and unwanted, you learn instead to *metabolize* through a process of inner digestion.

Like recycling literal garbage, alchemical transmutation often involves procedures that don't look especially mysterious. What makes these actions magical is their motive, the state of mind that gives rise to them. You are taking what you instinctively wish to reject as bad, embracing it, and working with it until it is transformed into something good. If to transmute rather than to reject has become your first impulse in most negative situations, you might be doing ordinary things, but you are not an ordinary person. You have already transmuted *yourself*, reversed the knee-jerk reaction to negativity that you, along with every other human being, were born with. You have developed the metabolism of a magician.

This fundamental change in "spiritual metabolism" is what it means to attain the philosopher's stone. Once you have achieved it, you won't need step-by-step instructions on how to transmute phenomena any more than you presently need instructions on how to digest your food. To address ordinary situations in a magical way will come naturally to you. This book will be primarily concerned with what alchemists call the "Great Work"—the preparation of the stone. This is the part that took Flamel twenty-four years to achieve. (With Anselm out of the picture, you may have better luck.) Once he had accomplished it, the rest was obvious and easy.

The philosopher's stone is not a metal or a mineral. It's not a material object at all. So what is it? Here's a hint from Mahatma Gandhi: *Be the change you wish to see in the world.* Maybe right now you read that as just a bumper sticker slogan. But one day you may be astonished that you've heard it for free, that it isn't buried deep in some Himalayan cave, guarded by high priests, dragons, vestal virgins, and blood-guzzling Tibetan deities. For Gandhi has let the cat entirely out of the bag, given away the most mysterious and potent alchemical secret of them all. There is in it the power to overthrow an empire. Take that literally.

Hermes and Hermeticism

The many esoteric traditions that contributed to Western alchemy have a common ancestor in a small collection of writings that survived the destruction of the great library of Alexandria. Known as the Hermetica, the writings were attributed to someone called Hermes Trismegistus or "thrice-great Hermes." This was probably a brand name applied to the works of a number of different writers over several centuries, rather than the name of a particular person.

The story usually goes that the texts were written by ancient Egyptians and discovered later by the Greeks, but some scholars believe it was the other way around. Conventional historians have trouble figuring this out because they assume that the author's namesake—the Greek god Hermes (known as Thoth to the Egyptians)—exists only in mythology. If you accept the premise that Hermes is an actual being whose job is to impart messages from the spiritual world to humans, it is much easier to understand how not only Greeks and ancient Egyptians but Jewish Cabbalists, Muslim Sufis, Gnostic Christians, Tibetan Buddhists, and Chinese Taoists kept coming up with variations on the same ideas. The Greeks and/or Egyptians applied his name to their alchemical texts because he was the actual source of them.

A hermeticist—literally an associate of Hermes—is one who seeks to understand the mundane world in light of the spiritual world. My dictionary defines "hermeticism" as a synonym for alchemy. During the Middle Ages this was true and perhaps it will one day be true again. At present, most people who call themselves hermeticists would not call themselves alchemists.

Alchemy is the practical application of what the hermeticist understands. To do something useful with spiritual knowledge was, for ancient and medieval hermeticists, the point of acquiring it. During the Renaissance, this pragmatic impulse shifted to the natural sciences. Hermeticists, by and large, stopped expecting their studies to bear practical fruit. They stopped trying to do magic. Some even ceased to believe that magic was possible.

Contemporary alchemists are indebted to hermeticists for preserving and advancing alchemical theory. But that theory is of little worth unless it's tested through practice. Approaching knowledge of the spiritual world with neither religious faith nor scientific rigor, the hermeticist can all too easily become a pretentious crackpot. It is the practicing magician who puts hermetic findings to the test of workability.

2

Unlocking the Secret Codes

NICHOLAS FLAMEL was not the only alchemist to be stumped by the question of the *prima materia*. In *The Canterbury Tales*, Chaucer wisecracks about alchemists trying "powders diverse, ashes, dung, piss and clay" all to no avail. Many alchemical texts seem to be speaking in deliberate riddles on the matter. According to the *Sophie Hydrolith* (1619), "it is found potentially everywhere, and in everything, but in all its perfection only in one thing." The *Gloria Mundi* (1526) tells us:

> It is familiar to all men, both young and old; is found in the country, in the village, in the town, in all things created by God; yet it is despised by all. Rich and poor handle it every day. It is cast into the street by servant maids. Children play with it. Yet no one prizes it, though, next to the human soul, it is the most beautiful and the most precious thing upon earth and has the power to pull down kings and princes. Nevertheless, it is esteemed the vilest and meanest of earthly things.

If alchemical texts are not mere allegories, if they are practical instructions that their authors wish their readers to act upon, why do they speak in riddles and symbols? Why do they so elaborately describe the roadside scenery while failing to direct you to the on ramp?

Alchemical traditions exist in all the major world religions. Practitioners believe alchemy to be the deeper meaning of every religion. Since the keepers of orthodoxy have rarely agreed, alchemists have often been persecuted. Christian practitioners of the art, for instance, had the Inquisition to worry about. Their alchemical findings were often disguised as stories, poems, and games. More direct instructions were sometimes presented in code and might include deliberate disinformation to throw off the casual or hostile reader. One could understand the texts only if initiated by another practitioner, as Flamel was initiated by Canches.

To be initiated means to be clued in, to catch on. The practice of formal initiation still persists in Sufism, Tantric Buddhism, and esoteric Christian orders such as the Freemasons, Rosicrucians, and Templars. When it works as it should, the teacher guides the student through preparatory exercises, practices, and tests—a process that may take many years. It culminates in either a ceremony or a spontaneous encounter during which there is a kind of intuitive communion between teacher and student. It is as if the student suddenly shares the teacher's "take," perceives as the teacher perceives.

In settings where the knack of teaching in this way has been passed from person to person and retained its vitality, initiation can be very effective. Unfortunately, you may also run into sects where the outward forms have been reified and lost most of their inner power. At their worst, initiatory orders can be snooty, elitist, and ungenerous, putting needless obstacles in the student's way. Freshmen are hazed merely because freshmen have always been hazed. Difficulty comes to be prized for its own sake.

I should also point out that many alchemists prize *blarney* for its own sake. The guiding spirit of alchemy is Hermes who, in Greek mythology is the god of seers, messengers, and travelers and also of thieves, charlatans, and con artists. Even a highly reliable source may succumb now and again to the impulse to pull your leg. Part of a magician's initiation is learning to recognize a joke when you see one.

But deliberate misdirection is not the whole explanation for the difficulty of alchemical literature. In a number of baffling texts, the author has expressed an earnest intention to be clear and to tell all. Consider

Artephius, a twelfth-century alchemist who, rumored to have lived a thousand years, felt qualified to pen a manual entitled *The Art of Prolonging Human Life*. He wrote:

> As I have seen, through this long space of time, that men have been unable to perfect the same magistery on account of the obscurity of the words of the philosophers, moved by pity and good conscience, I have resolved, in these last days, to publish in all sincerity and truly, so that men may have nothing more to desire concerning this work. I except one thing only, because it can be revealed only by a master, or by God. Nevertheless, this likewise may be learned from this book, provided one be not stiff-necked and have a little experience.

If this "one thing" that Artephius isn't saying can nevertheless be learned from his book, why doesn't he just spit it out? Pretty much for the same reason that a joke isn't funny if you have to explain the punch line.

Like Artephius, Basil Valentine was doing his level best to spill the alchemical beans. He meant for others to act on his lab notes and replicate his experiments. Nevertheless, even trained chemists are mystified by his writings. For every procedure, he appears to eliminate one key step. But, as the modern writer Archibald Cockren has observed, the key "is invariably to be found in some other part of the writings, probably in the midst of one of the mysterious theological discourses which he was wont to insert among his practical instructions." Nicholas Flamel made a similar discovery after "pondering the words of the philosophers and proving various operations suggested by their study." That is, the philosophy suggests the operations. In alchemical writings, the abstract implies the concrete, and vice versa. Procedures imply metaphysical principles, and principles imply procedures. If you don't know what to do, study what they're telling you to think about. If you're not sure what to think, study the instructions on what to do.

Sometimes alchemists wrote in code, either to conceal information from unintended readers or as a kind of shorthand to communicate more efficiently with colleagues. Both types of code are easy to crack once you have the key. It's similar to how you decode e-mail by knowing what ASAP, LOL, and :-) mean. In codes of this type, a symbol means one thing and one thing only. You simply substitute the concept for the symbol (e.g., © means copyright) and you've unlocked the entire meaning.

The alchemical pictures and diagrams we'll be concerned with in this book are not that simple. Symbols such as the caduceus, the Ouroboros, and the rose cross communicate many meanings at the same time. They are employed not to hide, but to reveal. But if you attempt to crack them as you would crack a code—if you think that the caduceus stands for such-and-such and that's that—you will be misled, as Flamel was misled by Anselm. Alchemical symbols imply procedures. You have to *do* something with them, add something to them, before their many layers of meaning will unfold.

Consider this symbol:

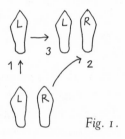

Fig. 1.

The enfolded meaning is the box step. To produce this step, you need to add three things: movement, time, and relationship. The footprints show you where to place each foot in relation to the other. The arrows indicate movement (where to go) and the numbers indicate time (when to go there.) If you correctly understand and follow these indications, the result is a waltz.

Alchemical symbols work the same way. Consider the pentagram and the Seal of Solomon, figures 2 and 3 respectively:

Fig. 2.

Fig. 3.

Suppose I tell you that one of these figures includes a circle. Which one is it? You can stare at the two diagrams for twenty-one years, and you won't be able to answer, so long as you consider them as static objects. But suppose that like figure 1, they are instructions on how to move. You could try dancing them (not a bad idea) or you could just try drawing each figure a few times on a piece of paper. Getting any closer to an answer? If you're still stumped, try drawing some circles as well.

You might remember learning to draw a five-pointed star when you were a child. Kids like drawing this type of star because it's fun. You zigzag in five different directions and return to the starting point without having to lift your pen. The movement is pointy, but also circular. But why is that fun? You can't explain why. It just is. It satisfies something in you that you can't name. As a kid, you felt that "something" instinctively and enjoyed exercising it.

Now concentrate on what it's like to draw the six-pointed star. You have to draw the two triangles separately and take care to properly align the second one with the first. In principle, you only have to lift the pen once—between the two triangles—but you probably make all six strokes separately because it's difficult to draw an equilateral triangle freehand. You have to think about the length of each line and its relationship to the others or your triangle will come out lopsided.

Keep drawing five- and six-pointed stars, without trying to think anything deep or important about it. Just notice the mental atmosphere that seems to go with each one, the slight shift in your consciousness as you move from one to the other. Don't expect to be thunderstruck by some huge revelation. What you're looking for is extremely subtle, and you can't really describe it in words. That's why it's expressed by symbols.

Let me give you another tip about geometrical figures, for you'll find a lot of them in hermetic texts, and they might start showing up in your dreams as well. Suppose that in our pentagram, each of the five points stands for something. (Don't worry about what exactly. It's not important at the moment.) The line between one point and another indicates a relationship between the two. In a pentagram, each of the five points has a direct relationship with two of the others. Now look again and notice that besides the five original points that were connected to form the pentagram, there are an additional five points where the relationship lines intersect. They form a pentagon within the pentagram. These five points are five additional somethings that result when you connect one relationship to another relationship. In the pentagon, each point is already connected by lines to the two points adjacent to it. Try adding some more lines so that each point in the pentagon connects with all of four of the others. What do you get? It's another pentagram.

The Tree of Life from the Cabbala is another figure that works on the same principle.

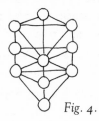

Fig. 4.

The circles indicate attributes of the divine. Each of the connecting lines represents a relationship between two attributes.

Now let's consider the caduceus.

Fig. 5.

Imagine that this picture is telling you a story. To reveal the narrative in a static picture, you once again need to add the elements of time, movement, and relationship. You have to turn a snapshot into a movie. At the moment, two snakes are twined around a staff of some kind. Where do you suppose the snakes were before they slithered up the staff? How did the staff get there? How are the snakes related to each other? Are they moving or holding still? What are the wings for? You have no doubt seen this symbol many times in medical contexts. Can you see any relationship between the story it tells and healing?

Don't get hung up on whether your answers are "right," i.e., similar to what other alchemists have seen in the caduceus. If you attempt the exercise again tomorrow, you might come up with a different story, and yet another story a month from now. Just animate the picture as the spirit moves you, for the movement of your spirit is ultimately what you're after.

What you've been doing with these symbol exercises is what Artephius meant when he said "be not stiff-necked." You might have skimmed right over that offhand remark of his, but it turns out to be one among those keys that are hidden in plain sight—a key to discovering what "can only be revealed by God" yet "likewise may be learned from this book." Artephius isn't trying to obfuscate for the sake of obfuscation. He intends to be perfectly clear, but that clarity requires your participation. If you read as a passive recipient of information, you won't get it. You need to move your mind. Alchemical symbols, stories, and procedures are all intended to set your mind in motion. That's why crucial information is so often displaced, why the answer you need is located some distance away from the question. The movement you have to make between the question and the answer is an essential part of the answer. It is the difference between mere information and meaning.

Now that you're on a roll, you might want to reconsider some of the elements in the story of Nicholas Flamel. While trying to discover how to prepare the *prima materia*, he got stuck for twenty-one years. Some things he tried got him more stuck. Other things he tried eventually got him unstuck. Try listing the procedures that worked for him and the procedures that didn't. See if you are able to make sense of any of them in the light of what you've discovered so far. As for those that still baffle you, bury them for now in the cemetery of the Holy Innocents.

Naming as an Alchemical Procedure

In the Quran, God assembles the angels and demands that they prostrate themselves before his latest creation, Adam. The angels respond

(I'm paraphrasing here), "You've got to be kidding!" To them, Adam just looks like a glorified animal. They can't see anything in him that would command their respect. So God asks the angels to tell him the names of the animals he has previously created. The angels are unable to do it. "How can we know the names of these things if you haven't told us?" they protest. But when God sets Adam the same task, out come words like tiger, rhinoceros, and jellyfish. Duly impressed, the angels prostrate after all. For some reason, naming is a very big deal in the spiritual world.

It's also a big deal in school. If the words we use to describe inner and outer phenomena are similar to the words used by our teachers, our statements are deemed true, and we get good grades. Social agreement about the meaning of words is essential if we are to communicate intelligibly. Should you use the word "five" to mean what others mean by "four," you will think that $2 + 2 = 5$. One could argue that the difference between your thought and that of your arithmetic teacher is merely semantic. But if you and your teacher can't agree on the semantics, you will probably flunk, because your teacher has no way of understanding what you're trying to say.

Sometimes you learn a name for something *before* you have perceived the thing itself. Being told the name clues you in to look for the phenomenon. When children are taught the word "five," they learn to see five-ness. This is how a lot of alchemical thinking works. Its object is not necessarily to make thoughts correspond to outward phenomena that you already perceive. It is more like building a road that will carry you to what you *don't* presently perceive. The test of a good road is whether it takes you where you want to go. When alchemists assert, "As above, so below," they are not offering it as a proposition for debate. Rather, they are describing a mental pathway that has led them to new perceptions and insights.

As Einstein and the theoretical physicists who followed him began to illuminate the relationship between energy and matter, scholars noticed the pronounced similarity of these theories to the metaphysical teachings of Buddhism and Taoism. If you substitute scientific words like "matter" for Buddhist words like "form," Buddhist metaphysical discourses sound very much like the theories of modern physicists. Based on this observation, someone had the brainstorm that you could substitute the word "energy" for "spirit," and "Universe" for "God."

The idea caught on. It proved especially appealing to people who were drawn to the "spiritual" yet felt turned off by the religions in which they'd been raised. They had no use for the judgmental patriarch of monotheism, but the Universe has a nice way of minding its own business. If you want to sleep in on Sunday morning, the Universe won't object. Not only that, but with a simple semantic shift—substituting "energy" for "spirit"—the whole disconnect between science and religion pretty much disappears. The discoveries of theoretical physicists begin to shed light on everything from providence to prayer. Magic, too, begins to look logical. If thoughts are a form of energy, then it must be possible to get things done by directing that energy.

Equating spirit with energy is certainly workable for people who like their scientific explanations and their metaphysical explanations to match. But this way of naming may create some new mental obstacles for the alchemist. You see, if matter is just energy in another form, the converse is also true. On its own, neither matter nor energy has much to say for itself. Both are, from a human point of view, impersonal. It follows that if you don't take lightning personally, you shouldn't take the "energy" of another's affection or anger personally either. Much of the richness of human experience gets lost in the translation.

To conceive of spirit as pure energy suggests that, when this energy separates from your body at death, it must be no more human than the stuff that turns on your desk lamp or runs your dishwasher. How, then, can you tell one person's spirit from another? Assuming this pure energy reincarnates, why would it do so in the form of another human as opposed to, say, a comet or a hippopotamus? And if the energy you call "I" does take form as another human, what do you have in common with that new person?

The Tibetan lama, Chögyam Trungpa, had a good answer for this. Asked how Tibetans recognize one lama as the reincarnation of a previous lama, he replied, "They have the same style." The word "style" in this context says something different from the word "energy." Style is how energy takes one form and not another. You could say that style is like an idea or an intention. Or you could say that it is like personality. Style is the essence of the matter. Style is also where names come from, why such disparate forms as the gnat and the praying mantis are both called "insect."

In our mundane perceptions, the style of a thing is identical to its form. We don't usually perceive chair-ness as separate from the chair, or Dalai Lama-ness as separate from the Dalai Lama, or kiss-ness as separate from the particular kiss we are engaged in. Yet there are times when we find it useful to consider style apart from form. A furniture designer wishing to come up with a brand new form of chair has to perceive what chair-ness is. Otherwise he will end up with a desk or a bed. If you want to be a better kisser, it helps to contemplate kiss-ness. And if you want to identify a being who is not manifesting in a physical form (such as an angel or the spirit of someone who has died), you will have to recognize him by style alone.

Style, for the alchemist, is a workable concept because it can be used to expand one's perceptions. Starting with the hypothesis that there is such a thing as style—that all phenomena have some sort of essence or personality—you can go looking for it. Style is also the link between sensory and extrasensory perceptions. If you would like to have more of the latter, begin by learning to distinguish the style of things from their physical forms. (On page 36, I've given you some exercises that may help.)

The law of correspondences is an elaboration of the style concept. It is an attempt to understand phenomena by means of analogies—a kind of metaphorical thinking that we usually associate with artists rather than scientists. The basic idea is that disparate objects in the universe—such as planets, elements, minerals, flora and fauna, organs of the body, etc.—have stylistic similarities. We express this all the time in our figures of speech. Our clichés about plants—"cheerful as a daisy," "strong as an oak," "regal as a lily"—draw an analogy between a plant and a human quality or feeling. Alchemists would say that these expressions have become cliché's because there's something universally true about them. Plants actually do embody qualities similar to those found in the human soul. In the system of remedies devised by the alchemist Edward Bach, stoic people are offered a medicine made from oak, while those suffering from excessive self-pity are advised to take one made from willow. How a plant might be described by a poet is relevant to its medicinal effects.

Let's contrast this with what biochemists do when they want to make medicine. Observing that people living in the Amazon rain forest munch on a certain type of leaf when they are suffering from gas, biochemists might analyze the sap in the leaf, breaking it down into its chemical components, trying to isolate and eventually synthesize the molecular compound that aids digestion. They're trying, in other words, to *eliminate* relationship, to separate the active ingredient or relevant variable from the context in which it originally appears. What the plant looks like, where and how it grows, and what poets might have to say about it are, to the biochemist, irrelevant variables. There is no disputing that medicines devised by this method actually work. Yet the rain forest dwellers who have always chewed on that leaf discovered it by means of perceiving, rather than eliminating, relationship.

A common activity of hermeticists is to work out tables of correspondences between one group of things and another group of things. Astrology is the most familiar example of this kind of thinking. Planets correspond—that is, have a similar style—to particular organs of the human body and qualities of the human personality. These correspondences enable astrologers to make predictions about people based on the movements of the planets.

When correspondences are perceived correctly, they have practical applications. Instead of trying to force change on a phenomenon that is resisting it, you could apply your efforts to a corresponding phenomenon that is more amenable to influence. Let's say, for example, that a correspondence exists between the state of your mind and the state of your closets. If you throw away items you no longer use and reorganize what remains, you might find that your thinking becomes clearer and that you are more open to new ideas. You will have to determine whether or not this particular correspondence holds true by experimenting with it yourself. I just offer it as a simple example of the potential magic of analogy.

Boarding Platform 9¾

Having been raised by muggles (non-magical people), J. K. Rowling's orphaned hero, Harry Potter, learns on his eleventh birthday that he was born of magicians and that he has been admitted to Hogwarts Academy, where all the finest magicians are educated. His first challenge is to get there. The train for Hogwarts departs from London's King's Cross Station, on Platform 9¾. From a muggle perspective, there is no such platform. Harry can't see it either. So how does one get to Platform 9¾? In the world of Harry Potter, this is the equivalent of the *prima materia*— what the magician must find before he can make any further progress.

Just as you would expect, Platform 9¾ is between Platform 9 and Platform 10. *Between*. Grammatically, *between* is a preposition. But suppose you think of it as a noun: *the* between. Platform 9¾ is not located anywhere in the three spatial dimensions perceived by the physical senses. It exists in an alternative dimension, and that dimension can be called "the between." Like style, the between is one of those names that is meant to prompt you to go looking for something subtle, something you don't normally notice, though it's always around.

Two words you'll hear a lot in alchemy are *fixed* and *volatile*. To be fixed is to be matter-like. To be volatile is to be energy-like. Through various alchemical operations, the fixed can be made volatile and the volatile can be made fixed. In other words, the alchemy is happening *between* two states—matter and energy. The magic isn't in the energy any more than it is in the matter. The magic is in *the between*.

The between is not a midpoint. It's not an average or a compromise. Those are abstractions we make up in our minds. The between has a life of its own, born of whatever is on either side of it. It is a quality of relatedness and also a quality of potential. It is what differentiates random sounds from music. Between the notes of a song or symphony, there are spaces, silences. But these silences are not merely the absence of sound. The surrounding notes give the silences a distinct flavor. The pause between one musical phrase and the next feels pregnant with something.

Picture two people who are so angry with each other that they are about to come to blows. What is their between? Is it the energy of anger?

Not exactly. Two people who are very angry might also decide to shun and avoid each other. Do you see how, even though the emotion is still anger, this second situation presents a different kind of between? The between of angry people who are fighting has a quality of "toward-ness." That of people who are shunning has "away-ness." It is toward-ness or away-ness, rather than anger, that describes the potential latent in the between. Perceiving such subtle differences in potential—and knowing what to do with them—is a key to transmuting situations.

That is why, to be a magician, you must not only locate Platform 9¾, but also find a way to board it. Harry Potter and his friends take a running leap of faith toward what appears to be a solid barricade. At the last possible moment, the between opens to let them in. But if muggles attempt the same feat, they just crash into the barricade. There is some quality magicians have that muggles don't that enables them to enter the between. What is this quality?

Suppose we start with what it is *not*. Choose an object some distance away from wherever you happen to be sitting right now. Pretend that your aim is to make the object move without touching it. You're going to do this by directing the power of thought. Put yourself in whatever state of mind you imagine might accomplish that.

Don't be concerned if you fail. To succeed would be impressive, but pointless. (To move objects is why God gave you hands.) Just get a feel for the mindset that goes with this type of procedure.

Even when it works, trying to get one's way by bombarding the world with thought energy is a pretty muggle thing to do. The problem is that you are trying to change the object without being changed yourself. Of course, we do that with objects all the time. When you pick up a pencil, you're the boss and, as far as you can tell, the pencil doesn't resent you for it. What makes the action mundane rather than magical is the absence of a living relationship, of anything interesting happening in the between. At best, you can only manipulate. You can't transmute.

Now let's try to imagine what it would take to enter the dimension of the between. If you happen to be incarnate as a male right now, this should be easy, since you no doubt spent much of your youth obsessed with gaining entrance to a between, and learned, by trial and error, to accomplish it. If you are presently female, you know a between as its gatekeeper. Either way, your experience in that context is relevant to other kinds of between. What approaches have gotten the best results?

I am by no means the first writer to employ this somewhat racy analogy. Wooing was a frequent metaphor in medieval alchemy. The troubadours' ballads of courtly love can be read as coded instructions on how to get to Platform 9¾. The suitor was admonished to become infinitely patient, gentle, and attentive to the lady's fluctuating moods and whims. To win her, he must learn to empathize with her, tone down his boisterous masculinity, and attune to her feminine style. The central paradox of these stories is that to attain a magician's power, one must relinquish the impulse to force and conquer. To change anything in an alchemical way, you must allow *it* to change *you*.

On the first night of an extended visit to Marrakech, I dined at a rooftop restaurant overlooking a very busy intersection at rush hour. The streets were teeming with every sort of conveyance: cars, trucks, municipal buses, bicycles, horse-drawn carriages, and donkey carts. As far as I could tell, the lane markings and traffic lights were purely decorative. They had no discernable bearing on what anyone in the street was doing. The whole setup looked both dangerous and insanely inefficient, yet traffic was moving along at a pretty good clip—much faster than in downtown Chicago, where there are no donkeys to contend with. There were no accidents, no near-misses, no altercations.

Marrakech traffic became even more mystifying to me when I joined it as a pedestrian. Since traffic signals were rare and universally ignored, crossing a busy street was a matter of choosing the right moment. Americans do this by crossing from a corner, and looking both ways before stepping off the curb. That didn't work at all. A car or bicycle would come careening out of nowhere when I was halfway across and I, freezing in terror, would inevitably cause a screech, a swerve, and a near collision. I noticed that my fellow tourists were getting similar results. Compared to Moroccans, visitors were always moving either too fast and bumping into people, or too slow and getting in everyone's way. Moroccans never seemed to get in each others' way. Nor did they look before crossing the street. They just dove in blindly and the traffic somehow wove itself around them.

In other words, there was a *between* to the Marrakech streets that natives knew how to enter and tourists didn't. It was almost like an invisible vehicle itself. If you managed to board it, it would carry you along safely, efficiently, and at the right speed. But to board it, you had to perceive it, attune to it, get in sync with it. By the end of my six-week visit I was jaywalking across busy streets with the insouciant blindness of Mr. Magoo. What had changed? *I* had.

Boarding Platform 9¾ is like that.

Finding Your Companions

The word "hermit" comes from the same root as "hermeticist," for in the eyes of the world, hermeticism is a lonely endeavor. But appearances, in this case, are deceiving. You can't make much headway with alchemy if you are working in complete isolation. You need helpers and friends. You might think right now that you've never met an alchemist. Yet I wouldn't be at all surprised if, a few years hence, you reported that you were surrounded by them.

When we want to meet like-minded people, often we look for an organization to join. While various official societies of hermeticists exist (some very secretive, others clearly labeled and advertised), you may find them disappointing. The spirit of Hermes seems to have a pronounced aversion to formal organizations. As soon as a group of humans establishes bylaws and begins collecting dues in his name, he's out of there.

Hermes works instead to weave a network that is unofficial, inconspicuous, and free of charge, yet robust and highly efficient. When your doctor or plumber or next-door neighbor "just happens" to be an alchemist—and don't be surprised if you discover this—you can thank the network for bringing you together. It also enables you to stumble upon ideas, books, and various other items you need in your magical endeavors—often by means of the wildest coincidences.

Actively looking for the network is of little use, for its members rarely hang out a shingle. But don't worry; it will find you. The beings who identify you and perceive your need are, quite often, non-incarnate. Many of your teachers and colleagues are likely to be body-free as well. I'm a little wary of calling them spiritual beings—though that's what they are—because the religious connotations of "spiritual" are likely to mislead you. Spiritual beings are not always holy, or virtuous, or lofty, or wise, or interested in religion. In all these respects, they are as various as people. The only thing they all have in common is lack of a physical body. To avail yourself of their help, you will have to learn to recognize and communicate with beings who do not appear to your physical senses. In the next two chapters, I'll be going into much greater detail about these contacts. Here, I just want to give you a couple of preliminary hints.

When you enter a room in the material world, you can tell immediately whether there are any other occupants. Even if you have no relationship with them, you can see that they are there, because they take up space. First you have an objective perception of them, and then you decide whether you'd like to engage with them. In the nonphysical world, it's the other way around. The engagement happens first. If you have no relationship with a being, you can't perceive it. As far as you are concerned, it's not there. That's why attuning to the between is important. With non-incarnate beings, the between is what manifests first.

Imagine you woke up one day feeling that you were in love and then had to look around to find out who in the world you had fallen in love with. Imagine you found yourself in possession of a gift that you couldn't remember anyone giving you. Or say you felt an intense wave of nostalgia without knowing what you were nostalgic for. That's approximately what it's like.

Sometimes a feeling of gratitude is the first intimation of a friendly being. When, by apparent coincidence, we stumble upon exactly what we've been needing, we feel as if we have received a favor. We have an impulse to thank someone even if we can't figure out who that someone is. Or we may, in a moment of acute distress, find ourselves feeling mysteriously comforted. A sense of peace comes over us, and we have no idea where it's coming from. If we're feeling consoled, there must be a consoler. If we're feeling gratitude, there must be someone to thank. What I'm saying here is not an argument, not a proof. It's not going to convince a person who doesn't believe in the existence of such beings. But if you are inclined to believe in them yet don't know how to meet them, start by attending to these feelings of unknown origin that sometimes come over you. Think of them as a between that signals the possible presence of a being.

Another very common signal that you have company is a fresh thought coming into your mind—one that seems different from your usual thoughts. I can't tell you exactly how to distinguish your own thoughts from those of other beings because I don't know the unique flavor of your mind. Elsewhere in these pages, you'll find a procedure for knowing that flavor yourself. For now let me just suggest that if a thought doesn't sound like you, it probably isn't you.

In order for a relationship to happen, perception has to be mutual. The other being has to perceive you, too. This isn't a given. People tend to assume that anyone who doesn't have a body is omniscient. Nothing could be farther from the truth. Like incarnate humans, some are knowledgeable and some are clueless. Like us, they gravitate toward what interests them. They don't tune in to every human thought any more than you and I tune in to every station on the radio. Indeed, the vast majority of our mental activity is just white noise to them. We become perceptible to spiritual beings when we are thinking about the sort of thing that interests them, and doing so in a manner that is comprehensible to them. The kind of thoughts I've been describing in this chapter—contemplating symbols, geometric figures, style, and correspondences—are readily recognized by beings of the hermetic network and good for attracting their attention.

Years ago, I corresponded with a hermeticist who was violently allergic to the word "spiritual." He pointed out that humans, too, are spiritual beings and that the so-called "spiritual world" includes *this* world. Since our entire correspondence revolved around the spiritual (you know what I mean), avoiding the word was quite a challenge. Apart from being clumsy, "non-incarnate" sounds a bit euphemistic, as if I were calling angels, devas, and the deceased "differently abled."

In my effort to correspond about the spiritual without actually using the word, I was challenged to become a lot more precise and specific about what I really meant. Sometimes the right term was "inner."

Sometimes it was "subtle." "Vertical" is a hermetic standby that works beautifully in certain contexts. On other occasions, what I really wanted to be talking about is the nontemporal, i.e., the world of nonlinear time. Each change in terminology brought about a change in perspective. So in each of the next three chapters I will be employing a different vocabulary, offering three different perspectives on the whatchamacallit world.

Learning to Perceive Style

If you're still trying to get a handle on what "style" means, here are some exercises that should help.

EXERCISE 1

Make a table of correspondences. Begin choosing two different categories of phenomena (flowers, foods, animals, colors, emotions, famous personalities, geographic features, weather conditions, etc.). Then try to pair items from the first category with items in the second.

Let's say your two categories are parts of a house and parts of a human body. What, in a body, corresponds to a furnace? What, in a house, corresponds to the eyes?

Go ahead and get silly with this. There are no right or wrong answers. At the same time, don't be surprised if you come up with something that has magical possibilities. Correspondences between human moods, emotions, personality traits, or physical symptoms and nonhuman phenomena such as colors, weather, music, architectural features, and so forth might give rise to a system of self-healing that works for you, even if it baffles everyone else on the planet.

EXERCISE 2: *Avant-garde Design*

Think of a common man-made object such as a spoon, a pitcher, or a chair. Picture as many different examples of that object as you can, getting a feel for what they all have in common. What features of a

---

chair can you alter and still have a recognizable chair? How far can you go in changing each feature before a chair ceases to be a chair? Try picturing a chair that is different from any chair you've ever seen yet is still, indisputably, a chair.

EXERCISE 3: *Style in the Abstract*

Begin this exercise as you began the last—by picturing many different examples of a common object, such as a chair. Then erase the pictures from your mind while still mentally holding the idea of chair. If the pictures are gone but you're still thinking of words that define or describe chair, make those go away, too. What you're attempting to hold in your mind is the pure concept of chair, without any specific examples.

Wordless and imageless concepts are extremely slippery, so if you get to it at all, you probably won't be able to hold on for very long. A full minute is doing quite well. If you manage to get to it once, see if you can find your way back to it later without using specific examples of chairs to get there. See how long you can stay with it before it slips away.

Apart from being frustrating, this exercise is pretty boring. I'd be surprised if you could stand to work at it for more than five or ten minutes at a time. But there's a big payoff for persevering, even if for just five minutes a day. More than the previous two exercises, this one is very good for awakening extrasensory perception. By the time you finish this book, you'll understand why.

When you get tired of the chair, here are some other concepts you can try: flower, male, insect, frame, youth, home, machine.

3

Separate the Subtle
from the Gross

IN THE PREVIOUS TWO CHAPTERS, I alluded to charlatans and pranksters in the hermetic community. By now you might be wondering whether I'm one of them. I suggested that in your pursuit of the philosopher's stone you would be guided by a network of intelligent beings who are invisible to the average person. I described the signs of their presence in rather elusive terms, while at the same time hinting that I possessed a specific and intimate knowledge of them that would be imparted to you later. In its bare outlines, all of this resembles one of the most successful hoaxes ever perpetrated, a practical joke dating back to the 1870s that has continued to hoodwink seekers and sustain the careers of bogus gurus up to the present day.

Its context was Spiritualism, a fad for séances that swept the United States in the aftermath of the Civil War. The apparent proof séances offered of life after death was comforting to the bereaved, despite the rather odd implication that the soul's principle activity in the afterlife was rapping on tables, banging on pots and pans, and causing common household objects to fly around darkened rooms. Even genuine mediums felt it necessary to supplement their channeled messages with special effects. A clever variation on the routine was to denounce the sensationalism of one's fellow mediums, demonstrate how their illusions were achieved, and then, having won the confidence of the skeptical, conjure "genuine" physical manifestations of the spirit world. This debunk-then-dazzle maneuver continues to be a standby of stage magicians today. Madame Helena Petrovna Blavatsky (HPB) was an adept at it.

Blavatsky's career as an occultist took off in 1874, when she met and captivated (in a platonic sort of way) Colonel William Olcott, a reporter doing a series of articles on Spiritualism. Her biography prior to that date is a dizzying and often contradictory collection of tall tales that historians have not been able to confirm or categorically refute. A daughter of a minor Russian aristocrat, she fled from her much older husband at the age of seventeen and embarked on a globe-spanning series of adventures, supporting herself through such diverse occupations as concert pianist, circus performer, spirit medium, and interior decorator. She claimed to have trekked across the American West in a wagon train, fallen in with bandits in Mexico, gotten shipwrecked off the coast of Greece, and fought alongside Garibaldi, sustaining both bullet and saber wounds. Her spiritual training included encounters with Cabbalists in Egypt, voodoo magicians in New Orleans, and, most improbably, Himalayan masters in Tibet. While most of this sounds like pure invention, the flamboyance of her well-documented adventures after meeting Olcott suggests that her implausible early history might occasionally touch base with fact. Blavatsky had a knack for making her personal mythology come true.

HPB expressed disdain for the mediumship that she herself displayed, dismissing it as trivial and sensationalistic. The real work of an occultist, she maintained, was to commune with higher beings, not ghosts. Such contacts were too esoteric to be appreciated by the rabble who attended séances, but she was willing to confide about them to a man of such evident discrimination as Olcott—and, it turned out, to the general readership of her massive works, *Isis Unveiled* and *The Secret Doctrine*.

At the center of Blavatsky's visionary world is the Great White Brotherhood, a group of immortal and sketchily incarnate Masters who guide the spiritual destiny of humanity from some remote Himalayan outpost. Its members include the Buddha, Maitreya, Manu, Jesus, Plato, Lao Tzu, Confucius, and the Comte de Saint-Germain. Headed by the

Lord of the World (who originally hailed from Venus and now manifests as a sixteen-year-old boy living in the Gobi desert), the Great White Brotherhood is opposed by the Lords of the Dark Face. Dispatches from the Masters to human initiates are delivered by a couple of celestial gofers: Master Morya and Koot Hoomi—a being who incarnated as Pythagorus prior to becoming a handsome Brahmin and attending the University of Leipzig.

Soon after meeting Madame Blavatsky, Olcott began receiving letters from two of the Great White Brothers—Tuitit and Serapis Bey—inviting him to become a candidate for initiation. Flattered, Olcott accepted, and was somewhat perplexed when their subsequent letters proved short on spiritual teachings but rich in advice on how to deal with HPB. They encouraged him to support her in founding the Theosophical Society and later advised him to divorce his wife and escort Blavatsky to India. Though the letters manifested by seemingly magical means (sometimes falling into his lap from the ceiling), Olcott remained a bit doubtful of their provenance until the night when one of their authors showed up in the flesh—or whatever it was that, in the Bey brothers, passed for flesh. The apparition sported a red-and-gold-striped turban and a long black beard and had eyes that were, as Olcott later related, "alive with soul fire . . . at once benignant and piercing . . . the eyes of a mentor or judge." Olcott fell to his knees and bowed his head as the visitor spoke of his (Olcott's) mysterious and unbreakable tie to Blavatsky and of the great work on behalf of humanity that the two were destined to undertake together. Even this did not entirely silence the faint voice of doubt, for it occurred to Olcott that Blavatsky might have hypnotized him. As if in answer, the master disappeared, leaving behind his embroidered turban cloth as proof of the visitation. That settled the matter. The pair set sail for India shortly thereafter.

Five years later, in an attempt to extort money from the Theosophical Society, HPB's former maid Emma Cutter threatened to reveal how this and other stunts had been done. When Society representatives hesitated to pay up, Cutter showed them concealed wall panels, holes in the ceiling through which letters had been dropped, and the puppet whose eyes had appeared to be so alive with soul fire. Blavatsky was obliged to resign her office in the Society and return to England, her friendship with Olcott in ruins. Yet the scandal had little impact on the growing membership of the Society, over which Olcott continued to preside. Nor did it put an end to Blavatsky's influence. For decades afterward, whenever the Society was disrupted by scandal or schism, a new "Back to Blavatsky" movement would arise. It was HPB herself who anointed Olcott's eventual successor, Annie Besant.

Besant was a well-known feminist and social activist, an intelligent, forceful and fetching woman whose admirers included George Bernard Shaw. Soon after falling under Blavatsky's influence in 1888, she herself had a vision of one of the Masters. This was apparently an inner experience, not one of HPB's stunts, for Besant never asserted that any of the Masters manifested physically to her. By her own admission, her dreams and visions of them were vague and impressionistic. While well qualified for the outward leadership of what had become a worldwide organization, she felt less secure in her ability to fill HPB's shoes as an occultist. For help in contacting the Masters and interpreting their messages, she turned to C. W. Leadbetter. A charismatic self-mythologizer in the Blavatsky mold, Leadbetter was privileged to receive vivid and elaborate visions of the Masters, as well as lengthy verbal messages from them, dictated by Koot Hoomi. Under Hoomi's guidance, Besant and Leadbetter authored many volumes of occult research into science and world history (or what, in the Theosophical milieu, passed for these disciplines).

Leadbetter's weakness was young boys. When he took a shine to one, his seduction procedure was to "recognize" the boy as the incarnation of some high being with an important destiny on earth and personally supervise his spiritual education, sometimes even gaining legal custody of the boy. It was rumored that this spiritual tutelage included lessons in masturbation. For years, Besant played deaf to these allegations, but in 1906 hard evidence surfaced in the form of a letter sent by Leadbetter to one of his protégés. This put Annie in a bind. Every major decision in the running of the Society was based on her astral encounters with the Masters, as mediated by Leadbetter, or on the letters he channeled from Koot Hoomi. It had always been understood that communion with the Masters was granted only to celibate initiates. As a pederast, Leadbetter could not possibly be one of them. Thus the very foundations of Annie's spiritual authority in the Society were shaken.

Or so it would seem to someone who was troubled by logic—an affliction to which most Theosophists were happily immune. Within a few
months, Besant and the Society as a whole had managed to shrug off
the affair. Leadbetter survived with his influence intact. In fact, it was
soon to grow.

Among his extraordinary abilities was something he called "reading
the Akashic Chronicle." This, according to Leadbetter, was a written
record of everything that had ever happened in the past and would ever
happen in the future of the cosmos. He began to publish the results of
his Akashic investigations in a sprawling serial entitled *Lives of Alcy-
one*. It recounted the epic past and future incarnations of prominent
Theosophists, with starring roles for his favorite boys. Anyone who opposed or displeased him soon found their way into the saga as minions
of the Dark Lords. Cosmic history was, it turned out, subject to amend-
ment. George Arundale, one of Leadbetter's young favorites, was put
very much out of countenance when his role as the future Buddha of
the planet Mercury was reassigned to a kid named Raja.

Reading auras was another of Leadbetter's attainments. It was the
extraordinary glow emanating from a young and, some said, half-witted
Indian boy named Krishna that caused Leadbetter to recognize him as
the Maitreya Bodhisattva, future World Teacher and Second Coming
of Christ. With Besant's cooperation, the Theosophists won custody of
the motherless boy from his baffled and uneasy father, sending him to
London to be educated. For Rudolf Steiner, president of the German
branch of the Society and one of its more sober thinkers (relatively
speaking), this was the last straw. He resigned to form the Anthroposophical Society, taking many Theosophists with him.

But Besant and Leadbetter were not to be deterred from their propri-
etorship of the Second Coming of Christ. Torn from his family and his
native culture, shunned in England on account of his dark coloring and
bizarre deification, and smothered by Theosophical matrons who alter-
nately bossed and worshipped him, the child who grew up to be Krishnamurti was a heartbreakingly lonely figure. But Leadbetter was not
altogether mistaken about Krishna's spiritual gifts, and Krishna proved
to be more cunning than he had appeared in childhood. As a young
man he extricated himself from his destiny by claiming to have lost his

memory. By then, guru was the only occupation he was fit for, so he became one of sorts. The gist of his teaching was to steer clear of gurus. That, I guess you could say, is the punch line to Madame Blavatsky's joke.

Grossed Out

A line in the Emerald Tablet of Hermes Trismegistus advises the alchemist to "separate the subtle from the gross, gently and with infinite sagacity." The story you have just read is an example of what Hermes means by "the gross."

In reading a brief synopsis of follies that took decades to unfold, it is easier for you to spot the errors than it would have been for the participants. Once people have moved in all their furniture, they tend to resist noticing that they're living in a house of cards. Immediately striking to the detached observer is the part human vanity played in the deceptions. When someone who purports to have a backstage pass to the cosmos awards you impressive credentials, you have a natural disinclination to consider that his own credentials might be bogus. Devotees who become enmeshed in cults give away their power to the spiritual teacher in the belief that the teacher will grant them marvelous new powers in return. Some teachers exploit this weakness in order to expose it. They deliberately jerk the student around until the student wises up. (Gurdjieff employed this tactic, as did the EST training popular in the 1970s.) The whole setup is based on the paradox that if you think you need the teacher, you haven't yet learned the lesson.

Let's give that head game a pass and focus instead on aspects of the debacle that aren't quite so obvious. In depicting Olcott and Besant at their most foolish, I haven't done them full justice. Both were intelligent, enterprising, and courageous, and did a lot of good in the world. The Theosophical Society boasted some estimable members, including William Butler Yeats, Thomas Edison, and Charles Darwin's collaborator, Alfred Russel Wallace. It continues to enjoy a good reputation in India as a result of its efforts to support and disseminate Hindu and Buddhist traditions at a time when Christianity was being shoved down Indians' throats. At crucial moments early in their respective misadventures, Olcott and Besant made honest mistakes that you or I might have made, too. The essence of those mistakes was a failure to separate the subtle from the gross.

The subtle is that which cannot be perceived by the ordinary senses because it is pre-physical. According to alchemy, before anything manifests on the physical plane (what alchemists call the "gross" or "dense"), it passes through a formative stage on the subtle planes. If you are able to perceive this formative stage, you become adept at guessing what will happen next.

When you predict rain because you see that the sky has filled up with black clouds, you are not seeing the actual future. Nevertheless, your prediction has a high probability of being accurate. A meteorologist can know that a storm is likely before the clouds even appear, by observing movements of warm and cold air that will cause them to form. Prior to the earliest cause of a warm or cold front that can be physically observed, there is a subtle phenomenon: the idea or the intention of a frontal system. A meteorologist who could perceive this phenomenon would be able to predict storms well in advance of his colleagues.

Alchemical magic never defies the laws of nature. Instead, it observes the workings of those laws at an earlier stage than is evident to the physical senses. Whatever manifests on a physical level begins with an idea or intention. While matter is too dense, too heavy, to be altered by mind alone, ideas and intentions are the mind's natural medium. If you can perceive phenomena at the formative stage, you can sometimes alter the intention that gives rise to them and thereby change the material outcome.

In the nineteenth century, the word "science" was a synonym for truth. Mary Baker Eddy named her movement Christian Science, while the Spiritualists, Theosophists, and Anthroposophists referred to what they were doing as "spiritual science" or "occult science." They were trying to get across the idea that spiritual phenomena are just as real as material phenomena. Yet these so-called scientists of the occult themselves tended to confuse the real with the material. The contemporary quantum physicist has a far less materialistic view of reality than did the average nineteenth-century spiritual scientist.

In Olcott's view, the turban cloth was proof positive that he had been visited by one of the Masters, because it was a material fact. He should have taken it as proof positive that someone was pulling his leg. Spiritual beings really do manifest to people, but they don't leave behind items of apparel. A spiritual being is a subtle phenomenon, while a turban cloth is a gross one.

Besant made essentially the same error when she gave Leadbetter's visions more credit than her own. Her description of her early encounters with the Masters as a vague inner impression is very similar to the description I gave in the previous chapter. A slight shift in your own consciousness—a feeling you can't quite put your finger on—suggests to you that someone else might be present. You're not sure who or what it is, and you half suspect that you might just be imagining the whole thing. Like the turban cloth, it was the vividness and specificity of Leadbetter's visions—not to mention the sheer long-windedness of his supposedly celestial visitors—that should have led Besant to suspect fraud. Subtle phenomena are just that: *subtle*. I am saddened to think that Besant suppressed what might well have been genuine subtle perceptions in favor of Leadbetter's comic-book cosmology.

Born Clairvoyant

In high school biology you probably learned how your physical perception works. Your central nervous system carries information from your physical sense organs to your brain. Perception hasn't happened until the brain responds to the impulses coming from the sense organs. If the brain is stimulated in a certain way, you might have the impression that you are seeing, even if your eyes are closed. This happens when you dream, and you can also cause it to happen at will when you remember or imagine.

Subtle perception likewise involves the brain, but the impulses come from a nonphysical source. Hermeticists used to call it the subtle body or etheric body. Now it is more often called the human energy field. Its perceptual centers are sometimes called chakras. While contemporary science has not yet reached a consensus that there is such a thing as a subtle body, Chinese and Indian medicine have always recognized it and attribute to it many of the cognitive activities that Western medicine assigns exclusively to the brain.

The subtle body isn't matter—isn't a thing—but neither is it pure spirit. It surrounds and interpenetrates the physical body, and you can more or less tell where it leaves off, even though the edges are fuzzy. The size of it corresponds roughly to the amount of personal space you need to feel comfortable around other people. If you are able to sense what proximity feels right to another person, you are already able to perceive subtle bodies to some extent.

It is the subtle body, not the spirit, that makes the difference between a living person and a corpse. Your spirit doesn't have to be in your physical body or anywhere near it for you to remain alive. In fact, it's nonsensical to talk about *where* a spirit is, since spirits don't have any location in space. For the spirit to "go away" simply means for it to turn its attention elsewhere, as it often does when you are sleeping. The subtle body, though, has a location. It has to stay with your physical body as long as you are alive. Ghosts are the detached subtle bodies of those who have died. If you have ever felt the presence of a ghost, you could probably say pretty clearly where it was, and approximately how big it was. By contrast, a meeting with a spirit feels more like it's happening in your mind. When a loved one dies, you might experience them for a while as a ghost. Then the subtle body goes away, and should you meet them again, what you will encounter will be their spirit.

If you enjoy music, thank your subtle body. It regulates movement, rhythm, timing, and relationship within the physical body and responds to these same qualities in the world around us. Remember when I invited you to draw pentagrams? The pentagram is a magical symbol in part because the gesture it describes is very pleasing to the subtle body. When I went on to talk about moving mentally with texts and symbols and about the between, I was addressing your subtle body more than your brain. Your subtle body understands that kind of stuff, even if your brain doesn't. It perceives the between because it *is* a between.

Subtle perceptions often have a quasi-physical quality. Whenever we use a body part or a body sensation to describe a mood or emotion, we are speaking the language of the subtle body. Say, for instance, you are feeling "heavy-hearted." You probably wouldn't consult a cardiologist about this, because it's not like the feeling you would have if something were wrong with your physical heart. Yet it's in approximately the same place—either in your chest or ever so slightly outside of it—and "heavy" is a good description of what it feels like. You might even walk around with your shoulders stooped and your chest caved in, because this "heart" is so heavy you can't quite hold it up.

When you're having an inner conflict, you might say, "My head says _____, but my gut is telling me _____." Try to recall the subtle sensations you were having the last time you said something like that. What feeling or activity seemed to be in the head? Was it actually in the head or just in the general vicinity? Where exactly did the gut message come from? How would you describe that sensation? If you can't remember right now, try asking yourself these questions the next time you feel torn between reason and intuition. (The expression "feel torn" is another example of what I'm talking about.)

Subtle impressions also come to us in the form of mental pictures. They tend to be rather vague. Sometimes they seem to have a shape (blob-like, or streaky, or pointy), a texture (rough, or silky, or feathery), a consistency (dense, or airy, or gunky), a color, a temperature, or several of these qualities combined. You might also sense movement. The combination of quasi-sensory qualities might suggest to your mind a more concrete image, which becomes a symbol of the feeling—for example "tiptoeing over thin ice" or "a pressure cooker about to explode" or even "a little demon sitting on my shoulder." When we dream, these symbols arise automatically. While awake, we are more conscious of thinking them up. Dreams and waking metaphors are how your subtle body conveys what it knows to your rational mind.

So what *does* the subtle body know? It is good at perceiving moods and emotions, qualities, meanings, trends, and connections. Compared to your physical senses, it's not so good at perceiving hard facts. It can usually tell when someone is lying to you, but it can't always discover the exact truth. It's better at telling you how you lost your confidence than where to find your keys. If you were a lawyer, it wouldn't be much help in passing the bar exam, but you'd want to consult it when selecting a jury. If you were a doctor, it wouldn't be a substitute for X-rays, but it might help you know what part of a patient you needed to take a closer look at. A construction engineer has little need for subtle information. An artist or therapist couldn't function without it.

Have you ever wondered why psychics have to do readings for a living? You might think that, being psychic, they could just choose the winning lottery number and be set for life. The reason they can't is that the subtle senses can only arrive at factual information by combining qualitative impressions. They might correctly guess that a client is recently widowed by sensing sadness, loneliness, and a lingering connection to the subtle body of the deceased. But they couldn't tell you the widow's social security number, because that has no qualities, no meaning. When mentalists ("mind readers" who perform on stage) astonish their audiences by guessing such specific data, they are relying on carefully guarded tricks of the profession. They're getting the information through their *physical* senses. In fact, too much fact-like information is a tip-off that a "psychic" is phony or that an occultist is a charlatan. A genuine clairvoyant might be able to tell from Krishnamurti's aura (the impression given by his subtle body) that he was spiritually gifted. But to predict exactly what he would do when he grew up was overreaching. As history demonstrates, no one knew.

While I have been contrasting physical sense perceptions with subtle perceptions, we don't experience a firm border between them. Perception is more like a continuum. Take the sense of hearing, for example. The range of audible frequencies varies somewhat from person to person, as does the ability to perceive sounds at very low volume. All of that depends entirely on your physical equipment. Some people are tone deaf, others have perfect pitch, and there is a range of accuracy in between. Here we are getting into a more subtle area: an ability to discriminate fine differences in quality. Yet you still need ears to have perfect pitch. The sense of rhythm is more subtle still. While it is usually combined with hearing, you could still have an excellent sense of rhythm if you were deaf. Rhythm is actually a subtle rather than a physical sense. Even more subtle is the ability to "hear" words that haven't been spoken aloud, as some poets "hear" when they are inspired, or as Muhammad "heard" the angel Gabriel.

Our responses to other people are another example of a subtle continuum. At the most physical end of the spectrum, you recognize a face by its features: this is Joe. Then you observe that the face is smiling: Joe is happy. Perhaps, despite the smile, you sense that Joe is worried. How can you tell? Your subtle body is picking up something about Joe's subtle body that contrasts with the physical smile. More subtle still is to pick up on Joe's worry when he is not physically present, as you very well might if you are his parent or spouse. If your subtle perception is especially acute, you might continue to receive impressions of what Joe is feeling after he has died. We think of people who perceive at the far end of the subtle continuum as psychics or clairvoyants. They have the same perceptual equipment everyone else has; they're just better at using it. Subtle perception is a learnable skill. You can get good at it, too.

The Myth of Pure Perception

If everyone has a subtle body, why isn't subtle perceiving as universal as seeing, hearing, and smelling? Our eyesight goes on working whether we believe in it or not, yet those who question the existence of the "third eye" tend not to have the sort of perceptions that are attributed to it. They would argue that if perception depends on belief, it's not really perception at all. What we truly perceive is objectively *there*, regardless of how we feel about it.

This notion of objectivity conceives of the physical senses as passive recording devices, like video cameras or tape recorders. We grant that what we wish or hope to see might cause us to hallucinate, or to misinterpret what is before our eyes. But if desire and expectation are eliminated, we tend to assume that our eyes are just taking pictures like a camera, and that pictures don't lie. In other words, we equate perceptual passivity with objectivity. If we eliminate all other cognitive activities and just fix our eyes on something, we assume we are having a pure and unadulterated sense perception.

Stage illusionists expose the fallacy of this belief and exploit it for the amusement of their audiences. Let's take a very basic sleight-of-hand maneuver as an example. The magician holds up his left fist and places a small foam-rubber ball atop the circle formed by his thumb and fore-finger. With his right index finger, he stuffs the ball into the fist. Then he holds up the fist and blows into it. One by one, he opens his fingers. The ball has vanished.

It's done like this: While the right index finger is descending, the magician uses the middle finger to slip the ball into the palm of the right hand. This action is all but imperceptible, but it's happening in plain view. If you caught it on film and replayed it in slow motion, you'd see the palming of the ball. Does this mean that the hand is quicker than the eye? Not exactly. It doesn't actually matter what the eye sees or doesn't see, because the magician is leading the mind to *misremember* what is seen. While the middle finger is doing its inconspicuous job, the index finger is making a big fuss of pushing its way into the left fist. The mind interprets this as stuffing the ball, and so "remembers" that the ball is in the left hand.

Physical perception involves a slight time lag. Visual impressions reach our eyes at the speed of light; auditory impressions come to us at the slower speed of sound. From eye or ear to brain is a journey so swift as to be barely measurable, yet it does take some infinitesimal unit of time. Thus, whatever we perceive with our physical senses is already in the past. Your first glimpse of a thing is your earliest memory of it. By alter-ing your memory, the illusionist alters your perception. Even if the trick is explained to you afterward, you will not be able to recall seeing what actually happened. In effect you *didn't* see it, for what occurred before your eyes left no impression on your brain. What you remember instead is your interpretation of what occurred.

We loosely agree that the account of an honest eyewitness to an event gives us the objective facts about it. Yet if multiple witnesses are interviewed separately, their accounts may vary so drastically that they scarcely seem to be describing the same event at all. Interview them as a group instead and their stories tend to converge. Perception is socially mediated. Cues from other people help us to decide whether we should believe our eyes.

If you know any small children, you will have observed their efforts to adjust to the perceptual consensus. By the age of seven, most kids grasp the distinction between "real" and "imaginary" and are busy sorting everything they encounter into these two categories. A friend that other people can't see is an "imaginary friend." An ache in the physical body is real, while an ache in the subtle body is "psychosomatic" (i.e., imaginary). When adults agree that a perception is real, they tell the child the name for it. They may also interpret it by analogy to something already familiar to the child. Without this interpretive help, kids can't make much sense of their subtle perceptions and eventually come to ignore them.

This is not to imply that adults are to blame for the loss of subtle perception, for it happens to children even in cultures where adult clairvoyance is widespread and taken for granted. No matter how they're raised, children over six or seven exhibit a strong preference for the physical senses. During the time when we are learning to survive in the physical world, the physical senses must necessarily predominate. The renewed stirring of subtle perception in adolescence contributes to the awkwardness of our teen years. We feel crazy when we sense things that we've never learned the names for.

Think of brain-based cognition as a filing system. New items of information are filed with similar items to facilitate later retrieval. Where no similar items exist, the brain tends to discard the information rather than create a new file folder. Have you ever noticed that, right after you add a new word to your vocabulary, you hear it or see it in print several more times? A word you considered obscure before you looked it up in the dictionary suddenly seems to have come into common use. In fact, it always was. You just weren't hearing it before. Since to perceive a thing is, in a sense, to remember it for the first time, we often fail to perceive the unfamiliar. Our brain doesn't know where to file it. It is said that Eskimos have many different words for "snow" because they observe snow more closely than we do. You could just as reasonably say that Eskimos are better at observing snow because they have more file folders for it. That is also one reason why people who believe in a subtle world are more likely to have subtle perceptions: they've got the folders to hold them.

I've already given you a handful of empty folders ("style," "subtle body," and "the between"), and there are more to come. You'll notice that I seem to circle around such terms rather than defining them succinctly.

You might be feeling that your intellect can't quite get a handle on what they mean. That's because the names refer to phenomena you might not have noticed yet. Learning the names will help you to be on the alert for subtle perceptions that your brain would otherwise discard. A year from now, you still might not be able to define a word, but your folder will be fat with the experiences it names.

Your Attention, Please

Some mentalists and pseudo-psychics employ a method called "cold reading." One of their techniques is to prompt the subject to divulge information without quite realizing that they are doing so. For instance, the reader might say tentatively, "You don't like to cook, do you?" If the subject replies, "I love to cook," the reader continues, "Yes, I was getting an image of you in a kitchen." If they say, "No, I hate cooking," the psychic replies, "Right. I was picking up that you're not really the domestic type." Given this sort of spin, even a wild guess can wind up looking like uncanny accuracy. But skilled cold readers do not guess wildly. They base their speculations on precise observation of the subject. Some practitioners of cold reading eventually come to believe that they actually are psychic. I'd be very surprised if they weren't. Everyone possesses subtle senses, and one of the best ways to activate them is to pay close attention. If you start at the physical end of the perceptual continuum and persist until you've exhausted it, the subtle senses begin to pick up where the physical ones leave off.

Attention is selectivity applied to perception. It is an inward decision, usually made unconsciously, about what is worth perceiving and what isn't. Attention both finds meaning and creates meaning. When we adopt the principle of "separate the subtle from the gross," we are deciding on purpose where we want our attention to go, temporarily withholding it from what is obvious and bestowing it instead on what is inconspicuous and elusive.

In the world of spirit, attention is the equivalent of physical movement. It carries us toward the knowledge and acquaintances we seek and away from influences that we have determined to be harmful or useless. If you can't control your attention, you can't move properly, can't get where you want to go when you want to go there. To the extent that you allow your attention to be jerked around by whatever happens to be manifesting most insistently, you look to other spiritual beings like a spastic. Control of attention is thus the first skill an aspiring magician must master, and perhaps the most important.

Let's return to the rubber-ball trick as an example. The illusionist makes you believe that the ball is in his left hand by drawing your attention to the left. That will only happen if his own attention is directed there as well. The difficult maneuver of palming the ball in what the magicians call the "guilty hand" must be practiced incessantly until muscle memory alone will accomplish it. If the magician's attention is at all distracted by what the guilty hand is doing, the illusion doesn't work. Another way to put it is that the magician must ignore what is happening on a gross level and concentrate on an imaginary reality that, if all goes well, his own concentration renders convincing. If you attempted the chair exercise on page 37, you were doing something quite similar. You were dismissing all the interesting mental pictures that "chair" evokes and focusing instead on a subtle reality that only emerges when the chair pictures have been made to disappear. Difficult, isn't it? What we apprehend through the physical senses is vivid, interesting, and reassuringly real. By comparison, perceiving the subtle is like watching paint dry.

Contemporary students of alchemy enjoy many advantages over alchemists of the past. We have easy access to a staggering wealth of resources from every spiritual tradition on the planet. Yet we are poor in a resource that medieval alchemists would have considered too obvious and abundant to mention: free attention. Our whole culture seems to have come down with a case of Hyperactive Attention Deficit Disorder. Most of us live in an overstimulating environment. We are bombarded by abrasive, insistent, and often meaningless claims on our senses. To the extent that we allow our attention to be jerked around in this way, we are allowing our inner world to be created by others. We are permitting them to decide for us what is meaningful and what isn't. It's odd that Americans, who are so fierce in defense of freedom of will, raise no objection at all to this incessant trespassing on their freedom of attention.

If you think of attention as a form of wealth (a currency we rightly speak of "paying"), the average American gets robbed several times a minute.

Our attention gets hijacked by inner stimuli as well. How many of your thoughts do you actually decide to think? And, when you do consciously choose the topic, how long are you able to stick with it before the mind gets carried away by a chain of associations? Most of our thoughts are involuntary. We don't make them. They just show up. Our mental freedom consists in deciding which thoughts to pursue and which to let drop. Our individuality is expressed by the bestowing and withholding of our attention, rather than by the various thoughts that vie for it.

To appreciate the splendor and the wonder of watching paint dry, a person has to be more than a little bored. In fact, "boredom" is just a negative way of labeling free attention. It's what we say we're feeling on those increasingly rare occasions when our attention doesn't know what to do with itself. One simple way to free up some attention is to eliminate superfluous entertainment. Even a very busy life has moments in which nothing much is happening. The trick is to let nothing be nothing instead of trying to embellish it. Let your attention go naked while engaged in boring activities like commuting. Approach a long wait— on hold, in line, or at the dentist's office—without an amusement backup plan.

The best practice I know for developing control of attention is mindfulness meditation (see appendix 1 for instructions). It opens a space in which subtle perceptions can arise by teaching you to make friends with boredom. It also helps you to become intimately acquainted with your own mind. Self-knowledge is extremely important when you begin to encounter other beings in the subtle world. It's how you distinguish self from other when there are no physical bodies to define who's who and what's what.

Perception and Imagination

The biggest difficulty beginners seem to have with clairvoyance is that they don't know how to recognize a subtle perception when they're having one. It escapes their notice because they are expecting the subtle senses to be like the physical senses. Subtle impressions are difficult to put into words, so clairvoyants often describe them by analogy to something physical that has the same style. This could lead you to discount your own subtle perceptions—as Annie Besant did—because they are less concrete and vivid than the descriptions you've heard from others.

The human aura (a visual impression of the subtle body) is a good example. It is usually described as streaks of color surrounding the physical body. If that doesn't sound like anything you've ever seen, you probably conclude that you are unable to perceive auras. Nevertheless, you might have accurate intuitions about other people that you can't trace to anything they've said or done. If you're good at picking up "vibes," you are, in fact, getting information from the subtle bodies of others, even if you have no visual impression of them.

Each of the physical senses has a subtle counterpart. Imagination is the subtle sense of sight. It is an inner experience that has the same style as eyesight. What is perceived this way is usually described as "seen." Inspiration is akin to the sense of hearing. Subtle experience is described in terms of sounds or words that one has "heard." There are also subtle senses that correspond to taste, touch, smell, and temperature.

Let's say that three different people are attempting to practice energy healing by placing their hands on the part of the patient's body that most needs attention. One might see a particular color in the area of affliction. She is exercising the faculty of imagination, "seeing" the aura in visual terms. Another might have the thought, "Something is amiss with the liver." She is "hearing" words that convey what the aura "means." That's inspiration. The third might simply find her hands moving to the right side of the patient's torso. That's intuition. Whether the information is received through images, words, or the impulse to act, all three forms of perception get the job done.

So why do some people see colors? When a clairvoyant describes an aura as "blue" she is perceiving something that has the same *style* as blue, that evokes in her the same feeling as blue. When that feeling arises in her mind, the literal color arises simultaneously. You probably experienced something similar if you attempted the third style exercise in chapter 2 (see page 37). When you try to think the style of "chair," your mind keeps filling up with images of chairs you've actually seen.

You're not trying to make these literal chairs appear, but your brain is so used to associating the concept with the image that you keep getting chair pictures whether you want them or not.

Let's try a slightly different approach to meditating on the style of chair. Focus first on the process of sitting. When you sit, your weight shifts from your feet to your bottom. Your knees bend, and the back of the chair supports your own back, enabling it to relax. So think of "chair" not as an object, but as a process that facilitates the act of sitting. When I approach it this way, I find that I am able to hold the concept of "chair" without visualizing any particular examples.

If you practice this often enough, the pictures become less automatic. Between the thinking of an abstract concept and the viewing of a mental image, you will start to notice a slight time lag. If you focus your attention on that gap, you will witness the birth of your inner pictures, the fleeting moment in which the abstract gives rise to the concrete. You discover that you yourself are the creator of these images.

You can come to the same insight by watching what your mind does when you read a novel. When the author describes a tall, dark, handsome stranger, you get a mental picture. That picture is not identical to the one in the writer's imagination. It is conjured out of whatever previously seen images the words "tall, dark, handsome" evoke in you. The author might be picturing Clark Gable but you (okay, *I*) see Adrien Brody. The mental image is a co-creation of the author's words and the pictures your brain already has on file.

What would it be like to read a novel without making mental pictures? Would you enjoy it? Would the story move you? Would you still remember it a year later? Would you even be able to follow the plot? The physical senses help us to comprehend, to remember, and to *care*. Pure abstraction doesn't engage us for long. If the chair exercise required you to remember every chair you've ever owned or mentally design the perfect chairs for your dream house, you could stick with it for a long time. But the *style* of chair holds little human interest. You're doing very well if you manage to concentrate on it for three minutes.

When sensory input is absent, as it is in the subtle world, we use our imaginations to simulate it. We render the subtle a little *less* subtle so that, as physical beings, we can focus on it, remember it, and care about it. In this way, the imagination builds a bridge between the physical body and the subtle body. For the hermeticist, a lively imagination is a great asset. It is what makes the subtle world feel as real to you as the material world. It is how you eventually come to feel that your spiritual life is your *real* life.

We are used to making a firm distinction between what we see and what we imagine. But physical seeing also involves the imagination. When I look at what I'm wearing, my eyes send impulses through the optic nerve to my brain, which interprets these impulses as "blue jeans" and presents me with a mental picture. I am actually perceiving my brain activity, not my blue jeans, just as I would be if I "saw" blue streaks in somebody's aura or daydreamed about a blue moon. In the case of blue jeans, the information comes to the brain by way of my physical eyes. In the case of the aura, it comes by way of my subtle senses. In the case of the blue moon, it is produced by a deliberate act of imagination. In all three cases, the end result is a mental image.

But, you protest, the blue jeans are really *there*. I could be an episte-mological smarty pants and ask, "How do you know?" All one can really perceive is one's own brain activity, not the jeans themselves. But I won't persist with that argument because, to be perfectly frank, I, too, am convinced that the blue jeans are really there. (If they're not, I want my money back.) We feel sure that a thing is really there when we know that we did nothing, mentally, to put it there. When my deliberate imagining stops, the blue moon disappears. The blue jeans don't.

And what of the blue aura? It is more like the blue moon than the blue jeans, because I can make the blue appear or disappear at will. Yet, should I imagine blue, it would be because something was coming to me through my subtle senses that had the style of blue, that seemed more blue than green, or yellow, or black. In translating a subtle perception into something more like a physical perception, I am interpreting it. If I can make the blue come and go, I am aware that it is an interpretation. I recognize my own role in putting it there.

But what if I *can't* make the blue go away? By the standards we apply to our physical senses, that would mean the blue is "really there." We know that we're not just imagining a physical perception because it stays put. With the subtle world, though, it's exactly the opposite. Unthinking

a mental picture *should* make it go away. If the object of a subtle perception appears to be as solid, permanent, and fact-like as a physical object,
the seer is hallucinating.

Some people hallucinate because they're physically or mentally un-
well. But hallucinations can also be a function of what hermeticists call
"atavistic clairvoyance." Atavistic clairvoyants are overtaken by visions
that seem very solid and real because they don't consciously experience
the mental translation of the abstract into the pictorial. It happens too
fast. Since they don't notice that their brains are interpreting subtle
input, they can't correct a mistaken interpretation. Their subtle perceptions are *too* convincing.

It's not unusual for the subtle faculties to get off to an atavistic start.
Assuming there's no underlying pathology, the problem is easy to fix.
The conversion of subtle impressions into mental images needs to be
slowed down or suppressed altogether for a time, so that it stops happening automatically. (Alcohol is the traditional suppressant of choice.
Mindfulness meditation is more reliably effective, if not quite as much
fun.) It's a bit like closing your eyes. The eyes themselves still work, but
they've temporarily stopped sending messages to the brain. Then you
can start over, learning to imagine on purpose.

What I'm saying might disconcert you, for many people assume that
the more "psychic" you are, the more solid and fact-like your subtle perceptions will be. But the subtle world is just that: *subtle*. Nothing there
can be seen, heard, or touched. These sensory qualities are supplied—
consciously or unconsciously—by our imaginations. When you imagine on purpose, you are less likely to be misled by your mental pictures,
because you know you're making them up. When you understand how
the conversion process works, you are also less likely to be misled by the
mental pictures of others.

Let me give you a personal example. It seems that every time I meet
a clairvoyant, she hauls off and tells me about one of my previous incarnations. The first of these accounts, set in medieval times, was especially vivid. I was some sort of spiritual leader who ran afoul of the
Inquisition. A former boyfriend in this lifetime was, back then, my archenemy. He presided over my torture and sentenced me to be beheaded.

Another clairvoyant set her story in the American West of the nine-teenth century. This time I was a healer, having learned herbal medicine from Native American shamans. Again, I had an archenemy, his wicked face adorned with a black handlebar mustache. He had me condemned to death for practicing alternative medicine. That time I was hanged. A third version of the story was set in seventeenth-century England. Then, too, I was a healer, and I got hanged for witchcraft.

If all three stories are true, martyrdom would seem to be my customary method of leaving the planet. It's a wonder I have the nerve to reincarnate at all! Actually, I doubt that any of the stories are true in a factual sense. From a historical perspective, the first two are implausible. Victims of the Inquisition generally died by burning, not beheading. As far as I know, the practice of alternative medicine has never been a capital crime in the United States. What interests me, though, are the common elements in all three tales: spiritual teaching or healing, an enemy, opposition by the Establishment, and an unjust death involving trauma to the neck. The plot of my first published novel (which, to my knowledge, none of the psychics had read) contains these elements as well. What arose in the imaginations of three different clairvoyants as they perceived my subtle body, arose in my own imagination while I was writing fiction.

If I were to take literally the lurid tales of my past incarnations, I could only conclude that I have every good reason to keep a low profile in this one. But I regard them as highly imaginative ways of describing anxieties that are apparent to anyone who can perceive my subtle body. The fifth chakra, located in the neck area, is associated with self-expression. Fear that speaking out will get me in trouble dates back to my childhood in *this* lifetime. I feel terribly guilty when I believe I've said something wrong. This is the subtle reality that the psychics were picking up. All three stressed in their stories that my punishment had been unjust. By understanding the stories as symbolic communications, I am able to get the message that my guilt is inappropriate and that I should work on overcoming it.

Madame Blavatsky's cosmology is another example of true subtle perception decked out in fictitious imagery. The notion that all the great spiritual philosophers from Plato to Jesus to Lao Tzu should be camped out together somewhere in the Himalayas is absurd. The myth was nevertheless compelling to intelligent people because Blavatsky didn't invent it out of whole cloth. You will find some version of it in nearly every culture and religious tradition on earth. The essential idea is that great spiritual leaders continue to influence humanity after they have died, not just through their written works and the memory of their deeds on earth, but by directly inspiring the living in real time. In other words, you can meet them in your head. Many people who have had such encounters report that these great spirits appear to be acquainted with one another. If you meet one, you are likely to be introduced to others. Raphael depicted this inner reality in his famous painting, *The School of Athens*. I am alluding to something like it when I speak of the "hermetic network." Unfortunately, many of Blavatsky's followers took her stories literally. One of them even set off on foot to meet the Himalayan Masters on his own. His frozen body was eventually discovered by Nepalese sherpas, a casualty of the failure to separate the subtle from the gross.

The imaginations that we create deliberately or that arise spontaneously in response to subtle perception are not facts, but they can nevertheless be true in the way the best works of fiction are true. Good fiction writers know that they can't just make up any old thing they please. There are true fictions and false fictions, and only the true ones are believable and moving. Take for example, the screenplay for a romantic comedy. The basic formula couldn't be simpler: a man and a woman get off on the wrong foot, go through a series of conflicts and misunderstandings before discovering, at the very end of the movie, that they are in love. Many such movies fall flat, because the formula is not so easy to execute in a believable way. If the conflicts are more convincing than the romantic chemistry, we begin to suspect that the characters are truly all wrong for each other, and we don't buy the happy ending. If the chemistry rings true, but not the conflicts, we become exasperated with the characters for failing to see the obvious. Either way, the audience can wind up feeling manipulated by the formula. In a really great romantic comedy, though, both the attraction and the obstacles feel real. We are in suspense about how it will turn out, and we also laugh our heads off, because the movie is saying something about man-woman relationships that resonates with our own experience. It feels true. Not true fact, but true meaning.

Unreliable Sources

A few years ago, the Bey brothers made an appearance in an online discussion group. Their channeled posts, written in a pompous and antiquated style, were annoyingly irrelevant to the hermetic discussion at hand, so we expelled the authors on the grounds that membership was open only to the incarnate. Since the Beys were a fictional creation of Madame Blavatsky, it is logical to suspect their channeler of a deliberate hoax. But I am inclined to believe he was sincere, because he misspelled their name as "Bee." This suggests that it had been "heard" rather than read. The channeler was having a genuine subtle perception of beings who originally existed only in the imagination of HPB.

That sort of thing happens a lot. Remember the collective thought atmosphere I described in chapter one? Another name for it is the "astral plane." Think of it as the lost and found of the human psyche. When thoughts, feelings, and fantasies become detached from their original owners, they end up in the astral. Often this is because they have been discarded as junk. Other thoughts are projected into the astral deliberately—as advertising, propaganda, or art. How long and how vividly a thought lingers there depends on the concentration and imaginative force of its original thinker. Great artists, leaders, and magicians are particularly adept at creating astral phenomena. Madame Blavatsky was a genius at it. Her fictional creations live on not only in her books and in the oral tradition of Theosophy, but in the astral.

When I was nineteen and going through a phase of atavistic clairvoyance, I "saw" the Akashic Chronicle. The border between dreaming and waking was a bit fuzzy for me in those days, so I'm not sure whether I was asleep or in a trance. I was doing homework in my apartment on a sunny afternoon and next thing I knew I was in some room I'd never seen before. There was nothing in this room except an old-fashioned manual typewriter with a long roll of paper coming out of its carriage. Though no one else seemed to be present, I was somehow given to understand that if I read this document, I would know the history of all my past incarnations and those of everyone else in the world. Something about this felt bogus to me, so I decided to give it a pass. Next thing I knew, I was back in my apartment doing homework.

The typewriter with its roll of paper was a fixture of my own imagination. I'd read that Jack Kerouac had devised such a setup because he wrote very fast and didn't like stopping to put a fresh page in the carriage. But the notion of what the typewriter was recording could not have come from me. In those days, I was a Catholic. I didn't believe in reincarnation, had never heard of the Akashic Chronicle, and wasn't even curious enough to read the thing when given the opportunity. The perception existed independently of my desire or previous expectation. It was really there, a fact. Yet, as I vaguely sensed back then and now know for sure, it was also a falsehood. I was having a genuine perception of a fraud.

It is reason, not perception, that tells me the Akashic Chronicle is bogus. Every document must have an author, and every author has a point of view. Each person who knows me well would tell a different story of my life. My own memory of it shifts with my moods and with my audience. As time passes, my notion of what life events were significant changes, and I forget a lot. I am not competent to record a complete and accurate account of *yesterday,* much less the rest of this lifetime, or all the hypothetical lives I might have led. So who in the world is the author of this so-called Akashic Chronicle? Who is qualified to tell not only my complete story but that of every other human being? It would have to be God, for only God is omniscient. Now, think about it. Is it likely that God would submit such a document for review by a nineteen-year-old space case? Or offer it to a sexual abuser of children such as C.W. Leadbetter? The Akashic Chronicle is a scam. But don't be surprised if you run into it in the astral. If you go looking, you'll probably find Saddam's weapons of mass destruction there as well.

Some of our subtle perceptions are direct, as when we pick up feelings coming from the subtle bodies of other people. We might also pick up thought forms that have become detached from their original thinkers and are floating around in the astral, "breathing them in" from the collective thought atmosphere. Other subtle perceptions are personally communicated to us by subtle beings. You won't always be able to tell that a being is involved, for they may communicate by stimulating the subtle body. Your brain processes this just as it does any other subtle stimulation: by forming a verbal thought or mental picture. We perceive the message, not the messenger.

Mediated information is only as reliable as its source. Some messengers are misinformed, and some are outright liars. Even those who are knowledgeable and truthful can be quite opinionated: what you learn from them has a definite slant. This is especially true of ghosts, who are the easiest beings for the neophyte clairvoyant to perceive. Since they themselves are subtle bodies, they're plainly evident to the subtle senses. Once they realize you can perceive them, you become very popular. Complete strangers may start throwing Halloween parties in your head.

Ghosts tend to have issues. A lot of them are unhappy that their presence goes ignored. They feel left out. If they're still hanging around years after the physical body has died, it's usually because they feel they have unfinished business or some attachment to their former life that they can't seem to relinquish. Some of them are still trying to live through the living. Others just like to be helpful. Meeting one of these can be a boon. (An accountant friend of mine was accompanied to an audit by the ghost of a former IRS agent who gave her excellent advice.) A common tactic of ghosts who crave attention is to render their human subject impressively psychic, for ghosts are privy to a lot of gossip. I might have wound up dependent on such a ghost had I taken the Akashic bait.

Channeling is all the rage these days among ghosts who enjoy showing off. If you find that some being is attempting to hijack your voice or your pen, you can be certain it's a ghost. Beings of the hermetic network don't channel themselves. They consider it rude to monopolize the conversation and treat an incarnate human as a stenographer. If a living person attempted such a thing, we'd never stand for it, yet channelers seem to regard it as an honor. This misapprehension is the result of believing that every subtle being is a spirit guide, and every spirit guide is transcendently wise. I have also noticed a tendency to assume, as Madame Blavatsky did, that all good spiritual beings share the same agenda, and that the proper role of incarnate humans is to get with their program. Actually, the spiritual world is like this one, only more so. There are lots of different cultures, different personalities, and different agendas. Very little that an individual subtle perceiver learns of it can be said to be universal.

Suppose aliens send three different expeditions to planet Earth. One group lands in Antarctica, one in the Amazon rain forest, and one in Amsterdam. Each explorer returns to the home planet purporting to be an expert on ours. Imagine how their descriptions differ! Yet each sounds authoritative, and deservedly so, because his knowledge is based on firsthand experience. Whatever each of these aliens says is quite true—*as far as their particular location goes*. Still, it would be most unfortunate if the Amsterdam expedition launched a jihad against the Amazon crew, or the Amazon team subjected the Antarctic explorers to an inquisition. The same goes for our experiences of the spiritual world. If yours differs drastically from someone else's, it doesn't necessarily mean that one of you is wrong. You're probably just visiting different regions.

When it comes to the physical senses, social consensus helps us to keep our perceptions within accepted norms. What they tell us is either true, or so widely believed that it will serve as a workable stand-in for the truth. There are fewer such norms for subtle perception. In a world where many people regard *all* subtle perception as flaky, how can you tell whether your *particular* perception is flaky? How can you tell if it's coming from a reliable source?

There are no easy answers. Discernment is the work of a lifetime and along the way you will make many errors. My own whopping bloopers are too embarrassing to commit to print. But I will pass on three helpful hints that I learned the hard way. I hope they will spare you some trouble.

1. *Use your physical senses to check the facts*. If you want to know facts, look to the material world. Your physical senses are the best equipment for determining what's true on a factual level. What the subtle world has to teach us is the *meaning* of facts—their significance, their implications, and the relationship of one fact to another. In the mundane world, academic disciplines that deal with meaning are not subjected to the same laws of proof as the sciences. We evaluate thoughts about meaning based on their logical consistency, persuasiveness, and helpfulness. Subtle intuitions about meaning should be evaluated in the same way. You can regard them as trustworthy if they are helping you to make

sense of your life. But fact-like information obtained clairvoyantly should be treated skeptically until confirmed by ordinary material methods of investigation. If a subtle intuition contradicts material facts, it is false.

A well-regarded hermeticist once asserted, based on his clairvoyant research, that the Jesuits were "the driving force behind the Spanish Inquisition." This rumor, which has been floating around the astral for centuries, is not supported by historical evidence. The Spanish Inquisition began in 1478. Ignatius of Loyola, the founder of the Jesuit Order, was born thirteen years later, in 1491. Ignatius and his early followers were frequently harassed by the Inquisition and were even imprisoned by it on several occasions. In this matter, clairvoyant intuition must yield to the findings of ordinary historians.

It is important to make a distinction between what scientists and other scholars haven't affirmed or explained *yet* and what they have definitively disproved. The intuitions we receive from the subtle senses often leap ahead of scientific or scholarly work. Indeed, most scientific hypotheses arise from intuitive leaps. In the past, healers discovered many botanical remedies through the use of their subtle senses. While the contemporary biochemist and the medieval herbalist offer very different explanations of *why* these medicines work, science has begun to demonstrate that the herbalists were indeed on to something. The fact that an intuition has not been proven true by science is not grounds for discarding it. But once an intuition has been proven *false*, the clairvoyant, like the scientist, must defer.

2. Enlist a guide. Beings perceived through the subtle senses rarely introduce themselves by name. Usually they just drop unsigned messages into your subtle in-box. An intuition pops into your head, and you have no idea where it came from. That's fine when it happens spontaneously, but if you're seeking advice on a matter of importance, you would like the source to be wise and to have your best interests at heart. Some people ask for guidance from "the Universe." That's like standing on the fifty yard line during half-time of the Super Bowl and shouting, "Would someone please tell me what to do?" Ghosts and other astral opportunists are sure to take the bait.

Eventually you will develop relationships with invisible friends and teachers. Even if you never give them any name but "you," both you and they will know which "you" you mean. Until then, it's a good idea to enlist a guide to help fend off unwanted attention, just as you might when traveling in a country where mobs of people are pestering you and hoping to rip you off. If you're Catholic, this is easy, for the church has an official guide corps called the saints. You don't have to be Catholic to avail yourself of their services. Just get a book of lives of the saints, pick one you like, and invoke him or her by name. In polytheistic religions, devotion to a particular deity serves the same purpose, while the spirit guides in many Native American traditions take the form of totemic animals. You could also ask Archangel Raphael to put you in touch with your guardian angel or request that Archangel Michael protect you from bad influences. Just be sure to use a specific saint or angel or deity name that you've heard of from some reputable tradition (i.e., *not* Koot Hoomi). The names are traditional because they've been proven to work. The one exception is your personal angel who will answer to any name you choose. The safest way to make initial contact, though, is to call on Raphael who will ensure that the guide you get is really your angel and not some ghostly imposter.

3. *Mind your own business.* Beings who truly have something to teach are drawn to incarnate people who know how to ask an intelligent question and have some practical use for the answer. Esoteric knowledge of healing is imparted to those who work in a healing profession. Scientific hypotheses are suggested to scientists. Artistic inspirations are offered to practicing artists. Insights into child development are given to parents and teachers.

It is much easier to perceive messages in your own field of expertise because you know the sort of thing you're looking for. You've got the file folders. And because you know your field, it is easier to distinguish a genuine insight from a bum steer. You can test the idea you've been given to see if it works.

When clairvoyants stray into falsehood and flakiness, it is almost always because they are attempting to investigate matters that are none of their business. Do you really need to know the history of the root races or the previous incarnations of your next door neighbor? In the unlikely event that you were to be given genuine insights into these matters, what would you do with them? How would you go about confirming or refuting them?

In the material world, too, we are curious about all sorts of things that are really none of our business. We don't need to know about the personal life of our favorite movie star, yet it's hard to resist reading headlines about it in the supermarket checkout line. The journalists who pander to our voyeurism are notorious for their lack of allegiance to the truth. The same holds true for informants in the subtle world. Those who indulge our idle curiosity are, for the most part, misinformed show-offs.

The most reliable informants are spirits, not ghosts. Communicating with them requires that you connect with your own spirit. In the next chapter, we will be approaching this connection through abstract thinking rather than through the subtle senses. These two approaches are largely independent of each other. Many psychics and mediums are excellent subtle perceivers yet have little or no access to the thoughts of spirits. The reverse is also true. People who excel at abstract thinking often move freely in the world of spirit even if their subtle faculties remain dormant. So don't worry about how the next chapter fits with this one. They're not meant to fit. This one was addressed to your subtle body. The next one is addressed to your spirit.

Your spirit, like all spirits, is a genius. Its IQ is off the charts. In order to comprehend what it knows and what other spirits know, you have to teach your ordinary mind to keep up. That's what we'll be working on in the next chapter. Don't be discouraged if you find it heavy going. What you read will jump-start a process that occurs mainly in sleep. If you reread the chapter a few months from now, it won't seem so difficult.

Cultivating the Imagination

We all imagine well when we daydream because our fantasies are enlivened by the wishes they fulfill. A hermeticist, though, needs to be able to imagine vividly in the absence of emotion or desire. A traditional exercise for doing this is called "composition of the place." The idea is to establish a physical setting within your imagination—

someplace entirely made up—experience it with all five senses, and return to it repeatedly.

Start small—a single room, modest house, or walled garden. As your powers of concentration improve, you can always "build" an addition or acquire more land. Furnish or landscape this space to your taste and with great attention to detail. If you mentally hang curtains in the windows, be sure to design the curtain rods as well. If there are bookshelves, see the titles and bindings of the books. A garden will need bird, animal, and insect species as well as plants. Since it's a made-up garden, you're free to have both parrots and polar bears if you like, so long as you provide each with imaginary food and habitat.

Bring all of your senses to bear on this imaginary place. Feel its temperature, notice the ambient sounds, the smells, the textures, and so forth. Walk around and view it from different vantage points. (Notice what your feet feel as you are doing this.) Discover how things look from the back as well as from the front.

Return to this place in your imagination for a few minutes every day. Visit it at different imaginary times—dawn, noon, dusk, midnight, and in different imaginary seasons. Note changes in the temperature, background sounds, intensity and angle of the light, and so forth. Also make some changes of your own. Rearrange the knick-knacks on the coffee table, prune a shrub, or paint a fence. Upon your return, try to find the place exactly as you left it.

4

Levity and Gravity
Navigating the Vertical World

SUPPOSE YOU GOT LOST in a wilderness where there were no trail markers and no one to ask for directions. You'd probably want to climb to the highest point in the landscape and look down. When we're disoriented in the physical world, our first instinct is to try to get an overview.

The same thing happens in our inner lives. Here's how Dante described it in the opening passage of his *Divine Comedy:*

In the middle of the journey of our life, I came to myself within a dark wood where the straight way was lost. Ah, how hard a thing it is to tell of that wood, savage and harsh and dense, the thought of which renews my fear! So bitter it is that death is hardly more.

I cannot rightly tell how I entered there, I was so full of sleep at that moment when I left the true way; but when I had reached the foot of a hill at the end of that valley which had pierced my heart with fear, I looked up and saw its shoulders already clothed with beams of the planet that leads men straight on every road.*

*Trans. John D. Sinclair (New York: Oxford University Press, 1939).

Having become lost in his earthly life, Dante feels a stirring of hope when he looks *up*. He realizes that the "true way" can only be discovered by moving vertically.

When we stop to think about it, we know that the spiritual world is not really above us in the geographical sense. In the physical universe, as modern people conceive of it, nothing is higher or lower than anything else. At best, celestial bodies can only be described as closer in or farther out, relative to our subjective position as occupants of planet Earth. When we regard Earth from some arbitrary reference point elsewhere in the universe, it's just a speck orbiting another speck.

We know full well that God is not in the sky. Yet when speaking of God, modern people, just like the ancients, tend to cast their eyes upward. Our everyday language is full of expressions that associate the spiritual with the vertical—*up* expressions like "high-minded," "uplifting," "raising consciousness," and "head in the clouds;" *down* expressions like "base motives," "fall from grace," and "down-to-earth." When making value judgments like these, we instinctively locate them on an imaginary vertical axis. We intuit something in the spiritual world that has the *style* of up, even if it isn't up in the literal, physical sense.

Some years ago, I was studying with a hermeticist who offered a correspondence course in how to perceive the spiritual world. His method of teaching was to e-mail you a riddle. If you gave a bad answer, he'd hint at what was wrong with it, but apart from that, you were on your own. You couldn't move forward until you'd returned an answer that he found satisfactory.

The first riddle went like this: "There is a door to the spiritual world. Find the words that open it."

I was stumped by this for a good two weeks and obsessed with finding a solution. I tried every form of meditation I knew. I pored over spiritual texts. I tried writing as fast as my pen would move in the hope that the answer would somehow spill from my subconscious. I took long walks, but could not have told you where I'd been or what I'd seen, for my concentration on the riddle rendered me oblivious to the outside world. At night I slept fitfully, alert to my dreams lest the answer appear there. I stopped returning phone calls, lost my appetite, and wore the same outfit for days.

As so often happens, the solution finally came when I gave up looking for it. A friend cooked me a very nice dinner, and I suddenly realized I was famished. I ate a lot, drank a lot, and became so drowsy that I conked out while he was washing the dishes. When I came to, maybe a half hour later, these magic words were dancing in my head: "We hold these truths to be self-evident, that all men are created equal."

From a mundane perspective, nothing could be *less* evident than the equality of people. What immediately strikes us when we look at others are their differences. According to any standard you can think of—beauty, health, intelligence, athletic prowess, wealth, talent, virtue—some are quite obviously better than others. Yet we all have a sense of what "all men are created equal" means, and no amount of contradictory evidence will dissuade us from *believing* what it means. When we see it as true—and not merely true, but perfectly obvious—our perspective is not mundane. We are seeing human life as it appears from *above*.

I had always thought the words were penned by Thomas Jefferson, but I recently learned that Benjamin Franklin was responsible for the magical part. Jefferson's first draft had read, "We hold these truths to be sacred." Franklin crossed out the "sacred" and substituted "self-evident." His stated rationale was that "sacred" sounded too much like an appeal to religion. "Self-evident" had a more secular ring, an appeal to nothing higher than human reason. To my way of thinking, his edit rendered the sentence *more* spiritual. The sacred is something we perceive when we are looking up. We are below, and it is above us, making us feel awed. When a truth appears self-evident rather than sacred, when it strikes us as nothing more than ordinary common sense, we are on the same level with it. We ourselves are "up." We are looking down on earthly life as the angels do and perceiving, as they do, the equality of the people there. With that seemingly minor edit, Franklin lifted an entire nation into the vertical dimension.

If you can understand what is meant by a statement like, "All men are created equal," you are already acquainted with the vertical world. You know it with that portion of your consciousness that you consider to be higher—your ideals, your values, your inspirations and aspirations. If you are capable of admiring—anyone or anything at all—you know the inward direction of *up*. This sense of "up" refers to the movement of the soul, not movement in physical space. Yet no matter how many times I repeat that the spiritual world is not really a *place*, you and I will both go on imagining it as such—the place we came from, the place we'll return after we die, the place we're often homesick for in the meantime. This inner sense of place is imbedded in our vocabularies because it is deeply imbedded in our psyches.

The ancestors from whom we have inherited this way of speaking didn't believe that God lived in the sky any more than you and I believe it. If anything, their inner sense of place was more sophisticated than our own. Ancient and medieval scholars, who could not afford to own many books, used it as a memory device. One of their tricks was to build a "memory palace" in the imagination. For each subject, they envisioned a room. Within each room were shelves, cupboards, chests of drawers, and so forth in which to store individual items of information. When they wished to recall something, they would imagine themselves retracing their steps in the memory palace to the exact spot where they had put the information away the last time they used it. Every idea had an inner "location." Many alchemical teachings come down to us from people who ordered their thoughts in this way. They understood the power of a good spatial metaphor to advance inner development and the power of a faulty one to hinder it.

In our own age, the predominant spatial metaphor for inner development is "the path"—an Asian import that accords well with American notions of getting ahead. Picture a path right now and consider its implications. What's at the end of it? Can you see the endpoint from the starting point? If not, how can you be sure you want to go there? Is there one path for everyone or are there different paths for different people? If a path is unique and individual, how would it come exist in the first place? (Real paths get made by many different feet following the same route to the same destination.)

Put some other people on your path. Where are they situated in relation to you? If the path is a straight line, some will be ahead and some behind. It is easy to perceive others' progress relative to your own. But suppose that instead of a straight line, the path describes a spiral. Advancing along a spiral entails a lot of doubling back. You might have to look behind you to see someone who is actually farther along. While both the straight line and the spiral are just metaphors, it matters which one you choose.

Another very common spatial motif is the circle. A mandala, for example, represents the spiritual world from the point of view of the figure at its center. The relative importance of other symbols or figures is indicated by their size and their spatial relationship to the central figure. You could picture your own spiritual life as a mandala with you in the center, filling the rest of the circle with other beings, significant experiences, and so forth.

Man-made structures can also be metaphors for the spiritual world. It might be imagined as a temple, a school, a palace, or a city. The "inner castle" of St. Teresa of Avila combines both structure and circle metaphors; its rooms are arranged in concentric rings. One advances by moving from the outermost to the innermost room.

The cross—a vertical axis transected by a horizontal one—is yet another way of describing inner space. While the Christian connotations of this shape are neither accidental nor irrelevant, the cross predates Christianity in the hermetic imagination and in the human imagination in general. As long as anyone can remember, people have been seeing the spiritual world in terms of up, down, and sideways. It is the spatial scheme underlying many important alchemical teachings.

You probably already have some mental images, however vague, of the spiritual world as a place. To sharpen and develop them will be of great benefit. A sense of "inner geography" helps us to connect the life of the body with the life of the spirit. It makes the inner life feel more concrete and real. It also helps us to stay oriented. When a spiritual problem crops up, knowing *where* it is may clue you in on *what* it is. It's similar to feeling confused by another person and asking, "Where are you at?" or "Where are you coming from?"

In this chapter, I'm going to be encouraging you to develop a very detailed and specific imagination of a cross-shaped world, a "geography" in which every inner event has a specific location. At the same time, you will be learning how to move within this inner world, how to operate the vehicle of your own consciousness so that it reliably takes you where you want to go. Later you might decide to replace this map with one that better describes your own inner experience. But the effort to imagine this one—even if it is not ultimately to your taste—will help you to understand the many alchemical teachings that are based on the idea of verticality. You will begin to recognize the procedures implied by the principle, "As above, so below."

One more thing before we begin. If you get tuckered out by this mental journey, it's not because you're unfit. Up-and-down movement is as tiring to the mind as it is to the body. In places, the climb is steep and the air thin. When you come to a section break, you might want to pitch a tent, roast some marshmallows, and get a good night's sleep. We're not in any hurry.

The Straight and Narrow

In Chicago, where I live, the streets are laid out according to a grid system. Madison Street marks the center of the north/south axis. If an address is 2100 North, you know that it is twenty-one blocks north of Madison. Hermeticists use a similar scheme to navigate the vertical. Picture a horizontal line. That's your Madison Street. It represents ordinary waking consciousness. Departures from ordinary consciousness carry us above or below the horizontal baseline. To travel safely, you need to know which direction you're going, for the "rules of the road" below the horizon line are different from those above it, and what happens below is different from what happens above.

In a cross, the horizontal dimension is represented by a line, but our subjective experience of it is more like a plane. The mind has lots of room to move around and many different objects of consciousness from which to choose. Our thoughts can spring ahead or double back, shift from side to side, or wander around in circles. Stop for a moment and imagine that your mental activity is being recorded as a doodle on a page. Or imagine that you're in a supermarket and your movements through the aisles are being drawn on its floor plan. Assuming your mind was entirely on your shopping, the squiggly line on the floor plan would pretty well map the sequence of your thoughts. This is what I mean when I describe an inner space as plane-like.

The vertical dimension is different. It truly is a line in the geometrical sense. But if that's too abstract, you might imagine it instead as a very narrow tube with an opening at the bottom that you can only just squeeze through. Once you're in the tube, you can't move at all from side to side. The only ways to move are up or down. You can look down through the hole at the bottom and see the horizontal plane below you. The higher up you go, the better your perspective of it. But you can't get a broad view of the vertical itself, because you're stuck in the tube. When you look at the vertical from ground level, all you can see of it is the narrow entry point.

The vertical extends below the horizontal plane as well as above it. If you're in the lower vertical and look up toward the horizontal, what you see is its underside. If the light source is above the whole setup (and let's suppose for the moment that it is), then the horizontal casts a deep shadow on the lower vertical. It's dark down there. The deeper you go into the lower vertical, the less perspective you have on the horizontal.

Now I'm going to draw a contrasting image to give you a better sense of what the vertical is *not*. Imagine yourself in a space capsule, able to see Earth as an object in space. Keep panning out till Earth is just one of a billion specks in the night sky. Does this perspective tell you anything useful about the meaning of your life? Probably not. The fact that you are perceiving vastness does not mean that your consciousness itself has enlarged. On the contrary, it is, at this moment, rather cowed by an infinity that makes any personal concern of yours seem ridiculously trivial. When we view Earth from the vantage point of some distant galaxy, all men are created equally small and do not appear to be endowed by their creator with much of anything. To contemplate the vastness of the universe is an interesting variation on *horizontal* consciousness. The mind is moving *out*, not up. If you're truly moving up, you don't feel small.

Some people conceive of the vertical world as a series of "inner planes." The planes are stacked, so that one is higher than another. But on each plane it is apparently possible to move laterally, as if it were another horizontal. Looking down from any given plane would give you a panoramic view of the one below. A picture of it would look something like this:

The "inner planes" idea might be a useful way of talking about the vertical from ground level, since it makes sense to horizontal consciousness. You could organize your memories of past vertical experiences by mapping them on various planes. But such a map is of no more use in navigating the vertical than a globe would be in trying to find your way to the restroom. If you feel like you're actually *on* a spiritual plane, you are, by definition, not moving vertically. There is nothing plane-like about vertical experience when you're actually having one.

In our imagination of a plane, things tend to stay put. You can ignore them, walk away from them, and they remain as you left them. You can certainly imagine a spiritual world like that, and people do so all the time. But you can't directly experience it, because in the vertical, nothing stays put. It's as if you had no peripheral vision. If you are not completely focused on something, you don't perceive it at all. As far as you can tell, it has disappeared. Consciousness narrows to a single point. It's a bit dark and claustrophobic, but in a nice way, like kissing with your eyes closed. Imagine a world where, the moment your mind wandered away from a kiss, the person you were kissing would vanish. That's what vertical experience is like.

We often use the word "see" as a synonym for "understand" because, out of all our physical senses, sight is the one that feels the clearest and most objective. We imagine spiritual sight to be pretty much like physical sight, only better. But the actual onset of spiritual sight feels a lot like going blind. To move vertically is to enter what mystics have called "the cloud of unknowing." While we are kissing someone, we can no longer see them. And we can only kiss one person at a time.

Friends in High Places

As I've been describing it so far, vertical consciousness sounds about as exciting as being stuck in an elevator. But suppose your companion in that elevator were someone like Jesus or Confucius or Einstein, and that during the ride, you had this great mind all to yourself. In the upper vertical, thinking becomes a tête-à-tête with another conscious being. We learn about the world of above by communing with its residents.

The beings we encounter most readily are those with whom we have something in common. Christians meet beings who correspond to their idea of the saints and the angels. Polytheists meet gods. People from cultures that venerate ancestors meet ancestors. People who think in terms of archetypes meet archetypal beings. People who don't believe in non-incarnate beings at all experience the upper vertical as a realm of ideas and ideals rather than personalities.

Your point of entry to the upper vertical is situated directly above wherever you happen to be standing in the horizontal. Thus, it is unique not only to you, but to the particular moment of entry. Though you are always in just one elevator car at a time, your consciousness focused on a single point, you can expand the range of vertical experiences you have over time by establishing multiple points of entry. Each new interest or experience in the horizontal is potentially a new elevator. For instance, if you study Taoism, you create a corresponding point of vertical entry through which you might start to encounter the spirits of Chinese sages. Though each vertical experience remains narrow, you feel like the vertical world has widened, because you can reach it through multiple adjacent entrances. It's like social life on earth. Mostly you phone or e-mail or text message your friends one at a time. But if you have lots of them, and some of them know each other, you feel like part of a network, even though most of your contacts are one on one.

The upper and lower verticals do not correspond precisely to the Christian notions of heaven and hell. A being is not necessarily good because you meet it above, or evil because you meet it below. Up and down refer to weight rather than merit. Not physical weight, obviously, but something spiritual that has the same style as weight. Beings who dwell upward of you are lighter than you. That is why they are so often depicted as winged.

Of course, you have no objective means of measuring the weight of another being. You simply judge it in relation to yourself. A being is light if, in order to meet it, your consciousness has to become lighter than it is in ordinary horizontal life. It is heavy if you encounter it when your consciousness has become heavy. Changing your own vertical weight is how you move up and down. Alchemists refer to these movements as levity (getting lighter) and gravity (getting heavier). As in horizontal life, most people find it easier to gain weight than to lose it. That may be why the upper vertical tends to be held in greater esteem: getting there requires more of a conscious effort.

Spiritual beings can likewise change their weight. Like individual humans, they vary in their vertical range. When you encounter an angel— a being normally lighter than you—it can be because you have gone a long way up, because the angel has come a long way down, or because some combination of your up and their down puts you in the same spot. Some vertical beings have such a great range of movement that they can manifest both above the horizontal and below it. (You are one of them.)

Many of the beings you encounter in the upper vertical are human. These are the easiest beings to engage with because their psychology is similar to yours and because you don't have to go very high up to find them. Some, in fact, are currently incarnate.

Consider what it's like to have a conversation that you later describe as "mind-blowing." From the outside, it appears to be an ordinary horizontal meeting, since you and the other person are sitting in the same physical room. But at some point, the conversation achieves liftoff. Though you continue to exchange audible words, you almost don't need them, for your rapport is such that you can neglect to finish your sentences and the other person still knows exactly what you mean. You feel like your mind is soaring and your companion is soaring right along with you. That's levity. You might experience something similar while reading the work of a favorite author, listening to a brilliant orator or a great musician, or watching some other kind of performance. Whether you know the artist personally or not, you feel in sync with how their mind is moving. To move along with them is exciting, uplifting. You feel as if your consciousness has expanded. When something like that happens, you have encountered an incarnate human being in the vertical.

Other humans you will meet in the vertical are not presently incarnate. You may encounter the spirits of deceased friends and relatives as well as people you never knew when they were living on earth. When reading a favorite author, for instance, you might feel a meeting of minds that seems to be happening in the present and that does not depend entirely on the written word. It's as if something between the lines on the page is being communicated to you telepathically. Since spiritual beings are drawn to humans with whom they have something in common, it shouldn't surprise you that deceased authors gravitate toward their fans.

Because I was raised Christian, I tend to use "angel" as a generic term for all the other beings one finds in the upper vertical, but if you don't like that word you could just call them "lighter beings." In the monotheistic traditions (Judaism, Christianity, and Islam), angels are defined as higher beings who have never been incarnate. They were created from the beginning as something other than humans. In other traditions they are believed to have been an ancient race of humans who have long since ceased to incarnate, dwelling now in a higher realm from whence they serve as teachers and guides. The gods of polytheistic traditions are also lighter beings.

Whatever their origin, these beings either no longer remember or never knew what physical experience is like. Being lighter than human spirits, they dwell higher up. Contacts with them are more subtle and have a more ephemeral quality. One hermeticist I know describes them as "shy." The lighter among them tend to be a bit fuzzy about the practical aspects of human existence. If you've ever read the Old Testament, you'll recognize what angel advice is like. "Sell your flock, abandon your crops, and go forth this night into the land of Egypt." Hassle is not a concept for them.

Nevertheless, we do have something in common with lighter beings, and that's how we're able to connect with them. The higher reaches of our consciousness resemble the lower reaches of theirs. The extent of the overlap depends on how "up" a human individual is able to go, and how "down" a lighter being is able to go.

Achieving Liftoff

To define levity precisely would be to render it too heavy, so I'm just going to point you in its general direction. As leaven is what makes dough rise, levity is what makes the soul rise. In its moments of levity, your mind becomes more like that of a lighter being. This enables you to better perceive their thoughts and to communicate with them in a way that *they* can more easily perceive. You are, in a sense, cultivating a common language.

Throughout human history, spiritual seekers have tended to assume that it is the body that makes us heavy. This is the reason for ascetic practices like fasting. If you live on bean sprouts and herb tea, refrain from alcohol, caffeine, and so forth, and engage in special breathing exercises, you may start to feel a bit light-headed, or spacey, floaty, vaguely holy. It is reported that people who persevere with this tactic are even able to levitate on occasion. Though such a feat would impress me very much if I ever witnessed it, it is not what alchemists mean by levity. Altering your bodily experience is neither here nor there, because levity is not a physical sensation.

The needs and appetites of the body, per se, are not what makes us heavy. The problem is with our *thinking,* which, under normal circumstances, is bound to the physical. We are used to saying that we think with our brains. Thoughts feel like they're coming from the head, and neurologists have been able to associate various types of brain activity with various types of thoughts. When something goes wrong with the brain, like Alzheimer's disease or a cerebral hemorrhage, the sufferer has trouble with mental function. Yet if thinking depended *exclusively* on the brain, there could be no such thing as consciousness after death and no such thing as conscious beings who don't have brains. If your mind is truly nothing but your brain, death must be the absolute end of it.

The fact that neurological activity can be observed and measured while a person is thinking does not prove that the brain is *originating* thoughts. Rather, brain activity is a *response* to thought, in much the same way that stomach activity is a response to food. Physical digestion is a process of transmuting the foreign into the familiar. Your body sorts through what you have eaten, breaking it down into its various components, determining what to assimilate, what to discard, and what to transform into energy. You might try to change yourself by changing your diet, yet on the whole you remain the same person no matter what you eat, because of your body's preference for the familiar.

The brain handles thought in much the same way, breaking down new information into familiar components. To the extent that new information can be recognized by analogy to the familiar, it is assimilated. That which can't be assimilated is discarded. This is why our mental activity tends to be so repetitive, a hit parade of "golden oldies." What you are observing is the digestive activity of your brain—not thought itself, but the aftermath of thought. Though we are not much interested in what happens to our food once we've swallowed it, for some reason we find the digestive activity of our brains quite fascinating.

We are right to admire it. The human organism is, in and of itself, an alchemical vessel, transmuting the spiritual (pure concept) into the physical (pictures, speech, and deeds). Later I will have a great deal more to say about why this is so fantastic, but just now I want to point out the downside. The body's sense of the familiar is rooted in matter. Being a thing, it tends to turn thoughts into things. Left entirely to its own devices, the body transmutes the quicksilver of thought into something more like lead. Thinking becomes a sluggish exercise in moving the same old, same old solid material through the same old, same old convolutions. This is the heaviness you need levity to overcome. Levity is an ability to taste thoughts when they are absolutely fresh, before the brain's digestive activity has gone to work on them.

Have you ever found yourself searching for a word that you've used in the past yet can't for the life of you call to mind in the present? The technical name for this is aphasia. If the word is the name of an object, you might have an image of that object in your mind. You can't recall the word "flask" or "quill," but you can picture what a flask or a quill looks like. Consider though what it's like to space out the word for something more abstract, a word that doesn't represent a *thing*. Say the word you want is "flagrant" or "quizzical." You can't "hear" a word or "see" a picture, yet something is definitely hovering at the edge of your consciousness for which only the word "flagrant" or "quizzical" will do. What is that something?

When you're struck by aphasia in the midst of a conversation, you might say, abashedly, "My brain isn't working right." Precisely! Your brain is failing to transmute this mysterious something or other, this pure *meaning*, into a sound you can make with your mouth and throat. Your brain isn't working properly, and yet you are thinking. You are experiencing what a thought tastes like when it is fresh.

Apart from these occasional blank outs, we normally find that the sound of a word arrives pretty much simultaneously with its meaning. In fact, when we are thinking in words, we subvocalize—make slight movements with the larynx as if preparing to speak the words aloud. Thus, our silent verbal thoughts move only slightly faster than our speech. This makes communication with lighter beings difficult, since their minds move more quickly. Again, recall what it's like to have a mind-blowing conversation. You stop finishing your sentences because so many thoughts are coming to you at once. And you don't *need* to finish your sentences because the other person's mind is moving fast enough to get the whole idea long before you arrive at the period. The thrilling velocity of such conversations is an angel's normal speed.

When we are able (for short periods, at least) to abandon the habit of talking to ourselves in our heads, thought moves faster. By this I don't mean the speediness, the restless jumping from thought to thought that makes meditation so difficult at times. That subjective sense of speediness arises from the brain's *slowness* in relation to thought. You are feeling your brain rush because it is unable to keep up. It is as if a school of minnows is swimming by and you are trying to capture all of them at once. You're darting about as fast as you can, but can't seem to grasp any of the minnows, much less all of them. But suppose you were to stop trying to catch them. Then you wouldn't need to rush. Suppose that instead of trying to catch the fish, you joined the school and swam along with it. If you were completely surrounded by minnows and gliding along at the same speed, it might seem to you that you weren't moving at all. When the human mind approaches angel velocity, its subjective experience is stillness. This feeling of inner stillness is a sign that you have achieved vertical liftoff.

What human and angel minds have in common is the word behind the word, that elusive something or other we are groping for in a moment of aphasia. Coming from a lighter being, this meaning is highly concentrated. You could write a whole book and still not say everything they mean by a single word. It is as if every possible denotation and connotation is happening at once. The word of a lighter being is not just one minnow, but a whole school, and you are swimming in the midst of it.

Consider all the meanings of the word "light." Sometimes it is a description of physical weight. Other times it is a description of mental or emotional weight (as in "light reading" or "lighthearted"). It can also refer to color ("light blue"), subtlety ("a light touch"), physical illumination ("street light"), or spiritual illumination ("the light of reason," "divine light"). When, in a particular human language, a single word has more than one definition, it is often because the multiple meanings share some obscure connection in the minds of people who speak that language. For an English-speaking alchemist, "levity" refers to weight, yet also relates to illumination, to subtlety, and to playfulness and humor. It is at once the opposite of heaviness, of darkness, and of seriousness. When a lighter being communicates the word "levity" to an English speaker, all of these meanings—and how each meaning is related to the others—are being imparted. In Angelese, all puns are intended.

In human language, meaning depends not only on the words themselves, but on the order you put them in. "Dog bites man" means something different from "Man bites dog." The sequential nature of sentences is related to our experience of time and causality, which is linear: cause first, then effect. But time in the vertical is not linear or sequential. From a lighter being's perspective, all the words are happening simultaneously. Where we perceive a string of words, they perceive something more like a collage.

Lighter beings may also have trouble grasping the distinction we make between nouns and verbs. Where we perceive a thing, a solid object, they perceive a *process*. We know from quantum physics that when you get down to the subatomic level, objects aren't really solid at all.

Yet no matter how many times this is explained to us, we go on perceiving things as *things*. Any doubt we may harbor that a brick is really solid will be immediately dispelled if that brick happens to fall on our foot. Quantum physics brings an extreme level of subtlety to our understanding of the physical. That level of subtlety is where lighter beings habitually dwell. It's how the world actually appears to them. Grammatically, their experience of reality is all verb. To an angel, I am not Catherine. I am Cathering. (That's an actual example of an angel joke.)

For humans, mental pictures—even when they're purely imaginary—are variations on things we have previously seen with our eyes. Lighter beings sometimes communicate in mental images, but since they don't have eyes, or physical objects to see, their sense of the pictorial is different from ours. Never having seen a tree, they can't send you a photorealistic image of one. They perceive a process—a tree-ing—and send a sort of diagram of that process. Like the symbols we considered in chapter 2, the diagram shows how the angel's mind is moving as it contemplates the tree-ing, so that you can move your own mind the same way.

Exceptions to what I've been saying are probably springing to mind, for religious literature is full of Technicolor visions and grammatically correct angel quotations. This is due to a translation process that I will describe in the next section. For now, I'm just trying to convey a sense of what communications from lighter beings are like in their raw form. You will notice that while what I have described is different from the way your mind usually works, it is not so radically different that you can't imagine it at all. I can describe it because I have occasionally experienced it, and you can understand my description because you have, too. This is the area where the minds of lighter beings and the minds of humans overlap. What lies above that area of overlap is beyond my power to know or tell.

Coming Back Down

The movement that brings you back down from the vertical is called gravity. Like levity, gravity has many meanings in English. It is the pull of the Earth's energy field that renders us weighty and prevents us from floating away. It also means seriousness and suggests heavy consequences (as in "gravely ill" or "the gravity of the situation"). A grave is a place beneath the surface of the earth where the dead are buried. When we want words to last a long time, we engrave them. All of these meanings are related to the alchemical sense of the word "gravity." To move downward from the upper vertical is to reenter the Earth's gravitational field, to take on weight, to relate seriously to consequences, to make words last, and to become vulnerable to death.

Upward movement is not unique to alchemists. In most religions, it is a valued attainment, and the mystics found in every tradition can give you excellent advice on how to do it. They usually have a great deal less to say about how to land, partly because landing is an inevitability requiring no particular skill. What goes up must come down. By most accounts, mystics just sort of plop down with a happily dazed look on their faces and report that whatever they have just experienced is inexpressible. An unusually articulate one like Julian of Norwich might manage, "All will be well and all will be well and every little thing will be well."

Well, that's all very well, but I for one would like to know precisely *what* will be well and *when* it will be well and in what manner it will be well. This desire to make horizontal sense of what is perceived in the vertical is what differentiates mysticism (pure experience) from gnosis (higher knowledge). To come back from the vertical with something intelligible to report is the way of the sage or seer. For some people, even that isn't enough. In addition to knowing what will be well and why, they want to participate in making it so. They want vertical insight to inform horizontal action. This is the way of the magician.

If you have chosen the way of the seer or the magician, it won't do to just fall back to earth babbling about the inexpressible. You want to come back from the vertical with something to show for your trip. But vertical experience in its pure form is too perishable to survive the return journey. It needs to be converted into something sturdier if you want to transport it. This is where your physical brain gets back into the act, translating the abstractions of the spirit into words or sense-based images or both. The brain's digestive activity, which is such an obstacle to levity, becomes essential on the way back down. Without it, we can neither remember nor understand our vertical experiences once they're over.

The result of digestion is a souvenir. It might take the form of words, an image or symbol, a story, a dream, or a vision. People often mistake the souvenir for the vertical experience itself because, as far as they can tell, it's the first thing that happens. We notice we're having—or have just had—a dream, but can't recall the more subtle experience that inspired the dream. To put it another way, we don't notice we've eaten until digestion is already in progress. Our consciousness registers the digestive activity of the brain, but not what our spirit was tasting before digestion began.

The distinction I'm making might not matter much, for often our souvenirs are more than satisfactory. We come back with artistic inspirations, creative solutions to problems, stirring words, beautiful pictures, and edifying stories. These are the fruits of a digestion process that is no less successful for being entirely unconscious.

There are, however, two basic problems with digestion. First, it alters the quality of the experience itself. It tends to discard the novel and retain the familiar. We are more likely to end up with new variations on old thoughts than startling new revelations. Secondly, mental digestion is always in the past tense. You can't experience what's happening *while* it's happening. So here's our basic dilemma: If you don't digest, you can't remember, communicate, or apply vertical insights. If you do digest, you might alter those insights beyond recognition.

This is why mystics so often despair of words. The gap between what vertical mind is able to apprehend and what horizontal mind is able to express can feel insurmountable. To the mystic, every souvenir brought back from above looks cheap and vulgar. At the opposite extreme is the fundamentalist who, in a souvenir collection, finds a comfortable substitute for the rigors of vertical travel. Perhaps when hearing from fundamentalists, you have been tempted to say, "Lighten up!" Well, that's it precisely. Firmly battened down in the horizontal, the fundamentalist word is all gravity and no levity. It is *too* concrete, too literal. What began as a rhapsody solidifies into a rule.

One remedy for this is to teach the brain itself to function at a higher level of abstraction—to think more like the spirit thinks. If the brain is able to recognize a pure concept, the concept doesn't need to be converted into pictures or words to be remembered, and the message is less likely to get garbled. Mystics function at a very high level of abstraction, for they are able to remember experiences that they don't— and often *can't*—translate into words or pictures.

It is also possible to become more skillful at creating souvenirs and to improve on the ones you've already got. Benjamin Franklin did this when he edited Jefferson's first draft of the Declaration of Independence. He used Jefferson's souvenir to get back up to the vertical experience that inspired it, then chose words that described the experience better.

The people we describe as "gifted" or "inspired" have a particular knack for spontaneous souvenir creation. Take Martin Luther King, for example. He had written out a speech for the March on Washington rally, but he didn't deliver it verbatim. When he got to the podium, the immortal words of his "I Have a Dream" speech spilled out instead. In a person who can do that, the verbal center of the brain is perfectly in sync with the spirit. The souvenir and the vertical experience it commemorates are happening simultaneously.

While the process of converting vertical experience into brain-based souvenirs is usually unconscious, you can train yourself to become aware of it while it is going on. It's done by "remembering backward." You begin with what, from a vertical standpoint, is the last thing that happened. This is, in horizontal memory, the *first* thing that happened—the souvenir. Think of the souvenir as the bottommost rung of a memory ladder that you constructed (unconsciously) as you were coming down. You can grope your way back up the rungs above it and remember what came *before* your earliest memory. Once you become adept at this, you will be able to move up and down at will, shuttling very rapidly between vertical and horizontal consciousness. Technically speaking, that's what Martin Luther King was doing on the podium. Some people are naturals, but for those who aren't, it's a learnable skill. Probably the best way to approach it is through dream recollection. You'll find detailed procedural instructions in the "Night School" appendix.

So far, I've described levity and gravity in terms of single inner events. But levity and gravity also apply to more extended rhythms of the inner life. In our inner work, most of us go through upward-oriented phases. These are the times in our lives when we *feel* spiritual—thinking spiritual thoughts and engaging in activities that *look* spiritual. In a healthy inner life, these periods alternate with more downward-oriented phases. Our attention returns to the mundane and practical. Inwardly, we feel heavier, and we may judge this change to be a loss or a lapse in what we ought to be feeling and doing. It isn't. Teresa of Avila is famous for her levity, but the mystical ecstasies we associate with her only went on for two periods of a few months each. As she tells it, the majority of her early years (including some that came *after* the first ecstatic period) were devoted to frivolity. Her later years were devoted to teaching and business travel as she worked to reform her order and establish new convents. In any useful life, periods of gravity are more frequent and prolonged than periods of levity.

How to Speak Angelese

1. The first exercise is a variation on perceiving style. You begin with an abstract concept like *beauty*. Specific examples of what you consider to be beautiful will come immediately to mind. Let them flow for a few minutes. Then begin to banish each mental picture from your mind. Banish the word "beauty" as well. Try to hold the concept in the absence of any words or pictures—as if you were having an episode of aphasia. Other concepts to try are freedom, power, truth, generosity, justice, and harmony. (Yes, this exercise is as difficult as is sounds. It's teaching your brain to tolerate a much higher level of abstraction than it's used to.)

2. To analyze the meaning of uplifting words often has the effect of dragging them down. Instead, try to carry them back up to their source using this procedure:

Meditate on a favorite quotation, proverb, or line of poetry. After repeating the full quotation to yourself several times, remove from it what you consider to be the least essential words. Meditate on the truncated passage for a minute or two, trying to retain the full meaning of the original. Then take out a few more words and meditate again on the result. Keep going until you are down to a single word. Finally, eliminate that one, retaining whatever remains of the thought wordlessly in your mind. For example:

Blessed are the meek, for they shall inherit the earth.
Blessed meek, they shall inherit earth.
Blessed meek, inherit earth.
Blessed meek, inherit.
Blessed meek.
Blessed.

. . . . . .

3. Verbs are better than nouns at expressing how a lighter being perceives. Can you write an intelligible paragraph without using any nouns at all? Probably not. But here's a silly exercise you can do to make your thinking more verb-like. Imagine that the only noun you know is "thingamajiggy." Choose a paragraph at random from a newspaper or magazine and rewrite it, using action words to distinguish one thingamajiggy from another. For example:
"President Bush Declares War on Terror."
"Bossing thingamajiggy declares fighting and killing thingamajiggy on scaring thingamajiggy.

4. NPR once ran a story about a man who proposed to eliminate the verb "to be" from the English language. He asserted that "to be" in all its forms (especially the ubiquitous "there is") merely escorts a noun into a sentence, rather than describing an action and therefore does not deserve the designation "verb." Why should you care? Well, as he went on to argue, when our sentences don't move, neither does

our thinking. We use "to be" to introduce labels, then come to believe that what we have labeled remains forever and always as labeled. (Consider, for instance, the difference between saying, "He is a thief" and "He steals.") On the radio, this fellow managed to hold forth intelligibly for a good ten minutes without ever employing any variation on "to be." In fact, he was very well spoken. (Oops. I mean, he spoke very well.) Had he not mentioned the rule he imposed on his speech, you might never have noticed.

Try taking a fairly long passage of your own writing (a letter or an entry in your journal) and rewriting it without any instances of the verb "to be."

South of the Border

Shakespeare's *Hamlet* concerns a fundamental alchemical problem: how do we take action in the horizontal based on intuition from the vertical? A subtle being who appears to be the ghost of his father urges Hamlet to avenge him by killing the uncle who is now married to Hamlet's mother. Is the ghost an autonomous being or merely Hamlet's projection? Since the ghost is inciting him to murder, this is no idle metaphysical question. For Hamlet to avenge a crime that exists only in his own imagination would be a catastrophic error.

Beyond the question of whether to trust subtle perception lies an even deeper problem. Had Hamlet actually been present when his uncle assaulted his father, he would not have hesitated to act. To slay his uncle would have been an instinctive reaction. What Hamlet is being asked to do is to act in the absence of instinct, to do violence in the absence of violent feelings. Lacking an external provocation in the moment, how is he to get his blood up? How does one perform an instinctive act based on principle alone?

The problem is more universal than it might at first sound. What Hamlet is grappling with is the fundamental disconnect between intention and will. What most of us are used to calling our "will" is actually a form of thinking: our conscious intention. What we call "willpower" is our effort to make that intention stick, to force ourselves to act in accordance with our thought. The *actual* will is that which tends to subvert whatever we are trying to achieve by "willpower." If you've ever broken a New Year's resolution, you know what I'm talking about. The trouble is not that your will is weak. Rather, your will is strong in some direction that has nothing to do with your conscious intention.

Will is the most mysterious function of the body. It causes our lungs to inhale and exhale whether we intend to breathe or not. It circulates our blood without consulting our opinion on the matter. Our intention to move is merely the green light for a whole series of motor events that don't require our conscious participation. Decide to walk and walking happens pretty much automatically. Confronted with what our body perceives to be a threat, we prepare for flight or fight with a rush of adrenaline even if our mind is insisting that there is nothing to feel threatened about.

In everyday conversation we often use the words "instinct" and "intuition" interchangeably, for both refer to motives for action that we haven't thought about in a rational way. While reading this book, I'd like you to make a distinction between them. Intuition refers to impulses that come from above. Instinct refers to impulses that come from below. For instinct and intuition to wind up on the same page, both the spirit and the body must be transformed. This is what the alchemists' Great Work is trying to accomplish.

Animals may strike us as quite elegant in the way they are at one with their instincts. A cat preparing to pounce on a bird does not appear to be conflicted in any way. As far as we can tell, she isn't stopping to weigh the pros and cons or to consider the moral implications. She is a stranger to self-reproach. But this harmony comes at the expense of freedom, for the cat is unable to contemplate other options, unable to form any intention that runs contrary to her instinctive will. Pouncing is the one thing she knows to do about birds. It doesn't occur to her to paint pictures of them or imitate their songs or study their migratory patterns or stuff them with wild rice and glaze them with a cranberry-orange reduction. Our own biological instincts have to compete with the many creative possibilities we can imagine in any given situation. We are used to overruling our blood in pursuit of the good, the true, and the beautiful. Yet we may also find ourselves overruled in such pursuits by the mysterious instincts of our blood.

Above is the realm of conscious intention. It is there that we find our creative and moral intuitions, our best ideas of what to do. The catch is that to achieve levity and avail ourselves of those intuitions, we have to detach temporarily from the physical. While we are entertaining lofty ideas and ideals, our instinctive side is out of the picture. We are not very concerned about what an inspiration might cost us. We can even imagine the extreme of dying for an ideal, if need be.

If we could act out of higher consciousness all the time, we would all be great geniuses, heroes, and saints. But intention alone does not produce deeds. Action comes from the will, and the power of the will resides below. By ascending to the upper vertical and making a controlled and mindful descent back to the horizontal, we can bring back ideas that make sense and inspire others. We can become very capable seers. But in order to become magicians, we must descend deeper, into the realm of the unconscious will.

While mainstream religions have a lot to teach about going up, they often seem to be doing their utmost to prevent us from going down. They teach us to regard downward movement as a screw-up, a punishment for sin or error.

The masculine aspect of the divine, which dwells above, has long dominated monotheistic spirituality, while the feminine aspect, which we encounter below, has largely been repressed. Mistrust of magic—and an inability to do it—is the consequence. If you want the appliances upstairs to work, you have to go down to the basement to turn on the power.

When it comes to going up, I've offered a lot of procedural advice. I shall have a great deal less to say about descent, for there really isn't any procedure. You just fall. It happens by accident. The lower vertical is the realm of the unintentional. You can't intend the unintentional.

We are carried downward whenever we feel ourselves losing control. Anything that makes us feel helpless will get us there—illness, depression, grief, addiction, shame, rage, anxiety, PMS. In vertical terms, to be helpless is to be heavy. Surrendering makes the downward journey swifter and a tad less painful, but gravity is going to take you down whether you choose to surrender or not. No matter how hard you struggle, eventually you have to acknowledge your helplessness. At that point, you find you've landed in a surprisingly soft place. Benevolent beings gather up the pieces you've fallen to and put them back together in a new and better way. They heal you. What they repair, specifically, is your will. You can't repair it all by yourself because the part that needs fixing is inaccessible to your conscious awareness. When we go up, we are like students. When we go down, we are like patients.

Just like going down, getting back up to the horizontal after you've been below requires no instruction, no technique. Conscious attempts to employ levity don't work. (If you can make yourself light on purpose, you're not below.) Some describe it as a rebound effect: the bouncing up of whatever has hit bottom. You could also see it as a natural consequence of being relieved, at the bottom, of the weight that has carried you down. You float back up because something or someone has taken a load off. Others have a sense of being carried, borne back up to the surface in loving arms. Perhaps you have some vague memory of this. You might have gone to bed one night in an extremely troubled frame of mind then awoken the next morning to find yourself strangely at peace, your body suffused with a drowsy heaviness that feels so delicious you don't want to move. That lovely lassitude is how the will feels in the immediate aftermath of a healing.

Strange, isn't it, that the place where this happens got the name hell? That negative perception of the place is inspired by the panic we feel when we discover we are falling. The downward journey can indeed be most unpleasant, for while we are below, we never seem to remember our previous soft landings and safe returns.

Like the upper vertical, the lower realm is populated. The beings there (including you, when you are visiting), are heavier than horizontal humans. By "heavy" I mean that they experience less freedom, less choice. The humans in downward movement—whether currently incarnate or deceased—are stuck in some way, unable to see or exercise all their options. This stuckness is temporary. When it is resolved, the sufferer becomes lighter and moves up. There are also permanent residents, beings such as animal souls and elementals who, by their nature, have a more limited range of choices. Since freedom is a positive value, to call a being "heavy" is, in a sense, a negative judgment, but it is by no means the same as "evil." Contrary to fire-and-brimstone preaching, the lower vertical is not a place of punishment. Permanent residents are there because it accords with their natures, as the horizontal accords with our own. Visitors are there to be healed.

Within most spiritual traditions—and even among different traditions—you will find a lot of agreement about the beings of the upper vertical. Jews, Christians, and Muslims, for example, not only describe angels in the same way, but name specific angels such as Gabriel who have made appearances in all three religions. The Greeks immediately recognized Hermes in the Roman god Mercury and the Egyptian god Thoth, for the personality of this being is unique and unmistakable. But nobody seems to agree on how to name or categorize the denizens of the lower realms. Even within a single religion, you will hear umpteen different versions of who or what lives there. Descriptions of contacts with heavier beings most often appear in works of fiction, and even those that purport to be fact come off sounding pretty fantastical.

We can only recognize other beings to the extent that we have something in common with them, for we experience them at the point where their consciousness overlaps our own. Some heavier beings are so unlike humans that very few people ever encounter them. What the spirit of a rock might be thinking is so foreign to human thought that most human minds can't even recognize it as thought. Other heavy beings overlap only those aspects of human consciousness that most people find creepy and repellant. We're not all that eager to share a maggot's perspective on rotting flesh, or to look at the world from cancer's point of view. When the consciousness of the heavier beings who live in our bodies impinges on our own—as it does sometimes when we are sleeping or ill—we usually experience it as a nightmare and are relieved to wake up.

Other heavy beings are difficult to recognize because we have *so much* in common with them. When we are below, they appear to be parts of ourselves: our own human moods and emotions. In shamanic cultures, illnesses and other disturbances are attributed to the influence of "demons" or "entities." Contemporary Americans, though, are more likely to interpret an inner disturbance as some troublesome aspect of their own personality, or the murky contents of their own "subconscious." At the urging of a psychotherapist, they will attempt to integrate or "own" the offending part. Often patients resist this at first, wishing to deny a feeling or impulse that bears little resemblance to their conscious sense of themselves. It is this sense of otherness about the feeling that leads those who take the shamanic approach to label it as a separate being.

Actually, these seemingly opposite interpretations are both pointing to the same inner reality. In order to recognize a spiritual being as itself and no other, we have to be able to recognize ourselves as spiritual beings. When we are in touch with our autonomy, we can perceive the autonomy of another and know that we are not just making them up. This self-recognition is one of our higher faculties. We lose the use of it while we are below. The clear sense of self departs and, lacking it, we can't very clearly distinguish self from other, or this other from that other.

The heavier beings that humans perceive as demons are in the same predicament, only more so. They don't know what "I" means, so they can't say to a human, "I am not you." These beings are not us, yet neither are they wholly separate from us. They have a parasitic relationship to human consciousness. Their own consciousness resembles some little piece of human psychology that has become detached from the rest to run amok on its own. Often a single emotion, desire, or fixed idea is the sum total of their inner repertoire. It can only be given expression by lodging in a human psyche. A human host who adopts it unwittingly may feel carried away or "possessed" by some emotion or impulse that in human terms is disproportionate, if not downright mad. This is what often happens when we are below. We can't easily distinguish between ourselves and our little parasite. It feels like *us*, and we feel out of control.

From the perspective of these heavier beings, a descending human is like an angel. While to connect with such beings lowers your own consciousness, it raises theirs. It expands their perspective and their range of choices just as contact with a lighter being expands your own. So there you are in the midst of a really bad-hair day, spiritually speaking, and a host of heavier beings comes rushing at you like you're their savior. Maybe you're just drunk, but to the beings of drunkenness, you look like a prophet. Whatever ails you attracts beings who seem to want a piece of you. From your perspective, whatever has caused you to fall below gets intensified as these heavier beings glom on to you. You and your trouble get heavier, and you pick up downward momentum. When, at the bottom, you are healed, any beings who have attached to you are healed along with you. Either you "own" and integrate them, teaching them to live in harmony with a complete human personality, or you get over the heavy feeling that made you such an attractive host to them, and they go looking for another place to live.

In their fictional accounts of journeys into the lower realms, J. R. R. Tolkien's *Lord of the Rings* trilogy and C. S. Lewis's *Chronicles of Narnia* offer some good clues about relating to lower beings. If you want to return safely, it's best to conduct yourself like a child or a hobbit. Lower beings, like wild animals, act scary when they are scared. Human pride makes them feel terribly insecure, for they look up to us and can't perceive that pride is just a cover for our own insecurity. They are often amenable to being tamed if you approach them with gentleness and humility.

In fact, many of these beings are touchingly eager to serve us. Their helpfulness becomes more apparent if we look at what happens to people who succeed in banishing them entirely. Ascetics like the desert fathers wanted nothing to do with the lower realms and attempted to stay out of them by living a very pure life. Initially, this would create a lot of inner conflict, for the more the ascetic resisted, the more the lower beings insisted, hassling him day and night with temptations. But when the saint finally prevailed against these temptations and persuaded the lower beings to go away, a worse problem arose. Inner life became extremely arid, colorless, and cold, a world of pure abstraction in which there was neither pain nor joy. The pleasure we take in our senses and our emotions depends on the participation of lower beings. From above, you might get a great idea for a work of art, but in order to create a work that profoundly moves other people, you have to mine the depths as well. Below is where you find the feelings, the colors, the juice.

In alchemical work, downward movements of the soul are precipitated by what has occurred during upward movement. When you form a clear and conscious intention in the upper vertical, you are, in a sense, making a pact, requesting that your will be transformed in accordance with that intention. Soon afterward, events may ensue that are beyond your control. As these events carry you downward, you can't for the life of you see what they have to do with your intention. Often they seem to be carrying you in quite the opposite direction.

An example might make this clearer. "All men are created equal" expressed the conscious intention of the founding fathers. As you are probably aware, both the author and many of the signers of the Declaration of Independence owned slaves. While conscious intention embraced equal rights, the national will was barreling along in a more Darwinian direction, i.e., "Some people are fitter for survival than others, and I want to be one of them." Formally declaring the higher intention triggered a corresponding downward movement that would bring the national will into congruence with it. In signing the Declaration of Independence, the founding fathers were also signing up for the Civil War.

I shall have more to say about this when we come to the Great Work, for much of that work concerns the coordination of upward and downward movement. For the moment I want to concentrate on explaining what downward movement is *not*, because getting mixed up about this subject can lead to trouble.

Some Dubious Methods of Moving Down

Think of the vertical world as a tree. Its branches reach toward the light while its roots penetrate deep into the earth. To say, "as above so below" is to say that roots and branches are interdependent, not that they are identical. Suppose you were to dig up the tree and transplant it upside down. The light and air would desiccate the roots, while the soil would smother and rot the leaves. A tree only works when it's planted right-side up. This is a basic law of spiritual movement. Magic that disobeys it out of ignorance (by far the most common reason) is usually ineffective. When the law is disobeyed out of deliberate perversity, the results are both perverse and ineffective.

You might have heard that the efforts of the Nazis were assisted by occult experiments. While such experiments were indeed undertaken by a group of occultists who called themselves Ariosophists, the important thing to keep in mind is that they didn't work. Competent magicians do not require guns and gas chambers to achieve their aims. To resort to brute force is a tacit admission that magic has failed.

The Ariosophists recognized that the source of the human will is to be found in the lower vertical. At the same time, they were strongly influenced by heroic archetypes that manifest in the upper vertical. So, based on a warped version of the logic I have been describing, they attempted to draw powers from below and fuse them to the archetypes, producing what they conceived of as a "triumph of the will." This was planting the tree upside down, for to triumph means to rise above, and the will belongs below. They were, in effect, trying to conquer the world while standing on their heads.

To join will to archetype is an excellent idea, in and of itself. What the Ariosophists got wrong was the method. The goal of alchemical magic is to *align* the ideal with the instinctive, not to amalgamate them. Alignment is the cultivation of a lively *between*. It is accomplished through vertical movement of the human soul: going up to meet the ideal and going down to transform the will in accordance with it. The vitality of a personality is expressed by its range and grace of movement. The sanity of a personality is expressed by its ability to distinguish up from down and to operate within each according to its own laws.

The downward leg of the journey is accompanied by feelings of helplessness that connect us with the vulnerability of the human condition. It renders a person more humble and compassionate. This is obviously not a spiritual gesture that would appeal to the *Übermensch* wannabe. So instead of going down, the Ariosophists attempted to draw the instinctive forces of the will up to the surface. When removed from their native element, those forces become animalistic and stupid.

In trying to fuse an ideal that had lost its levity with a will that had lost its gravity, the Ariosophists failed at magic, but they did succeed in creating a very toxic mythology. I don't know whether he consciously intended this or not, but Tolkien concocted the specific antidote with his *Lord of the Rings* trilogy. In transmuting a toxic myth into a healing myth, he rendered humanity a great spiritual service. His story, like the Nazi myths, is a tale of quest, but the object of the quest is not to bring anything back from below. Rather, the quest is *to get rid of* something, to return what was wrongfully brought to the surface back to the depths. This is an essential truth of downward spiritual movement. You must return empty-handed.

Concerning downward movement, nearly every occult text I've ever read contains the same exasperating statement. It goes something like this: "Of the various other methods of accessing the lower realms—blood sacrifice, and the ritual use of sex and drugs and the like—nothing more need be said, as these practices are the domain of the Black Path."

"Nothing more need be said"—just when it's getting really interesting! I can understand well enough the decision to give blood sacrifice a pass, but the ritual use of sex and drugs sounds rather promising, doesn't it? Why descend by painful mischance if it's possible to go down at a moment of one's own choosing and by means of an orgy? Clearly a great deal more needs to be said if bright readers are to be persuaded to abandon such an attractive possibility.

Ritual practices that carry the soul downward through a shedding of inhibitions (sex and drugs are just two of the many methods) have been employed with apparent success by respectable magicians. Such practices are a prominent feature of some forms of shamanism. The problem they present for the contemporary Western student of magic has nothing to do with the morality of kinky sex or drug use, for you might undertake these activities in the horizontal (excuse the pun) without coming to any spiritual harm. Rather, the problem has to do with a particular quirk of the modern mind: we are excruciatingly conscious of being conscious. We are able not only to think, and to think about our thinking, but to think about what we think of our thinking.

Say for example you lose your temper. The first layer of awareness is your anger. A second layer observes the loss of temper and, perhaps, disapproves of it. In most modern people, this watcher, too, has a watcher. It observes layer #2 scolding layer #1 and thinks, "I shouldn't be so hard on myself." If, as you read my description, you recognize yourself in it, you've actually got a fourth layer going—the one who is able to observe layer #3. And here we seem to reach the point of diminishing returns as far as consciousness of consciousness goes. The mind in its excess plumage begins to resemble a flightless bird. We feel painfully convoluted and long for some real or mythical primitive age when human psychology was more straightforward.

It is probably true that human minds used to be simpler. In ancient times, drama was a religious ritual that also served as a kind of psychotherapy. It could work that way because the audience identified with the action on stage. They felt as if it was really happening, and to them, personally. When the action came to a climax, they experienced a catharsis. To attend the performance of a tragedy was to go down, in the spiritual sense, to be guided by the dramatist into the lower vertical.

In the works of Shakespeare and his contemporaries, one can see a shift in the psychology of the audience. Shakespeare frequently reminds us that we are watching a play. He even suggests that our own lives could be likened to a stage production. To the extent that you are aware that a play is just a play, you are no longer fully identified with it. Part of your mind is watching the rest of your mind as it watches the action on stage. You know you're not King Lear, and you know the actor playing him isn't King Lear either.

The works of D. H. Lawrence exhibit yet another layer of self-consciousness. Mellors, the gamekeeper hero of *Lady Chatterley's Lover*, is meant to be a sort of noble savage, but instead of just using four-letter words, he editorializes for pages on end about why one *ought* to use four-letter words. Actual noble savages—if such people exist at all—don't stand before a mirror admiring their noble savagery. Instead of being carried down, you're watching Lawrence watch his characters as they watch themselves mimic their notion of descent.

When we are conscious of being conscious, the deliberate attempt to shed inhibition produces the opposite result: we end up watching ourselves pretending to be uninhibited. Apply this to something like ritual sex magic and the effect is at once exhibitionistic and voyeuristic. We are trying to go down in a state of mind (i.e., consciousness of self) that belongs to up. We're trying to go to a dark place with our headlights on. Shining too much light in a place that's meant to be dark causes shame. At best, we feel silly and embarrassed. But we might also find our shame reflected back to us, leading us to experience the lower vertical as a place of depravity. That is a distortion which, if embraced, would carry us into very dubious moral territory.

So how do we shed all these layers of self-consciousness and go down for real? It's easy; slip on a banana peel. Trying to lose control on purpose is contradictory, and nobody can be 100 percent sincere in their desire to do so. We descend as the true innocents we long to be when we descend by accident. There is no need to make a project of it. The shocks and sufferings of ordinary life send us below quite reliably, if reluctantly. If nothing has occurred lately to take you down, you must not need to be there.

The Baggage Disclaim Area

The dawning of clairvoyance opens up a vast new world of opportunities to be wrong. Where once we were only misinformed by lazy journalists, deceptive advertisers, and Internet newsgroups, we now have access to a whole host of invisible beings who are eager to meet our misinformation needs. I alluded to these characters in the previous chapter. Now it's time to locate them on our inner map.

In Christian hermeticism, the place where we become spiritually confused used to be called the "Realm of Deception" or the "Band of Lies." It is the ambiguous region we end up in when levity or gravity is on the blink, and the source of every misguided, dysfunctional, or just plain silly notion that tries to pass itself off as spiritual truth. When people refer to the "astral plane," they are usually talking about this place. Experts on vertical travel tell us that a layover in this area is unavoidable, for it lies between our horizontal consciousness and the more edifying regions of the upper vertical. If you want to go up, you have to pass through it. Until you learn to see through the deceptions, you're bound to keep getting detained there.

I used to envision this area as something akin to cloud cover. Like an airliner taking off, you went through the clouds and then climbed above them. This, it turns out, was a faulty conception of the realm of faulty conceptions and contributed to my getting stuck there so often. Here's what I have learned the hard way: the Realm of Deception isn't up. That, in fact, is the fundamental deception from whence all its other deceptions spring. If you believe you're moving up when you're actually moving out, your entire sense of direction is thrown off. You can't tell the difference between inside and outside, or forward and backward.

The reason people mistake this area for up is that they usually arrive there as a result of *trying* to go up. While attempting to employ levity, they find themselves in a place that's different from everyday waking consciousness and that exactly matches their conception of the spiritual world. They naturally assume that this must be their chosen destination.

That this area feels more like a plane than a tube or an elevator is the first tip-off that you're lost. In the true vertical, a shift in attention causes a change in vertical weight—you either move directly above where you were, or you fall back to the horizontal. Staying up requires a concentration that is hard to sustain for more than a few minutes at a time. By comparison, astral movement feels easy. You have the sense that you can wander around at your leisure, for you are able to move laterally—your attention shifting from one being to another, or from one thought to another. You may have the impression that the area is crowded, with many different beings vying for your notice. It's a bit like being in an Internet chat room. In fact, "virtual reality" is another good name for the Realm of Deception.

You will have observed that in their online interactions, people easily lose their sense of proportion—falling in love with people they've never met in the flesh, engaging in flame wars, and so forth. The esoteric term for this phenomenon is "astrality." It is the same type of inner movement that lands us in the Realm of Deception.

Left to its own devices, the body is incapable of falsehood. To the extent that we remain connected with our physical experience, it grounds us in common sense, for the body is disinclined to go to crazy extremes. Take sex, for example. If our sexual appetite is anchored to the needs of the body, we stop feeling horny once the body is satisfied. But if sexual desire becomes detached from the physical, morphing into an appetite of the *mind*, it can turn obsessive and insatiable. The same is true of our survival instincts. The fear evoked by a physical threat dissipates quickly once the threat is removed. But if we interpret an idea or a personal slight as a threat, we can remain churned up about it for days.

Astrality refers to this tendency of impulses and feelings to take on a life of their own when they break free of their bodily origins. It is easily confused with levity, because both involve a temporary detachment of mind from body. In that sense, astrality feels "light." The difference is that in astral movement, consciousness is being propelled out of the body by the body's own energy, while in levity we are being drawn upward by the attraction of the spirit. Experientially, the difference is subtle and difficult for the beginner to perceive. Not only that, but for every step upward in the development of levity, we tend to advance three steps outward in astrality. Thus, astral detours are all but inevitable while we're learning to go up.

Recall that the entry point to the upper vertical is extremely narrow. You have to be skinny, spiritually speaking, to squeeze through. Your consciousness must narrow to a single point, leaving behind its hopes and fears, sympathies and antipathies, preconceptions and preoccupations. This is what Jesus was talking about when he said that it was easier for a camel to pass through a needle's eye than for a rich man to get into heaven. You can't take any of your inner baggage with you. But the astral plane is wide enough to accommodate you and a whole moving van full of your stuff. So if you're attempting to go up and can't because you're too "heavy," you will tend to move outward instead.

Possessing baggage is not, in and of itself, an obstacle to upward movement. The problem is *denial* of baggage. If you know what you've got and how much of it you've got, you can check it at the gate when you want to achieve levity. But if you're unaware of your baggage, you don't think to check it. That's how you wind up in the deceptive realm that I'm now going to rechristen "Baggage Disclaim." To make matters worse, the baggage you don't even notice you're carrying is plastered with stickers that tell everyone who sees it exactly where you're coming from. This makes you an easy mark for the con artists who hang out in Baggage Disclaim.

Take the Ariosophists, for example. The baggage they were denying was the pain they felt over the German defeat in the First World War and the humiliating terms of the Versailles Treaty. Had they acknowledged their pain, it would have carried them downward to the place of healing. Instead they attempted to "spiritualize" their dilemma, to transcend their way out of it on the wings of grandiose ideals. Neither light enough to go up nor heavy enough to go all the way down, they wound up in Baggage Disclaim. It is one of the most pernicious con games to pander to the victim's secret wish to feel superior. The Ariosophists were perfect marks.

For many years, I participated in a hermetic discussion group over the Internet. One of its most brilliant members was a guy I'll call Hank. A gifted writer and scholar, Hank had the makings of a successful college professor. Instead he had chosen, for reasons I don't fully understand, to become a social dropout. He held a series of marginal jobs—assembly line worker, night watchman, nursing home orderly—punctuated by periods of unemployment. None of these jobs afforded him any opportunity to exercise and be admired for his formidable intellect. In Hank, the natural human desire to shine and impress was disclaimed baggage.

One day, Hank astonished us all by announcing his candidacy for President of the United States. He went on to reveal that he was the incarnation of the next Buddha and that his destiny was to lead the nation into a new spiritual age. When another member of the group asked bluntly what in Hank's lackluster career had ever qualified him for such a task, Hank replied that the menial jobs were themselves proof of his exalted identity. In the spiritual world according to Hank, working on assembly lines is what bodhisattvas do with themselves until their Moment of Destiny arrives.

Part of what made this episode so embarrassing for those of us who witnessed it was that we could identify with it. Though most of us had better sense than to parade our fantasies so publicly, it is a rare hermeticist who has not, at some point, entertained delusions of spiritual grandeur. Very few people manage vertical travel without falling for this con at least once.

The most fundamental motive for seeking spiritual knowledge in the first place is to discover the meaning of life and our true role in it. We want to know that our lives count for something. Genuine vertical experience reassures you that you are important, for lighter beings take a lively interest in you and your personal development. You don't have to do anything special to earn this interest. Lighter beings are fascinated by human life, consider it extremely important, and feel honored when asked their opinion. Like the authors of the Declaration of Independence, you come back from the vertical with an enhanced respect for humanity in general. By contrast, excursions to Baggage Disclaim may leave you with the impression that you are superior to others and that your importance is connected to some special mission or destiny. Sometimes this delusion, like Hank's, is just plain silly. But it can also be dangerous. We hope and pray that airport security will screen out those who believe they are on a mission from God.

Like con jobs in the mundane world, the spiritual con is an offer that sounds too good to be true. You are invited to believe that you are a great deal better or more important than you had previously thought. Being tempted at any level to believe spiritual flattery is a sign that you are dissatisfied with yourself. That dissatisfaction is nothing to be ashamed of. All true seekers feel it very keenly at times. Just label it clearly with your name and address, and the con artists will leave you alone.

When thoughts and feelings remain connected with the body, we can easily tell the difference between our own and those of other people. We know that an emotion belongs to us because we can feel its physiological symptoms: the heavy heart of sadness, the stomach churn of anxiety, the flush of embarrassment. But when these energies are projected out of the body, we may meet them coming at us in the form of phenomena that appear to be external. Aspects of our own personality may manifest to us as apparently autonomous beings. For instance, if we are angry, we might have a nightmare in which we are being attacked. If we are feeling disappointed in God, we might hear the thundering voice of a God who is disappointed in humanity. These astral manifestations tend to confirm our most secret hopes and fears, which then get projected outward with renewed force.

What we find in Baggage Disclaim closely resembles our conception of the spiritual world because we keep encountering our own projections. "God's will" as perceived in Baggage Disclaim holds few surprises.

What God thinks people ought to do is uncannily similar to what *we* think people ought to do. The baggage that informs our conception of God usually has a lot to do with unfinished business from childhood. We project a God who, like a parent, approves or disapproves, punishes or rewards, cares or fails to care. Our personal projection is fortified by those of every despondent "inner child" who has ever occupied the planet. It has been imagined by so many and with such force that it can easily manifest as a vision or a voice. Thus it is possible to spend whole life-times lost in Baggage Disclaim, because our beliefs keep getting confirmed by our inner experiences. Conversely, people with enough psychological savvy to recognize the illusion and how it is being created sometimes conclude, mistakenly, that the entire spiritual world is just a product of wishful or fearful thinking. Out goes the baby with the bathwater.

The best way to recognize that you're in Baggage Disclaim is by sensing your vertical weight—that is, by learning to discern the difference between levity and astrality. Here are some simple tests:

- What happens if you try to change the subject? Levity requires control of attention. Beings of above fall silent as soon as you stop listening to them. When you'd prefer to have your mind all to yourself, they're quick to take the hint. You're free to forget all about them whenever you choose. By contrast, in the astral you may encounter both thoughts that have become detached from their thinkers, and thinkers who have very bad manners. Their claims on your attention tend to be insistent and repetitive. Intensity and obsessiveness are telltale characteristics of thoughts arising from the astral.
- What happens if you try to change your mind? Respect for human freedom is an inviolable principle of above. Beings there are not intent on pushing you around. If you've started spelling words like "Mission" and "Destiny" with capital letters, you're probably get-ting your info from Baggage Disclaim. Ditto if you feel that failure to heed some "Call" will be an irretrievable screwup. If you believe that the Book of Revelation pertains to the immediate future and that your marching orders are to be found therein, it's time to call in the deprogrammers.

- What happens if you laugh at yourself? Laughing won't cause you to lose your place when you're truly in the upper vertical. Humor and reverence coexist quite happily there. If a good laugh returns you immediately to the horizontal, you've probably been in Baggage Disclaim. If you can't see what's so funny, you're probably still there.

In and of itself, there's nothing wrong with visiting the astral plane. It can be quite interesting in the way that flea markets are interesting, and a great place to shop. Among the cast-off thoughts, feelings, and fantasies that abound there, you will find some that are useful to you, and many that are entertaining. Some forms of magic involve the creation and/or manipulation of astral phenomena. (I'll say more about them in the chapter on sublimation.) Whether by accident or by design, you will almost certainly learn to heighten and project your own astrality in the course of becoming an alchemist. The astral only becomes a Realm of Deception when we fail to recognize where we are, mistaking it for the true upper vertical.

Getting out of Baggage Disclaim does not, alas, transport us immediately into the higher realms. When we realize that we have mistaken our astrality for the world of the spirit, we feel a sense of loss. The shattering of an illusion makes us wary, on our guard against falling for another. Between forsaking the false vertical and entering the true, we may experience a gap in which it seems that we have no spiritual life at all. Mired in this gap, we may feel a great longing to return to the familiar, for we can see nothing with which to replace it. This longing, projected outward, conjures up a new and improved version of the Realm of Deception—one that we cannot so easily see through. Eventually we wise up to that one, too, and then have to face a redoubled sense of wariness and loss.

It might console you to read of the same recurring cycle in the lives of the great mystics. It might, but it probably won't—not if you're deep in the despair phase. (Did it console you, as a child, to be told that you were "just going through a stage"?) I don't have any easy solution to offer, but I do know of a difficult one. I will describe it later, in the chapter on separation.

What If Your Map Is Wrong?

In my description of the vertical world, there is an apparent contradiction. Did you spot it? I told you that the natives of below are beneath us in the evaluative sense of beneath—their consciousness less evolved than the horizontal consciousness of a human being. Yet I described a place of healing at the very bottom of this region. When we descend to this place, we are transformed for the better. So who is doing the healing? When our own levity is on the blink, who or what enables us to overcome the heavy gravity of the lower realms and return safely to the horizontal?

When you come up against a discrepancy like this, you have a choice to make. The mental map you've been using to navigate the spiritual world does not seem to fit with what you're experiencing. That could mean you've gotten lost, or it could mean that the map is faulty: the region you're in has been mislocated or misdrawn. (This is what I concluded when I realized that the area I now call Baggage Disclaim didn't fit the description of the upper vertical.) When you make the correction, you find the map as a whole still works.

Another option—which needs pointing out, because people rarely think of it on their own—is to remind yourself that your map is a mental construct that you yourself have created. It's your conception of the spiritual world, not the actual spiritual world itself. You don't necessarily have to abandon your inner map when you discover something that doesn't fit, nor do you have to *make* that something fit. You can just say, "I seem to have discovered an uncharted area." Recall that it is impossible to get a true overview of the vertical dimension. We can only approximate such a view by connecting dots, making generalizations based on multiple isolated experiences. Even the most gifted seers come up with some pretty flaky notions when they misconnect dots in an effort to draw up a Unified Theory of Everything.

Yet another possibility to consider is that neither you nor your map is wrong. You have indeed ended up where you thought you were going; it's just not quite what you were expecting. There must be some logical explanation for those palm trees you're seeing in Antarctica or those apparently lighter beings who come to the rescue when you plummet into the lower realms. Looking for that explanation can lead to some remarkable discoveries. For me, wondering who those lighter beings are and how they ended up at the bottom is, quite possibly, the single best question I've ever asked. So I hope you find the question interesting enough to pursue for yourself, and that it will prove similarly fruitful for you. The purpose of this book is not to tell you Catherine's Unified Theory of Everything, so I won't go into my conclusions. I will, however, offer a few observations that you may find relevant to your own investigations.

Americans have a deep-seated aversion to hierarchy, for it clashes with our allegiance to the truth that all people are created equal. We are descended from those who came to the New World to escape corrupt hierarchies in the old. In the hierarchies that have nevertheless arisen on our shores, position has more to do with power than with merit. Those at the top of the human organization chart lord it over those below by virtue of . . . well, by virtue of their *lack* of virtue, in many cases. When we succeed in toppling them, we rejoice and count it a moral accomplishment. For Americans, horizontality *itself* is the sum and substance of what we think right, just, and appropriate in horizontal relations.

The hierarchy we find in the spiritual world works differently from those we find in human institutions. It is founded on the principle of noblesse oblige. Nobility is power placed at the disposal of the powerless. It is the voluntary descent of that which is above in order to offer a hand up to that which is below. The lighter beings who come down a ways to meet us when we attempt to raise our consciousness are being noble in this sense. They are sacrificing the bliss of the heights in order to form a rapport with one who dwells lower. Such contact feels marvelous to us, but we can't know for sure how it feels to an angel. Perhaps they complain to each other, "I feel like I'm coming down with something."

Christian tradition tells us that there are nine different ranks of angels above us. Human beings are what is called "the tenth hierarchy." We are the lighter beings who serve all who are presently beneath human consciousness in their spiritual evolution. We are, in other words, the lowest rank of angels. By the logic of noblesse oblige, that is a most exalted position!

If the notion of the tenth hierarchy makes sense to you, you might find it productive to think more about who the beings below us are and what humans do, or could conceivably do, to serve them. Another very productive question to ask is how a lighter being becomes heavy enough to descend to the lower realms. According to the creed adopted by most Christians, during the time between his death and resurrection, Christ "descended into hell." Now, in terms of vertical weight, Christ was extremely light—perhaps the lightest human being ever to walk the earth. How did a being whose natural position was at the top become heavy enough to sink all the way to the bottom? What did he use for ballast?

Symbol Exercises

1. Lighter beings perceive objects as processes. When they communicate in pictures, they are sending a diagram of a process. Let's try creating some of these diagrams ourselves.

Suppose you wanted to communicate the idea, *tree*. The process might go something like this: Below, a spreading down and out (i.e., the roots). In the middle, many consolidating into one (the trunk). Above, a spreading out and up (the branches).

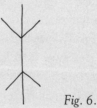

Fig. 6.

Next let's try to sketch the process of automobile. There is a circular forward movement and also a containing. A diagram of it might look like this:

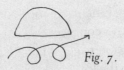

Fig. 7.

You'll notice that both of our process diagrams somewhat resemble the objects they're trying to describe. Gives new meaning to the maxim, "Form follows function," doesn't it? Try making process diagrams of other common objects and see if you get the same result.

2. Here's a picture of a *vajra:*

Fig. 8.

Tibetans use the vajra in ceremonial magic. It is an actual object, usually made of iron or bronze, that represents the magical will. Why do you suppose it has this particular shape?

3. Our inner map of the spiritual world—a vertical axis intersecting a horizontal axis—resembles a cross. Many alchemical symbols employ this cross. Their resemblance to the Christian crucifix is not accidental.

Try meditating on the crucifix (the cross with the body of Christ on it) as if it were an alchemical symbol instead of a literal picture of what happened to Jesus. Forget what you know of Christian doctrine and consider the picture as if you were seeing it for the first time. What is the relationship between the position of the body and the cross? Why is there such apparent suffering in this relationship? (Yes, I know the body is nailed, but *why* is it nailed?) When the cross is represented in the abstract—that is, without the body of Jesus—why is the horizontal beam toward the top instead of exactly in the middle?

Here is another alchemical symbol that employs the cross:

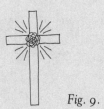

Fig. 9.

As you contemplate it, don't try to figure out what the rose stands for. Instead, consider the rose as a process. Try to feel that process happening inside you. How does it feel to be a rose? What happens when you place that feeling at the point where the vertical intersects the horizontal?

In some versions of this symbol, the rose is placed at the top of the vertical beam rather than in the center. Which version feels truer to you?

5

Living Backward

Time, Freedom, and Magical Intuition

A WOMAN I KNOW—let's call her Hannah—was losing her husband to cancer. Apart from her grief and horror at his steady decline, she felt overwhelmed by practical problems. She had been struggling to establish a small business at the time he fell ill and was under tremendous pressure to make a go of it now that she was the sole wage earner. The house was run down and the garden, which she had always loved tending, was weedy and overgrown. To be surrounded by all this mess that she had neither the time nor the energy to remedy made her feel even more despondent and helpless. One day she found herself wishing that another man would come into her life—someone who would help out like a husband without demanding any of a husband's privileges. But why would any guy want to do that? Might as well wish for an angel to appear.

The day after she had entertained this fleeting wish, Hannah took the subway downtown for a meeting with a potential customer. On the train, she noticed a remarkable man. He was wearing a tunic and loose pants of impeccably pressed gray cotton. A bag cut from the same fabric was slung over his shoulder. The whole ensemble appeared to be handmade. Its elegant simplicity suited the man, who was Asian and had an air of alert repose about him like a Buddhist monk. Just looking at him made her feel calmer.

Five hours later, her business successfully completed, she boarded the subway again to return home. Getting up to disembark as the train approached her stop, she glanced toward the far end of the car and noticed the same man she had seen in the morning. This seemed so wildly improbable that she wondered at first whether she was hallucinating. She stepped closer to make sure. He was there all right. His unlikely reappearance made her even more curious about him. Could it be that this coincidence had some special meaning? The moment she asked herself that question, he looked up at her in an alert, expectant way. He went on looking, longer and more directly than strangers normally do on the subway.

"I saw you this morning," she said.

"Yes," he replied, smiling.

"I noticed because of your clothes. You look kind of like a monk."

"I am monk."

"Well, that would explain it," she said lamely. She didn't know what to say next. But as the doors opened, the man got off, too, and kept pace with her as she made her way down the platform and out of the station. He continued to walk alongside her as she turned down the street toward her house. Since he wasn't speaking, she wasn't sure whether he was accompanying her or just going the same way. After a block, he finally broke the awkward silence: "Today my buffdy."

"I'm sorry, what?" He had a heavy foreign accent. "Buffdy" did not sound like any English word she knew.

"I bor this day." She still didn't understand. The thought of struggling to make conversation with someone who spoke so little English made her feel weary. She was a little sorry now she'd given him an opening. He stopped to fish an international driver's license out of his shoulder bag and showed it to her, underlining the date of birth with his fingertip.

"Oh, it's your birthday!"

"Yes. My buffdy."

Now it happened that this woman had a birthday cake in her fridge. Not just any cake, mind you. A cake with sugar roses and "Happy Birthday" inscribed in icing. The reason for this was sad. Some years before, her daughter had been stillborn. She and her husband always commemorated the anniversary with a little private party. She'd bought a cake as usual, only to realize that she couldn't bear to mark the occasion alone. So this must be the reason for the coincidence: the monk was there to eat the untouched cake.

"Come to my garden for tea, then," she offered. "I will give you a birthday party."

She had forgotten just then what a deplorable state her garden was in and felt a little embarrassed as she led him through the broken gate, thrashing through the overgrowth to a weedy patio where she bid him be seated on a rickety Adirondack chair. A few minutes later, she returned with a pot of tea and the cake. "See? It says 'Happy Birthday,'" she said, triumphantly pointing to the icing inscription. To her perplexity and slight disappointment, he didn't appear the least bit astonished. He seemed to take it entirely for granted that the pantry of a stranger should manifest a birthday cake on his birthday.

After a few futile stabs at conversation, the monk resorted to show-and-tell, pulling an envelope of color snapshots from his shoulder bag. "My home," he said, displaying several photos of a huge and ornate Buddhist temple. Another photo depicted him in elaborate ceremonial garb before a large crowd of monks and laymen who were prostrating. They appeared to be prostrating *to him*.

"Not just a monk," she observed. "You are an abbot, something like that?"

"What is abbot?"

"Like boss. Boss of monks."

"Not boss. Don't know English word. Like this: Many life. Always monk."

They fell silent. Hannah could think of many questions she'd like to ask of someone who'd been a monk for many lifetimes, but given the language barrier, there didn't seem to be much point.

"Why garden like this?" he asked at last.

"Like how? You mean a mess?"

"Yes. Garden very big mess. Why?"

"My husband is very sick. And I am very tired."

Carefully he set his mug and cake plate down on the wide arm of the chair and stood up. Then he fell to his knees before her. "I love you," he said.

She wondered if she should attribute this to his limited vocabulary. Maybe "I love you" was the only thing he knew how to say to a woman in English. But the ardor of his posture suggested that he did indeed mean something along those lines. Though normally such a brash declaration would have flustered her, she found herself receiving it as he had received the cake; as if strange men throwing themselves at her feet were something that happened to her every day.

"Thank you," she said regally. "But you are a monk. What are you doing?"

"I love you," he said obstinately. "Is good! I am happy."

He looked beyond happy. Downright beatific, yet oddly free of agenda, as if the accomplishment of loving her did not need to be crowned with any further attainment. In response, she felt oddly free to state her mind. "I am feeling very tired. Will you please go away now?"

"Yes," he said cheerily, scrambling to his feet. "Yes, is time. I come new day. I do garden. Okay?"

The next morning, Hannah was awakened very early by her doorbell. It was the monk, dressed this time in jeans and a tee shirt emblazoned with "TOMMY," and bearing a tool that looked like a miniature scythe. "I work now," he said.

Work he did, flailing away at the overgrowth with an energy that was almost violent. Five minutes into the task, sweat was already pouring from him. It made one hot just to look at him. She stood by, wringing her hands as he ruthlessly assaulted the skirts of the shrubs and the low-hanging limbs of the trees, beheading cherished perennials along with the weeds. "Too much. Too fast," she protested. "You're scaring me."

"Don't look," he said fiercely. "Go in house."

Torn between feeling grateful and wanting to call the police, Hannah cowered indoors, waiting for this tornado that loved her to blow over. Eventually she set about preparing lunch, carefully averting her eyes from the kitchen window. But he wouldn't stop to eat—or even to take a drink of water—until the job was finished.

"Okay, now look," he called finally through the screen door.

Dread turned to astonishment as Hannah took in what he had done.

The shrubs had been pruned into artful shapes, the vines tamed, the rose canes tied to their trellises. The flower beds were hoed clean of weeds and freshly mulched, the paths and patio hosed down and swept. He had even repaired the broken hinges of the gate and the wobbly arms of the wooden chairs. She could have worked all summer and not accomplished what he had managed to do in under four hours. The beauty of her own garden was a revelation to her.

After lunch, the monk set about making indoor repairs with the same vigor and expertise he had applied to the garden. Hannah found it very strange and humbling that a Buddhist teacher should be serving as her gardener and handyman. As he packed up his tools at the end of the miraculously productive day, she said, "You have helped me so much. I don't know how to thank you."

He clasped her hand in a gesture that was at once rough and courtly and bowed to her. "No thank. I love you." With that, he departed. She never saw him again.

Do you find this story credible? If you have doubts that it really happened, at what point did those doubts first arise? Did you buy the monk appearing in the same car of the same train Hannah was riding twice in one day? Was it the birthday cake in Hannah's fridge that first began to strain your credulity? Or was it the monk's eagerness to grant a secret wish she had conceived only the previous day? If this were a work of fiction, I'd never get away with such a plotline—unless, perhaps, the genre was Magic Realism. Fiction loses its aura of plausibility when the action is advanced by coincidences.

Strictly speaking, a coincidence is nothing more than the simultaneous occurrence of any two phenomena. When you and any other person happen to be in the same rail car at the same time, that is a coincidence. But it isn't worth noting if no relationship exists between you. You would only say, "What a coincidence!" if the other person's presence had some meaning for you—if it were a long lost friend, perhaps, or someone you had intended to phone later in the day. The surprising part is the meaning. Add a second layer of meaning—perhaps you and the long-lost friend are both traveling to the wedding of a third friend you never knew you had in common—and the coincidence becomes even more remarkable. Now add another. As you go on conversing you discover that each of you was, at one time, in love with the fiancé of the mutual friend. With each new layer of meaning, your astonishment increases. You move from "What a coincidence!" to "I don't believe it!" to "This is spooky!"

If you stop to think about it, what all this incredulity implies is that we're not expecting meaning. Our fundamental assumption is randomness. This assumption is the premise of probability theory and of statistical approaches to the study of science. Muggles often rely on it when trying to figure out what to do. For example, if it is known that only one resumé out of a hundred leads to a job interview and that the average person goes on three interviews before landing a job, the muggle who wants one job will send out three hundred resumés! Isn't that extraordinary?

The probability that the day you first meet someone will be their birthday is 1/365. If it happens to you only that often—one time in 365—the statistician would classify it as random and seek no further explanation. Let's suppose that, on average, Hannah talks to one stranger per week. On any given day, the probability of her talking to a stranger on his birthday is 1/7 x 1/365, or one chance in 2,555. Hannah buys three birthday cakes a year: one for her husband's birthday, one for her own, and one for their departed daughter's. If each cake is purchased a day in advance, the probability of there being an untouched birthday cake in her fridge is 1/121. The probability that this will coincide with meeting someone on their birthday is 1/2,555 x 1/121, or one chance in 309,155. It is actually a great deal more likely than winning millions in a lottery.

Still, the statistical plausibility of this coincidence seems somehow beside the point, for there are other meanings in the story that are not so easily quantified. Part of the meaning of the cake on that particular day was that Hannah was sad that she had no one to eat it with her. Even more significant was the monk's fulfillment of her wish. I have no idea how one goes about calculating the probability of subjective states like sadness and desire. Yet, though we might not know how to prove it, we somehow feel that Hannah's previous wish makes her meeting with the monk *more* likely. Only the most diehard rationalist could avoid suspecting that, in some undefined way, Hannah's desire *caused* the monk to appear. With a single flick of the mind, we leap out of the realm of statistical probability and into the realm of fate, magic, or providence.

Your present incarnation began when one particular sperm cell out of—I forget how many, but *lots*—won the race to the egg. Had a different sperm cell edged it out, you would have different genetic material, which would have made your body different in countless unknowable ways. Some of these differences would have significantly altered your life. You might have been more or less attractive, healthy, intelligent, athletic, and so forth. Your personality would be different, too. Now, fertilization is not entirely random, since the race is to the swift. Still, there would seem to be a large element of randomness as far as which sperm are first out of the gate and what conditions are like on the track. Anyway, what I want to ask is this: Do you consider the matter largely or entirely accidental, or do you feel that there was something inevitable about it? Have you ever felt, or do you consider it possible, that the victory of the sperm that made you was somehow "meant to be"? What do you prefer to think? Is there a difference between what you prefer to think and what you actually believe to be true?

In the contemporary American mind, an assumption of randomness lives side by side with a theory of spiritual causality that, in many, borders on predestination. The insouciance with which we mingle faith in statistical randomness with faith that whatever is was "meant to be" is a testament to our mental flexibility, if not our reason. In day-to-day life, the blatant contradictions in our notions of causality don't bother us a bit. In our minds, the spiritual and the scientific live on two different levels. Shuttling between them is as easy as riding an elevator. Trying to get it all to fit into one coherent worldview is the work of egghead philosophers who, after several millennia of fevered debate, have yet to reach a consensus. We shrug, leave them to it, and get on with our lives, meeting each challenge with a dash of statistics and a pinch of superstition.

Thoughtless mingling of chance with the destined is the way of the gambler. Most religions frown on gambling, for it is driven by two contradictory metaphysical assumptions (i.e., outcome is random and outcome is fated) that, taken together, undermine freedom. That is how gambling can so easily turn into an addiction. Paradox is magical, but outright contradictions paralyze the will. (Try walking backward and forward at the same time. See what I mean?)

What you believe about causality has direct bearing on what you believe you can accomplish through magic and how you go about it. You can't succeed at it if you're hedging your metaphysical bets. So let's see if we can sort through our conflicting notions of causality and come up with a workable hypothesis.

How and Why

Suppose a man on a business trip misses his flight. If, at the moment he's watching the plane take off without him, you ask him *why* he missed it, he will probably describe the events immediately preceding. First he overslept his alarm, then he got stuck in traffic on the way to the airport, and then he had some hassle going through security. These are the material causes. What they actually describe is *how* the flight got missed. In this type of explanation, what happened before is the cause of what happened after.

Now imagine that, an hour later, the man learns that his intended flight crashed, leaving no survivors. If you ask him again why he missed the plane, he might say something like, "It wasn't my time to die" or "Because I need to be here for my children." This type of why is a meaning. Yet he is advancing it, in all seriousness, as a *cause*. He can no longer recall the trivial mishaps that detained him without seeing in them some grace or providence acting to save his life. What annoyed him while it was happening can only be remembered later with the deepest awe and gratitude.

Notice that in this type of explanation, the cause comes *after* the effect. In some mysterious way, past events were shaped by a purpose that lay in the future. This purpose is not to be confused with the man's intention. His intention to *catch* the plane preceded all the various steps he took that morning and was the reason for them. The intentionality was moving forward from past to future. But somehow it got reversed, overturned by a causality that was moving in the opposite direction, flowing toward him from the future. That's how he sees it, anyhow. Could he be right?

I recently met a couple in their eighties who, after twenty years of marriage, are still besotted with each other. Ruth, the wife, had previously endured an unhappy marriage of thirty-five years. She told me, "If I hadn't stayed with my first husband for all those years, I'd have remarried earlier and wouldn't have been available when Fred came along." She so adores Fred that thirty-five years of marital misery have come to be dismissed as nothing but a delaying tactic.

When we say that something has worked out for the best, we are seeing our present good fortune as the reason for ill fortune in the past. We had to be unhappy then, so that we could be happy now. Without noticing that we are doing so, we reverse chronology, make the present the explanation for the past. Ask anyone and they'll tell you that cause precedes effect. It is to the past that we naturally look when seeking the cause of what is happening now. But as events recede in time, we become more inclined to explain them in terms of meaning. The more meaning we can see, the less we care how something came about in a material sense. We care more about why than how, and the why usually turns up *after* the how.

Notice, too, that when we place the cause after the effect, our explanation tends to be cheerful. We feel the reason something has happened is benevolent and makes sense. Contrast this with how we feel when we seek our explanations in the past. If the cause lies in the past, we can't change it. We can't get the spilled milk to go back in the jug. To answer a *why* question with *how* tends to stir up feelings of helplessness, blame, and regret. If causes come only from the past, our lives can never be quite up to date, for while we may grow in wisdom, we are always trying to dig ourselves out from under the pile of our previous errors. Our circumstances reflect who we once were better than they express who we are now. The longer we live, the less room we have for possibilities in an existence overcrowded with facts.

When, in the Gospel of John, a blind man comes to Jesus for help, bystanders ask Jesus to explain why the man was born sightless. Was it caused by his own sin or that of his parents? Jesus replies that it was neither. The man had been born blind so that his sight might be restored. Now, something had to go wrong on a material level to make the man blind in the first place, and whatever that was happened before the blindness happened. Jesus wasn't denying the one-way chronology of material events. But that's not what he'd been asked. The question put to him was not *how* the man became blind, but *why*. According to Jesus, the answer to that lay in the future.

In Jesus's backward chronology, the solution explained the problem. The cure explained the disease. At the very least, this is a more upbeat way of regarding affliction. If the cause of your clogged arteries is all the bacon you ate in the past, there's not much you can do about it now. If you think instead that the cause is the future health of your arteries, you can stop reproaching yourself over past bacon and get on with your healing.

The power of positive thinking is certainly not to be despised, but I don't believe it's the whole story. Jesus was suggesting that a cause coming from the future actually has the power to reverse a cause coming from the past. He proved that this idea was workable by restoring the blind man's sight.

Remembering the Future

In the Arthurian legends, the magician Merlin is said to live backward. When he thinks of the future, he is remembering. When he thinks of the past, he is anticipating. This is not as outlandish as it sounds. You, too, might come to experience time in that way. As both the gospels and the Merlin legends suggest, this altered sense of time is a key to working magic.

In its pure form, we do not experience time. We can perceive and measure its movement only if we use something physical as a reference point, i.e., the hands on a clock, the transit of the sun, the growth and decline of our own bodies. Because physical objects are absent from the spiritual world, time cannot be marked there. In a sense, the vertical is a dimension of time alone. You could call it "absolute time" or you could call it "timelessness," for it lacks the forward march that we on earth regard as the very essence of time. It can't go forward, because there is nothing fixed to serve as a departure point.

Some people try to approximate this experience of absolute time by floating in sensory deprivation tanks. Of course, one could still use the pulse to mark minutes, and a rumbling stomach might eventually declare "dinnertime." Still, many report experiencing something close to timelessness. The same is true of excursions into the upper vertical. To an outside observer, the trance of the mystic appears to last only a minute or two, yet on her return she may feel as if she has been away for hours or days. Having no boundaries, the vertical moment can expand indefinitely. Past, present, and future are all one moment: the absolute NOW.

Does this mean that if you enter that NOW you can see the future? Yes and no. You can't see what's going to happen because "going to happen" implies a chronology. If time isn't moving in a linear fashion, you can't perceive a story line. You just see what *is*. When we return to the horizontal, we return to a linear time sense as well. Inspired by the NOW we have glimpsed vertically, we might make up a narrative about the future. Some people are very good at this. Their predictions turn out to be remarkably accurate. They might even insist that they have *seen* the future story line unfold. But strictly speaking, this kind of seeing is an act of the imagination triggered by vertical perception, not a direct vertical perception in and of itself. Right now that might sound like a distinction without a difference, but it will become very important later when we are discussing free will.

The mark of vertical inspiration in a horizontal narrative is that time flows toward us in two streams.

The ordinary movement of time from past to future meets a second stream that, from our perspective, appears to be flowing from future to past. How meets Why. If you find the point where the two streams converge and step into it, magic happens. The knack for finding that meeting point is called intuition.

You'll find a thrilling example of such a convergence in Shakespeare's *Henry V*. Massed on a battlefield near Agincourt, Henry's troops are outnumbered five to one. His cousin Westmoreland wishes they had at least ten thousand more men. Henry replies:

> No, my fair cousin.
> If we are marked to die, we are enow
> To do our country loss; and if to live,
> The fewer men, the greater share of honour.
> God's will, I pray thee wish not one man more.

Henry doesn't appear to know the outcome, since he is allowing for the possibility that it could go either way. Yet as he goes on speaking, loss of the battle is an abstract concept that soon falls away, while victory is vividly imagined. He describes that victory not as it will be experienced in the coming hours, but as it will be remembered on its anniversary, many years later:

> He that shall see this day, and live old age,
> Will yearly on the vigil feast his neighbours,
> And say, tomorrow is Saint Crispian.
> Then will he strip his sleeve, and show his scars,
> And say, these wounds I had on Crispin's day.
> Old men forget; yet all shall be forgot
> But he'll remember, with advantages,
> What feats he did that day. Then shall our names,
> Familiar in their mouths as household words,
> Harry the King, Bedford and Exeter,
> Warwick and Talbot, Salisbury and Gloucester,
> Be in their flowing cups freshly remembered.
> This story shall the good man teach his son;
> And Crispin Crispian shall ne'er go by
> From this day to the ending of the world,
> But we in it shall be remembered;
> We few, we happy few, we band of brothers;
> For he today that sheds his blood with me
> Shall be my brother; be he ne'er so vile
> This day shall gentle his condition.

And gentlemen in England, now a-bed,
Shall think themselves accursed they were not here;
And hold their manhoods cheap, whiles any speaks
That fought with us upon Saint Crispin's day.

In this moment, the two time streams converge. As the army steps forward in time, into the *how* of fighting a battle in which they are so greatly outnumbered, the *why* of that apparent disadvantage is coming to meet them from the future. They are few in number so that the honor of each man's share in victory will be the greater.

You might argue that Henry's speech is merely an effective pep talk. But I invite you to consider that its effectiveness resides in its truth. What Henry describes actually comes to pass. Not only is the battle won, but the majority of those who fight live to tell of it. Nothing that Henry can see in the material circumstances supports this prediction. It is preposterous, yet he describes it with a precision and confidence that far transcend a mere hoping for the best. It reads like an eyewitness account. It sounds more *remembered* than hoped. The extraordinary outcomes that we call magical are quite often accompanied by this sense of remembrance.

In a recent interview, Muhammad Yunus, founder of the Grameen Bank, which makes micro loans to the very poor, said that he expects world poverty to be eradicated within the next few decades. Not hopes. *Expects.* He predicted that our grandchildren will have to take their kids to a "poverty museum" to learn how people used to starve. This is no mere wish. It is a precise description of the future. When we look to the past, all we can see is how poverty happened. The causes coming from the past are so incontrovertible that we can't see how it could be any other way. Yunus is seeing that it nevertheless *is* another way. That's intuition. It's how anything unprecedented gets created or accomplished.

The story of Hannah and the monk seems to be about a farfetched wish coming true. But if you apply the logic I've been describing, the wish was not far-fetched. It arose because its object was about to manifest. In the NOW of absolute time, the moment when Hannah wished for a man who would serve her selflessly coexists with the moment the monk knelt at her feet and promised to do exactly that. You can't say which came first. Since there's no chronology, cause can't precede effect. It makes just as much sense to say that Hannah wished for the man because he turned up as to say that the man turned up because she wished for him. At the time she was wishing on earth, she was, in the vertical world, already in possession of that for which she longed. You could even say that her earthbound self was *missing* him.

That could be why, once they met on earth, they were able to come so quickly to the point. When they saw each other on the train, there was some quality of mutual recognition. It was as if they were attempting to recall why they had come together. When each spoke to the heart of the matter—Hannah by offering the birthday cake, the monk by offering his love—the other wasn't surprised. We rarely feel surprised when we're merely being reminded.

Any true desire is a kind of memory. By "true desire" I mean one that arises directly from the soul, not the myriad trivial wants induced by advertising, nor the ambitions to which we are driven by our own insecurities and the expectations of others. I mean a desire you can really feel in your heart. Such desires are often the distant call of something we already possess and have forgotten, something we are missing. They are a kind of nostalgia for the future. A future which, in the vertical world, is our NOW.

The attainment of such desires on earth still entails a material How, still requires the taking of steps in linear time. Yet often these steps feel akin to walking on the moon. There is a bouncy quality to them. You might even feel this in your literal feet. You are expecting a step to carry you the length of one of your usual paces, but instead you leap as if momentarily weightless and come down a great distance from where you started. Others might describe you as lucky. The energy of a normal step is being augmented by the *whoosh* that results when the current of Why meets the current of How. Another way to put it is that you are being drawn forward by the attraction of what already *is*.

Years ago the comedian Jim Carrey described in an interview how, at the time he was first struggling to make it in show business, he had written himself a check for ten million dollars, dated several years in the future. The ten million dollars actually came through (in the form of a salary for his first starring movie role) eerily close to the date on the check. I'm always on the lookout for a magical procedure to end my financial worries, so inspired by Carrey's example, I wrote myself a check for a huge publisher's advance. The date on that check has come and gone and I'm no richer. Why? I wasn't actually *seeing* the future wealth, just trying to will it into existence through the power of positive thinking. If the object of a desire doesn't exist in your NOW, visualization alone is unlikely to conjure it into being. That doesn't mean you can't still get to what you want by means of ordinary How steps. Often you can. But if the corresponding Why is absent, the desire seems to resist magical attainment. You have to plod toward it methodically instead of moon walking.

Destiny and Choice

Am I saying, then, that Hannah and the monk were destined to meet? Not if by "destined" you mean that the whole thing was planned and that it could not have gone otherwise. It very well could have gone any number of different ways. When Hannah noticed the monk the second time, she might have shrugged and said to herself, "Small world!" and thought no more about it. Instead, she chose to speak to him. And just as she was wondering whether she should ditch him when he was trailing her down the street, he mentioned his birthday. He invited himself to return after she had asked him to leave. All of these were choice points where they made free decisions. Neither felt any sense of compulsion, of being driven to speak or act. They were both doing exactly what they felt like doing at any given moment. That's what gave the encounter its goofy spontaneity.

Confusion on this point is almost as old as time itself. As soon as people discover that the future is, in some sense, knowable, they jump to the conclusion that it is fixed. The confusion arises from applying the narrative conventions of linear time to vertical time. The "future" glimpsed in the NOW is not that which has happened or will happen. From a vertical standpoint nothing has happened or will happen. Happening only happens in linear time. Events can't be predestined or foreordained because in absolute time, there is no "pre" or "fore." They can't be planned, because planning is strictly a horizontal activity.

I think that it is only on a superficial, intellectual level that people get confused about this. Intuitively, most of us know better. We just can't figure out how to explain it. Have you ever watched *The Bachelor*? Contestants on that show are constantly invoking some vague notion of destiny. They say, "I believe I am here [i.e., in a hot tub with the bachelor] for a reason" or "I believe I will be chosen if it's meant to be." They do not, however, rest complacent in the certainty that what was "meant to be" will actually transpire. Far from it! They go through all manner of exertions—applying makeup, wiggling their fannies, composing love notes, and bad-mouthing their rivals—to be chosen. The metaphysically inevitable must, one gathers, be helped along by French kisses and the right bikini. When it actually manifests, they profess astonishment: "I never expected to feel like this!" "I never imagined this contest would actually lead me to my soul mate!" It would also appear that destiny is capable of going on the blink. Fifteen out of twenty contestants might believe that marriage to the bachelor is meant to be but only one is chosen. In the departing limo, losers will sometimes tearfully assert that what was meant to be hasn't happened because, for some unaccountable reason, the bachelor has failed to take instruction from the Universe.

Though I can't resist poking fun, my point is that these fey young ladies are probably closer to the metaphysical mark than a lot of serious philosophers. In words, they might deny free will, but with every action they assert it. Intuitively they grasp a very subtle and difficult point: what was "meant" doesn't necessarily happen.

The vertical is the realm of meaning, the realm of *why*. The absolute NOW is *not* the sum total of every single event that has occurred or will occur on earth. Memory is necessarily selective, for to remember everything is to remember nothing. The sum of all possible facts is utterly meaningless. Can you recall how many times you blinked yesterday? Can you recall even a single instance of blinking?

By the same token, you can "remember" what has never been and might never be. Suppose you receive a wonderful gift and resolve to write a thank-you note to the sender. While doing so, you get distracted, and months later you find the half-written note under a pile of papers on your desk. The note was never completed or sent, yet it still exists as a meaning. The contrast between its meaningful existence in memory and its *lack* of existence in the intended recipient's mailbox is what makes you feel so mortified.

You could say that time forgets, and also that it remembers what has never been. What has been attained entirely by means of horizontal How might not register in absolute time if it lacks a corresponding Why. Time forgets, just as we forget, that which is insignificant. Conversely, there are Whys that fail to hook up with a corresponding How. The significant is "remembered" even if it has failed to happen. It persists in the vertical as a possibility or an ideal.

To remember and to forget are acts of consciousness. They require a knower, a thinker. There is, in the vertical, nothing that could be compared to an impersonal database. So when I say "time forgets" *whose* consciousness am I talking about? Who is doing the forgetting or remembering? Who decides what gets recorded in the absolute NOW? Don't let the absence of an immediate answer cause you to forget this very important question. You're going to need it later.

It is our ability to attain the meaningless and pass up the meaningful that demonstrates our free will. When "destiny calls," we are free to ignore it, and often we do. When vertical desire meets horizontal opportunity, we might let the moment slip away—by failing to notice or by neglecting to follow our intuition. Many people are unhappy because they sense that they have blown it. When an "as above" has failed to incarnate into a "so below," the gap between fills up with restless discontent, uncertainty, self-reproach, and a feeling that something is missing.

Still, we are entirely free to "blow it." Apart from our own unhappiness, there is no penalty for this. As Henry V said at the start of his prophetic speech, "He which hath no stomach to this fight, let him depart; his passport shall be made, and crowns for convoy put into his purse." Apart from our own selves, we disappoint no one who dwells above. In the vertical world, there are no expectations to disappoint. Expecting, like planning, is a horizontal activity dependent on linear time.

Remembering Backward

Reversing or otherwise mixing up the order of remembered events is an excellent way to loosen up your linear conception of time and to begin perceiving the convergence of time currents. The first exercise comes from Rudolf Steiner's *How to Know Higher Worlds*.

1. Just before you go to sleep, review the events of the day in reverse order. Start with the present moment and work back to the moment you first woke up.

I always used to approach this in small units of action and must confess that's still the only way I can manage it. For example, I see myself washing the dishes, then eating the meal, then cooking the meal, etc. Each unit either moves forward in time or is frozen in time like a snapshot. But those who are really adept at the exercise see the whole day as a video on rapid rewind. If they are cooking, the cucumber slices reassemble themselves, the wine flows back into the bottle, and the well-done hamburger gradually becomes raw. One guy I know even hears whatever music he has listened to backward. When I scoffed at this, he proved it with the backward recital of any melody I chose. Impressive! Still can't do it for the life of me.

2. This one goes back at least as far as the ancient Romans and was practiced by many medieval hermeticists. It combines memory with the "composition of the place" you learned previously.

You can use either an imaginary place or a real one such as your own house. The latter is probably easier for starters. Think of ten people you know and assign each one a different position in your mental location. For instance, your mother is standing by the kitchen sink, your best friend is perched on the arm of the couch, etc. Next, see yourself entering through the front door. "Walk" through the house, naming each person in the order they appear on the way to the back door. Then enter through the back door and name them all in reverse order.

Once you're able to do that easily, assign each person an object or a word. See them holding the object or a card with the word written on it. Again walk through from the front, then the back, this time naming both the person and the object or word. Increase the difficulty by adding more people or by giving each person two different objects, one for each hand.

3. When devising the plot for a novel, writers often begin with the climax. From there they work backward, figuring out what had to happen previously to motivate the characters and bring them together for the climactic event.

Imagine your own life as a novel, choosing a major event, decision, or turning point as your climax. Plot backward from that point, listing previous events and decisions that got you there. What had to happen to make those events or decisions possible? Keep working backward. See if you can trace a chain that reaches all the way back to early childhood.

Once you have a long list of plot events, try sorting them into two categories: How and Why. A How is a material cause; something that had to happen *previously* in order for the climax to happen. For instance, say your climax is getting a job as a special-ed teacher. Pursuing the college degree that qualified you for the job is a How. Putting it after the job makes no sense.

A Why is a meaning. Though it might have preceded the climax in time, it would still feel relevant if you put it *after* the climax. As you think back, you might remember being friends in second grade with a kid who was dyslexic. In fact, now that you're thinking about it, you can recall many occasions when you felt especially sympathetic to people who were struggling with learning difficulties. These memories belong on your Why list, because they remain meaningful no matter what order you put them in. You could say you became a special-ed teacher because you felt empathy for kids with learning disabilities, or you could say you felt that empathy as a child because a desire to help the learning disabled has always existed in your NOW.

This exercise can be especially helpful when you feel you've lost sight of your purpose in life or can't figure out what the next step should be. Work backward from the last time you felt as if your life was making sense. The Why list you get when you look backward from that moment may help you to recover a sense of direction in the present.

Drivers and Passengers

They might not have plans for us, but we may sometimes suspect that spiritual beings are involving themselves in our affairs. When the attainment of a vertical possibility entails the thwarting of our horizontal intentions, we feel that we have been acted upon. Something or someone has intervened in the normal chain of causality. Our businessman was ultimately happy that he wasn't on the plane that crashed, but missing it was not his own idea.

Or was it?

Suppose for a moment that the consequences had been different. Suppose the plane arrived safely at its destination. Because the man wasn't on it, he missed an important meeting and lost a major account. Regret prompts him to reflect on what he ought to have done differently. Perhaps he overslept because he neglected to set his alarm, or lingered in bed after it went off. Perhaps traffic delayed him because he decided to take a taxi instead of an express train. By the time he arrived at the security gate, he was very anxious, and looked it. The inspectors detained him because his anxiety aroused their vigilance. In short, the mishap was a result of choices of his own that worked against his overall intention. Regardless of whether the consequences are positive, negative, or neutral, the material How of it works exactly the same way: there is a gap between what the man intends and what he actually does.

Such gaps are bound to occur because every incarnate human enjoys dual citizenship. We live in the world of linear time and also in the realm of the absolute NOW. If we neglect the vertical aspect of our conscious-ness (i.e., the spirit), we may come to identify so completely with the "I" who lives in horizontal time that the spirit doesn't feel like "I" at all. When it asserts choices different from our conscious, horizontal choices, we might feel as if we are being helped—or jerked around—by a sepa-rate spiritual being.

In *The Soul's Code*, the psychologist James Hillman suggests that the spirit will often sabotage activities of the temporal self that, from the spirit's perspective, are inauthentic. (In other words, activities for which no Why exists in the NOW.) Sometimes behavior that looks self-defeating is indeed a defeat of the self by the Self. The man might miss the plane and consequently suffer a business setback because, as his spirit sees it, he's in the wrong career. Self-sabotage is a possibility that anyone who is halfway introspective considers when mishaps occur that might easily have been prevented. We ask ourselves if uncon-sciously we wanted to fail. Hillman is suggesting that what's going on in that "unconscious" might be smarter than we suppose. The saboteur might be our wisdom, not our neurosis.

Regarding this question, a great hermeticist who preferred to remain anonymous once wrote that there are two attitudes of soul. Some people conceive of themselves as passengers, and some as drivers.

Passengers are fond of the phrase "meant to be." This begs the ques-tion: Meant *by whom*? Passengers can't say, but they're sure it's someone nice. When passengers insist that "there are no accidents," they mean that they trust the drivers. Pressed to explain *why* there are no acci-dents, the passenger will often invoke the law of karma. Ask what that might be and you come full circle, for as the passenger tells it, the law of karma boils down to this: the stuff that happens is the stuff that was meant to happen.

From drivers, too, you may hear that there are no accidents. By this they mean that most collisions are due to driver error, and the rest are due to driver desire. Like the passenger, the driver might say, "I believe I am here for a reason." Unlike the passenger, the driver will go on to tell you what the reason is. ("I am in a hot tub with the bachelor because that's what I feel like doing.") As for karma, the driver will inform you, correctly, that karma is the stuff that was *not* meant to happen.

Karma is the moral equivalent of the physical law of inertia. Things keep going or not going in the direction and at the rate that they were already going or not going unless given a good hard shove in a different direction. In other words, karma is the force of habit. To the extent that we are unconscious, we keep thinking, feeling, and doing the same things over and over again. "Good karma" simply means a habit that tends to have favorable consequences. If you are in the habit of telling the truth, this is good karma because people will tend to take you at your word. Their trust is not a reward to which you can consider yourself entitled because you are virtuous. It's just what will usually happen as a natural result of what you usually do. Same goes for bad karma. You're not being punished. You're just in the habit of doing something that, more often than not, produces an unfavorable result. We carry over good or bad karma from past lives only to the extent that we keep doing the same old, same old in our present lives.

Nobody is in charge of karma. No one is judging and doling out rewards or penalties. Like the law of gravity, it is just a mechanical description of what goes down. Karma is how things happen when we don't consciously intend, or when our unconscious will is stronger than our conscious intention. In other words, karma is the stuff that wasn't *meant*. It is all How and no Why. It comes only from the past. Even when it is good, it is unmagical, because its time stream flows in only one direction. You don't get that *whoosh* of the two time streams meeting. To the driver, karma is a speed bump. To the passenger, it is the vehicle.

What exists in the absolute NOW is meant. It has meaning. And the meaning it has in the vertical takes on the other sense of "meaning"—i.e., intention—when it enters the horizontal. The Timeless Self *means*. The temporal self causes *to be*. Something is "meant to be" when meaning weds action, when the vertical "I" and the horizontal "I" are working in concert.

How does the meaning get there? Passengers don't know and don't especially care. They just hope to find it and mope when they can't. Drivers will say that the meaning is there because they themselves put it there. They regard meaning as something you make, not something you find.

When we say "I" from a driver's perspective, it refers to both the vertical and the horizontal selves, the spirit and the dweller in linear time. The more we regard ourselves as drivers, the less difference we feel between the two. As the two selves begin to merge, the very notion of two different selves comes to seem nonsensical.

This perspective is difficult to attain, for all of us start life as passengers. Being carried is the first thing that happens to us. We hope and trust that those doing the carrying are benevolent. As we get older, this sense of passive trust in grown-ups is often transferred to the spiritual world. We are over the illusion that our parents always know what's best for us, but persist in believing that lighter beings do. We want to be sure that we are thinking, feeling, and doing the right thing, and we are used to looking outside ourselves for this quality of "right." We try to align ourselves with some principle or moral law. We listen for voices or turn to other clairvoyants for a reading. We look for signs and portents.

When help comes in the form of a meaningful coincidence or a lucky break, the passenger interprets it as a sign: "I'm getting help, so I must be on the right track." Practical assistance is assumed to be *guidance*. It means the grown-ups approve. To the driver, help is merely help. The fact that someone has changed a tire for you has no bearing on whether

Driver's Ed

I've recently discovered a quick way back to the driver's seat when I fall into passenger mentality. Maybe it will work for you, too.

A year ago I found myself embarking on an enterprise that scared me. I wasn't at all sure whether I really ought to be doing this thing, and my desires were equally murky. "Destiny," though, was acting very sure of itself, maneuvering me through an uncanny series of coincidences into what "they" had planned for me. (Who "they" might be was undefined, as it so often is in passenger thinking.)

While describing my predicament in a letter to a friend, I found myself listing the events leading up to it in chronological order. The narrative was in passive voice, i.e., sentences that describe what is being done without naming the doer. Since good writers frown on passive voice, and I like to think of myself as a good writer, I thought I'd better correct this. Then I got the bright idea of recasting each of the sentences with *myself* as the doer. I described the entire sequence of events as if I were the mastermind behind each and every step. "First I arranged to be out of work. Then I arranged to owe more taxes than I had funds to pay. Then I prompted so-and-so to phone me with a job offer . . ." Ten steps later, the sequence concluded with, "And that's how I tricked myself into doing exactly what I want to do."

I suspect it's no coincidence that, immediately after I had edited my way into driver mentality, circumstances changed for the better. The doubtful enterprise took off, and I felt a lot more confident about my decision. You might want to try this technique the next time you're feeling jerked around by fate, destiny, karma, or whatever else you happen to call your passenger vehicle.

you're traveling in the right direction. Even lost travelers can usually find someone to mend their flats.

In the vertical world, human freedom is sacred. Even beings we think of as higher defer to it. They prefer that you relate to them as colleagues. Rookies get loads of help from them, but if you persist too long in being a passenger, you may suddenly find that all help has been withdrawn. Overnight, your teachers and guides stop returning your calls. One day you feel confident you're on the right track. The next day, you can't see *any* track. You haven't a clue what you've been doing or what you ought to be doing next. This impasse persists until you take a firm step in some direction—any direction—entirely of your own choosing. Your allies will go on absenting themselves until you learn to declare, "Because I say so, that's why." Those who have cleared this hurdle are sometimes referred to as initiates. It means, quite literally, one who initiates.

As the Worm Turns

Fig. 10.

The symbol above is called the Ouroboros. You will often see it in conjunction with the saying, "The end is the beginning."

If you only had the picture to go on, what would you make of it? Would you regard the situation it depicts as favorable? The snake is, to put it rather rudely, biting itself in the butt. If you try to add time and movement to the picture, what happens? Nothing! A snake swallowing its own tail can't do anything else. It is effectively paralyzed. Like the skull and crossbones on a poison label, this symbol is a warning. It is telling you what can happen if you construct a closed system.

No matter what we believe about causality, we will likely find that our beliefs are confirmed by our experience. This is because meaning shapes and is shaped by selective attention. People who believe that life is random experience a lot of randomness. People who believe there are no accidents tend to have fewer of them. While selective attention is an important skill for a magician, its downside is that you might overlook something important if you weren't expecting to see it. The Ouroboros warns against constructing a belief system so airtight that no new truth can come in. Another word for that is solipsism.

"Whatever happens is meant to happen" is a solipsistic idea. Do you see how it turns around and bites itself in the butt? The thought has no exit and no entrance, no way for you to get out and no way for anything new to get in. If you wanted to paralyze someone's will, convincing them that "whatever happens is meant to happen" would be an excellent way to go about it.

Now I'm going to give you a more complex example. See if you can spot the error in it.

> The past no longer exists, except in our memories. The future does not yet exist, except in our imaginations. Past and future are really just thoughts. And the present is merely theoretical. We can't actually experience it. All we can experience is our thoughts, which are either memories of the past or projections about the future.
>
> That being the case, we can conclude that there is no such thing as the so-called "real world." What we call "reality" is just our own mental construct. We create the world out of our own thoughts. Therefore, all we need do to change our world is to change our thoughts. If you have some complaint about the world, your own thoughts are to blame. You could inhabit a different world just by choosing to think differently. Anyone who is unhappy is choosing to think the wrong thoughts.
>
> Consider this the next time someone criticizes you. The message is not about you. It is about the person who delivers it. It is based on their own personal construction of reality, which has nothing to do with you. Any opinion another may have of you is just their own projection. There's no reason why you should take it on. When someone puts you down, just remind yourself that they are really describing themselves, not you.

The first conclusion you can draw about this speaker is that he is a stranger to vertical experience. What he says about the present is true enough if you're referring to linear time and the brain-based thinking by which we apprehend it. But nobody who'd ever met the NOW in person would assert that the present is "merely theoretical."

Metaphysical faults aside, let's examine the practical implications. What will happen if you actually take this teacher's advice? Nothing new will get in. Nobody can offer you meaningful feedback because what they call "you" is just their own mental activity. Only you can know you, and you're free to think anything you like about you.

To be sure, this philosophy is likely to render a person very confident. Its actual proponent positively gleams with high self-regard and charges a pretty penny to assist his devotees in becoming similarly complacent. I'm not sure why they go to the expense, since they could get the same message for free from any kindergartner. "I'm rubber and you're glue. Everything you say bounces off me and sticks to you."

This, like any closed system, is a trap. It traps by rendering its prisoner impervious to surprise. Some belief systems really do have that power. If you go into them and seal the door, your expectations are consistently confirmed, and you can't learn anything new. Any philosophy that shapes your life needs a hole, a gap, a slight flaw in its logic, because that's how fresh truth gets in. An airtight system will suffocate you.

In its bare outlines, the philosophy I've lampooned resembles the Four Noble Truths of the Buddha. He, too, taught that we construct our reality out of our own thoughts, that thoughts make us suffer, and that we can alleviate our suffering by relinquishing our attachment to thoughts. That is the path. If taken on a strictly intellectual level (which is not how actual Buddhists take it), this is a closed system. Its potential solipsism was corrected by the Mahayana—also known as "the open way."

The core teaching of the Mahayana is expressed by the Heart Sutra, which many practicing Buddhists recite at the start of the day. It goes, in part, like this: "There is no suffering, no cause of suffering, no end of suffering, and no path." This is a *negation* of the Four Noble Truths. When they sit down to meditate, the first thing these Buddhists do is to deny the very reason they're sitting down to meditate! Why? As the Buddha taught, belief systems cause suffering. So if the Four Noble Truths have become your belief system, you'd better stop believing them! It's a practical joke, this sutra. It's also a ventilation system, an emergency escape hatch. It's how the snake lets go of its tail.

The Occult Prison

When magicians feel like giving themselves—or you—the heebie-jeebies, one of the terms you'll hear them invoke is "occult imprisonment." For example, it is said that Madame Blavatsky was incapacitated for several years because her enemies had put her in occult prison.

As you might expect, this is a type of magical spell, not a physical jail. Over the years I have met more than a few incarcerated hermeticists. Perhaps it will reassure you to hear that the vast majority of occult prisons are constructed by their occupants.

Your mission, should you decide to accept it, is to construct such a prison by yourself and for yourself. Why on earth would you want to do that? Because knowing how to build one will render you forever immune to both the fear of occult prisons and the actual danger of them. No one else will ever be able to cast this particular spell on you.

An occult prison is a thought form that prevents its thinker from exercising freedom. The most rudimentary version—what you might call the county jail of occult prisons—is the "damned if you do, damned if you don't" proposition. It's a thought that renders you incapable of action because no matter what you do, you're screwed. If you're feeling more ambitious, you can erect an occult Alcatraz—an entirely closed belief system, such as the one on page 138.

After you have built your prison, your next challenge is to figure out how to escape from it. There are several possible methods. You could look for a tiny hole in the wall and scrape away at it until it's big enough to let you through. You could dismantle the entire thing, brick by brick. (Hint: look for the loosest brick and start there.) If you happen to possess a magic wand, you could just wave it and make the prison vanish into thin air. I'm rather given to explosive devices, but that's just me. The important thing to keep in mind is that if you have the means to build a prison, you also have the means to escape from it.

PART TWO

Procedures

6

Commencing the Great Work

I EARN MY LIVING as a ghostwriter of self-help books. Addressing the reader as "you" is a convention of the self-help genre and such a long-standing habit of mine that when it came time to write my own book, I just naturally fell into it. But occasionally I wonder whether you might be finding it presumptuous. After all, we've never met on earth. I really don't know beans about your inner life.

I bring this up because I'm about to get even more specific about the inner life of alchemists in general, and I would not wish this constant use of "you" to become overbearing. I write that at a certain stage you will feel thus and so—because I have felt thus and so and because many others have reported feeling thus and so—but perhaps *you* are feeling no such thing. I never mean to imply that you *should* be feeling thus and so. I just mean that one sometimes does. But, you see, I am not writing this book for "one." I am writing it for you. So I do apologize if you feel that I'm getting you wrong.

In each of the preceding chapters, I've given you a slightly different take on what the Great Work is trying to accomplish. Here is yet another: The Great Work is a process of reincarnating into your own life.

The notion of reincarnation implies that we need a do-over, that we don't get incarnation right on the first try. Part of us dives boldly into earthly existence while another part recoils from the brink, as if to say, "You want me to do *what?*" The one who dives is called the soul. As I am using the term, soul refers to the part of you that lives in space and linear time. It includes both the consciousness that is based in the brain and central nervous system, and that which is based in the subtle body. The soul is, quite simply, what you are used to calling "I." The one who remained behind in the realm of absolute time is the spirit. Though apparently too chicken to make the dive itself, it keeps wanting to tell you how and where to swim. It thinks it knows better. (Knowing better is easy when you're not the one fending off sharks!) Reincarnating into your own life means getting this vertical know-it-all to jump in with the rest of you.

Hermeticists usually put it more poetically than that. Some describe the soul as a grail—a cup or chalice that the alchemist is preparing so that it will be worthy of holding the spirit. The myths of the quest for the Holy Grail are allegories for the process of transforming the soul. Others use the metaphor of a wedding. Soul and spirit are a couple who meet, woo, and win one another. During their courtship, they have many conflicts and misunderstandings. Each has to learn to love, respect, and accommodate the other.

I don't believe that soul and spirit become estranged for lack of love, respect, or worthiness. The problem is rather that the soul can't see any way back to the diving board, and the spirit doesn't know how to swim. If the soul took some climbing lessons and the spirit took some swimming lessons, maybe they could jump back in together. That is what it would mean to reincarnate into one's current life.

Earlier chapters have already introduced you to some of the technical difficulties. The soul thinks with a brain; the spirit thinks without one. In order to accommodate the spirit's thoughts, brain activity has to change and so does the relationship of the physical body to the subtle body. The soul has trouble acting at the direction of the spirit because its will is driven by biological instincts and is not, for the most part, under conscious control. Because soul and spirit live in different versions of time, they have different priorities. The soul can't see the forest; the spirit has never climbed a tree. During the Great Work, both soul and spirit take independent initiatives to resolve these problems. Insofar as you are the soul, this means that sometimes you will be working actively and other times you will be just trying to recognize and cope with the activity of your spirit.

There are probably as many versions of the Great Work as there are alchemists. Seven seems to be a favorite number of steps, but some list ten, or twelve, or twenty-two. I chose seven because that seemed like a manageable number of chapters. I picked this particular version of seven—called "The Ladder of the Wise"—because I liked the quaintly scientific words used to label the steps. So don't let what were rather casual choices in my mind become monuments in yours. In time you will develop your own procedures and, perhaps, identify different or additional stages. Each alchemist's process is unique, but a book must necessarily generalize. I've used the seven-step model to elaborate on seven challenges that seem to recur in the inner lives of most alchemists. If you can't relate to something I'm saying, maybe it doesn't apply to you.

While I've arranged the steps in a logical sequence, to the extent that you experience them, they will be in "shuffle" mode. That's because they don't happen at your conscious initiative. You don't say to yourself, "I think I'll start work on sublimation today." Rather, you diagnose a stage that is already in progress when you notice its telltale symptoms. "I've got the blahs. Maybe I'm in fermentation," or "All hell is breaking loose. This must be calcination." Once you realize what process is occurring, you work consciously to bring it to a successful conclusion.

For each stage, I offer a procedural tip or two, along with warnings about known hazards and admonishments not to blow up the lab. Like Basil Valentine, I sometimes omit key steps and wander off into theological discourses. When you come to these, keep in mind that principles imply procedures. They are implied rather than spelled out because no one has ever transmuted *you* before. To do so will require procedures of your own invention.

As far as I know, nobody ever finishes with a stage once and for all. You will probably continue to cycle through them over and over for the rest of your life, even *after* the big initiation that comes at step 7. To be in a phase of conjunction does not put you ahead of someone who's going through separation, because neither of you is traveling in a straight line.

The "path," if one were to draw it, would look less like a road than like a plate of spaghetti. In other words, it's not a path.

The phases do, however, come to definite—if not permanent—conclusions. When you've finished with one for the present, your mood will change. In retrospect, you'll see that you've made progress in the form of new insights, new behaviors, and new capabilities.

Technical Overview

The number seven might already have led you to suspect that the Great Work has something to do with the seven chakras.

In their receptive form, the chakras are organs of subtle perception. Each one is attuned to a different type of information. The chakras are also points at which our energy can flow outward into the world. As such, they are organs of will. I know of no explicit references to the chakras in Western hermetic literature prior to the nineteenth century. Still, the correspondences between the seven-stage models of initiation in the West and the volitional aspects of the chakras are striking. These initiations were designed for a human being who, it would seem, has seven different "wills."

These wills are not always in agreement with one another. At any given moment, some could be aligned with others, some in conflict with others, and some altogether dormant. This is why our actions are so often contradictory and inept. Technically speaking, the Great Work is a realigning of the will centers so that they are all working toward a shared purpose.

You can't see your own chakras. Most of the time, you probably can't feel them either. This makes it difficult to check up on them directly. You can only infer how they're doing by noticing how you're feeling and how you're behaving. By the same token, the overview I'm about to present won't be of much use in checking your progress once the Great Work commences. I can draw you a diagram of what's supposed to happen, a picture of your inner alignment as it might appear if viewed from the outside. But you can't compare yourself to the picture because you can't see yourself from the outside. The picture won't tell you how you're doing. It will, however, help you to visualize what you're going for. You might want to try meditating on the diagram, moving inwardly with it as you do with other alchemical figures and symbols.

Here is the alignment of a person who can't do magic. You could call it "Muggle Alignment."

↑

Ideal

↑

Thought

↑

Word

♥

Territory

↓

Desire

↓

Fear

↓

The three lower centers comprise our instinctive will. They are the drives we need to survive as physical beings on earth. The names I've given them reflect our subjective experience of them. That is, we feel driven by fear, desire, or territoriality (the need to patrol our borders and rule our domain). These are our centers of gravity. Their natural orientation is down.

The top three centers represent the higher faculties that inform our conscious intentions. Ideal is our source of creative and moral inspiration, our point of connection with the spirit. Thought is deliberation and understanding. Word is declared intention. These are our centers of levity. Their natural orientation is up.

At the center of the picture, the heart is the point where up meets down and where the vertical intersects the horizontal. It is the *between* of the human being and the source of alchemical deeds. But no such deeds are happening at the moment, and the picture tells you why. If the arrows represent the flow of energy, the heart isn't getting any. The upper part of the person is streaming toward heaven; the lower part streaming toward earth. Isolated in the middle, the heart doesn't have much power. It is mushy and sentimental, like the heart on a Victorian valentine. It might *feel* love, but it's not much good at *doing* love. Its love manifests as inept good intentions and niceness.

The inner alignment that gives rise to alchemical deeds looks like this:

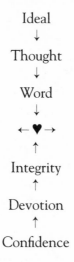

Notice that the labels for the lower three centers have changed. The survival instincts of the unconscious will have been transmuted into qualities. Fear has become confidence; desire has become devotion; territoriality is now integrity. They remain below, but their orientation has shifted upward. The energy they draw from the earth now streams toward the heart.

Changes in the upper will centers are less dramatic. They still have the same names. But something has happened to shift their orientation downward. It is as if they are bowing their heads. The energy they draw from above spills into the heart. The heart is now the meeting point between intention and will, between heaven and earth. Empowered by all the other centers, its energy streams outward into the world. It is brilliant with the intelligence of heaven-inspired intention and sonorous with the power of the earthy will. Like a diamond, it is indestructible, cutting, and radiant. It loves bravely, shrewdly, mightily, and *magically*. It has become the philosopher's stone.

On Messing Up the Kitchen

In many spiritual disciplines, the desired outcome is an ideal state, such as enlightenment or inner peace, that one strives to maintain consistently. In alchemy, the nearest thing to an ideal state is an ongoing state of disarray. At first you undertake the Great Work in order to be able to work magic. Gradually you discover that the Great Work *is* the magic. You are constantly transmuting yourself and, as a result, you are able to transmute other phenomena as well. If you were ever to declare yourself finished, all your magical influence would vanish overnight, for it is only in their *unfinished* state that phenomena are transmutable.

America is an especially favorable setting for the Great Work, for the American spiritual temper is, I believe, uniquely oriented toward the will. Our soil produces more magicians than mystics. We inherited part of this strong will impulse from a source that most of us now find repellant: the Calvinist religion of the early settlers. According to Calvinism, God likes some people better than others and expresses his approval through earthly gifts. Health, wealth, and happiness are proof of God's favor. Poverty and suffering are telltale signs of sin. Whether people will be favored or rejected by God is already decided before they are born. Some are predestined to be saved, and some are earmarked for damnation.

Contrary to what you might expect, this peculiar doctrine didn't plunge its believers into despair or stop them from making an effort. On the contrary, it spurred them on. By working hard, amassing wealth, and keeping their lives in good order, they could prove to themselves and others that they were among the elect. This was the source of the Protestant work ethic.

Nowadays, you don't find many card-carrying Calvinists. I've never met one personally. But I have known many who pursue yoga or Buddhism or even paganism in a Calvinist way. The Calvinist impulse has broken free of its Protestant origins and entered the collective unconscious of Americans. When I spell out its doctrine explicitly, you probably think it's the dumbest spiritual teaching you ever heard. Yet, at some level, you are almost sure to be influenced by it. Rare is the American who isn't.

You might say that you don't believe in predestination, but if you are fond of the phrase "meant to be," you're leaning in that direction. If you think that an unhappy marriage, poor health, or money troubles are a sign that you're on the wrong spiritual track, or that spirituality will fix it, you are making a Calvinist assumption.

In medieval Europe, people looked to the impoverished and emaciated for spiritual teachings. Austerity was the mark of a saint. In America, the prerequisite for any spiritual teacher is a life that works. We don't turn for guidance to someone who can't pay their electric bill. Consciously or unconsciously, we assume that the spiritually accomplished lead healthy, prosperous, and well-ordered lives. This assumption has a lot in common with the premise of alchemy, that spiritual insight can and should be applied to the material well-being of humanity and that workability is a good test of spiritual truth. Yet it will constantly trip you up if you undertake the Great Work.

The Tibetan teacher I used to follow required his students to practice generic Buddhism for several years before embarking on the Vajrayana, the Buddhist alchemical path. When trying to figure out the pecking order, newcomers to the scene often concluded that the students who'd been practicing only two or three years were the most advanced. These students had great posture, impeccable manners, and the kind of composure one associates with Buddhists. The actual senior students—those already deeply immersed in the Vajrayana—were taken by newcomers to be fellow rookies. They presented an emotionally disheveled appearance, bursting into tears or unstoppable giggles during meditation sessions, showing up drunk, losing jobs, getting into love triangles, and running up debt. Nothing about them looked advanced except, perhaps, their advanced state of disarray.

Alchemy makes a mess of the kitchen. If your intention is to transmute poison into medicine, you're going to have poison lying around. The raw instincts of the unconscious will have to come to the surface before they can be transformed into qualities. While this is going on, they will be evident to others as well as yourself. It's embarrassing. External conditions that used to seem well under control may suddenly fall apart. Don't undertake the Great Work if you want others to think you one of the elect.

A common error of the spiritual life is to confuse outcomes with procedures. For example, a well-regarded hermeticist, in his guide to inner development, admonished his students that without a feeling of reverence they would never succeed in making contact with beings of the upper vertical. That is an unworkable requirement. If you have never enjoyed contact with a higher being, what would you have to feel reverent *about*? Reverence is an outcome, not a procedure. When it is expected of beginners, the student's only recourse is to *simulate* reverence, which followers of this teacher do by wiping the smiles off their faces whenever an angel's name is mentioned. (The maneuver is especially unfortunate because humorlessness is off-putting to angels.) It is difficult to make any headway with the Great Work if you're trying to imitate some notion of what a person looks like when they've reached the advanced stages. Without evident faults and follies, the alchemist has nothing to transmute.

Think of feelings, moods, attitudes, qualities, and virtues as outcomes. Approaching them as procedures usually just leads to feeling down about yourself, because you're trying to control aspects of your personality that are meant to be spontaneous. If you happen to find your neighbor really annoying, the admonition "Love your neighbor as yourself" won't make you any happier to be living next door to him. Neighbor loving is an outcome. You need a procedure to get to it.

An effective procedure is an action you can take regardless of what you are thinking, how you are feeling, or what your personality traits might be. It is something you can conceive of doing whether you are in the mood to do it or not. It will work even if you approach it with a rotten attitude. Along the way I will suggest some procedures that I have found to be effective. But if, for you, a suggested procedure doesn't meet the criteria I've just outlined, then skip it. Make up a procedure of your own that suits you better while meeting the same objective.

Another common error is to assume that doing well means *feeling* well. When any emotion or situation moves toward an unpleasant extreme, we try to mitigate it, so as to achieve both the feeling and the appearance of balance. Alchemically, though, phenomena are most amenable

to change when in a volatile state. Inner upheavals are signs you're getting somewhere. The alchemist's strategy is to abet rather than to abate.
You push any process further in the direction it's already trying to go.
Balance is eventually reestablished when the process comes to its own
conclusion. As my physician—a practitioner of Chinese alchemy—
frequently reminds me, symptoms often intensify when an illness is on
its way *out*.

Alchemists abet because it's efficient and thorough. While it's going
on, though, it can be vexing and chaotic. You'll be swimming against
the American spiritual stream, this strange admixture of wind chimes,
yoga mats, and Calvinist complacency. Alchemy is not about feeling
good, looking good, or being good. It's about experiencing the world as
magical and oneself as a magician. You mark your progress not by evaluating how you appear, feel, or act, but by noting changes in the effects
you have on the world. It is your effects, not your inward state or outward demeanor, that should be held to the standard of workability.

7

Calcination

The substance is burned until
nothing remains but ashes.

BASE MATTER:

False roots

SYMPTOMS:

Anxiety
Loss, and fear of loss
External upheavals

TO ABET:

Avoid blaming self or others
Refrain from attempts to explain misfortune

TRANSMUTATION:

Confidence

I am the true vine, and my Father is the vinedresser. Every branch
of mine that bears no fruit, he takes away, and every branch that
does bear fruit, he prunes, that it may bear more fruit.

If a man does not abide in me, he is cast forth as a branch and
withers, and the branches are gathered, thrown into the fire and
burned. (John 15:1–2, 15:6)

If you were brought up Christian, sermons based on this passage from the Gospel of John may have given you an off-putting impression of it. Preachers often interpret the fire as hell and the branch's consignment to it as a punishment for not believing in Jesus. But as any gardener will tell you, Jesus is simply describing what happens to vines that are growing where they are not wanted. In my own garden, the Virginia creeper is welcome to take full possession of the pergola, where it provides summer shade and gorgeous autumn color. It is not welcome to conquer shrubs, trees, lawn furniture, or drowsing cats—as it invariably attempts to do. Every few weeks, I yank up the branches that have tried to set root where they don't belong. I would indeed throw them onto a fire, if city ordinances permitted. I'm not *punishing* the vines. The only judgment I'm passing on them is that they've wandered too far from their purpose.

Notice that Jesus says, "every branch *of mine.*" His own branches get pruned when they're fruitful and uprooted when they're not. When he says, "I am the true vine," he's not pulling rank on you. He's not saying, "I am the true vine, *and you're not.*" He is offering himself as an example of what you are, too—a true vine that sometimes produces wayward branches. The burning of these branches is the process of calcination.

Who is "I"?

Working as fast as you can, write down a series of statements beginning "I am." For example:

> I am female.
> I am blonde.
> I am of Scottish ancestry.
> I am reclusive.

The more of these statements you can think of, the better. Try to come up with at least fifty.

Next, go over your list and cross off any items that are impermanent. For instance, while I've been blonde all my life, some day my hair will be gray. Blondness is impermanent. Lately I'm reclusive because I'm working on this book, but I used to be sociable and might become so again. So reclusive is impermanent too.

After eliminating any conditions that have changed at some point in your life or might change later, go over the remaining items and cross off anything that will cease to be true after you have died. I will no longer be of Scottish ancestry or female, because those conditions depend on my DNA. Spirits don't have DNA.

This step will probably reduce your list to zilch. Pretty much any situation, condition, or adjective you might apply to yourself is subject to loss or change. Even personality traits are impermanent. Chronic illness can render a cheerful person crabby, or an active person listless. Alzheimer's disease could erase the memory of every insight you've ever attained. The only absolutely permanent thing you can say about I is "I am." That irreducible I, stripped of all relative and transient conditions, is the true I, the true vine. If you attempt to set down roots, to establish your sense of identity anywhere but that I, sooner or later you're going to be uprooted. It's not a punishment. It's just what happens.

No doubt you have already grasped the idea just by reading these few paragraphs and doing the exercise. On an intellectual level, it's not at all difficult to understand. Yet it will probably cease to be meaningful the minute you close this book. In everyday life, all sorts of impermanent conditions feel like "I." When they are threatened, we feel threatened. Some of them feel so necessary to our identities that we might kill to defend them and call it self-preservation. Our instinctive will is necessarily bent on staying alive. As basic survival gets embellished with various niceties—not just a paycheck, but a fulfilling career; not just reproduction but a happy marriage; not just a healthy body but an attractive one—the survival instinct enlarges to cover them. The loss of any of these embellishments can feel like a death.

This is the basic predicament that the teachings of the Buddha address. He said that we suffer because we keep attaching our sense of "I" to conditions that will eventually be taken away from us. We suffer because every time we set down roots in the transient, they get yanked up. The uprooting would hurt less if we didn't grow them so deep.

The alchemical process of calcination addresses the same problem, but for a different reason. In and of itself, the suffering caused by attachment is not an obstacle to magic. The problem is rather that attachment to transient conditions distracts us from who we really are. We get so caught up in the temporal How of our lives that we lose track of the Why. The meanings that exist in our absolute NOW are obscured by the clutter of our everyday preoccupations. The meaningless offshoots have to be uprooted and destroyed so that the true vine can bear magical fruit.

Calcination is going to happen whether you embark on the Great Work or not. Every human life is marked by a series of losses that escalate in their frequency and severity as we approach the end. Many old people are wise because, in suffering many losses, they have gradually learned to identify with the true vine. If you aspire to be an alchemist, you don't want to wait until you're old to be wise. You want to hurry the process up, so that your true vine can enjoy many productive years while you're still living on earth.

So how do you speed up calcination? Either you have to suffer greater and earlier losses than the average person, or relate to average losses with greater than average awareness and intensity. If we had it in our power to choose, most of us would probably choose the latter. But—let's face it—neither option is very appealing. Branches to which we have attached our sense of "I" do not go jumping into the fire of their own accord. To calcinate on purpose would be as bizarre as setting one's own hair ablaze. Calcination happens at the initiative of the spirit, not the soul. At the onset of the process, that spirit doesn't feel like you. It feels like your mortal enemy.

The Book of Job is a story of calcination. It begins when Satan challenges God to a bet. He proposes to test Job's character by afflicting him with one terrible misfortune after another. In accepting this sick wager, God comes off looking almost as bad as Satan. My own take on the story (which, I will admit, is not supported by any theologian I've ever heard of) is that the character of Satan is actually Job's own spirit. From the perspective of a soul undergoing calcination, both God and the spirit appear perverse. The spirit is an arsonist and God, for some inscrutable reason, is supplying it with matches. To feel infuriated with both of them is a perfectly natural reaction.

How to Burn

Follow the advice of the Buddha if you want to mitigate the suffering of this phase. He taught that, on its own, pain is just intense sensation. It turns to suffering when you add fear. Think of what it's like to cut your finger by accident while chopping food. That's pain. Then imagine that someone is going to cut your finger on purpose. They warn you that they're going to do it, and you have to hold still while you watch the knife slowly descend. That's suffering.

You can't eliminate pain, but you can alleviate suffering by subtracting the fear, which comes not from loss itself, but from our anticipation of loss. Say, for instance, that baldness runs in your family, and you'd rather not be bald. Each time you comb your hair, you find a few strands between the teeth of the comb. The loss of a dozen hairs or so isn't noticeable on your head. You only mind them on the comb because they're a reminder of what's coming. If one day you were to decide that a full head of hair didn't really matter, finding lost hairs on the comb wouldn't bother you any more. That's the basic logic of nonattachment. Stop clinging to what you're likely to lose and the losing won't hurt so much.

Attachment causes additional pain when we believe we can or should do something to prevent the anticipated loss. For example, suppose you have a feeling that your lover is going to leave you. Maybe it's an irrational fear or maybe it's an accurate intuition. Either way, you start doing everything you can think of to prevent the loss. You act clingy, or spy to discover whether your lover is being unfaithful, or even launch a preemptive strike, breaking off the affair yourself. These stratagems are likely either to cause a problem that wasn't already there or exacerbate one that was. They add to the suffering of the loss itself. If you could stop being afraid, maybe you wouldn't screw up the relationship. Even if the loss is inevitable, if you could stop worrying about it, you wouldn't suffer over it in advance.

Buddhists arrive at this kind of composure through meditation. As fearful thoughts arise in the mind, you witness them, then let them go. They come back, and you let them go again. If you keep this up long enough, you begin to wear out your fear. The offending thought stops producing such a rush of adrenaline. Then it becomes ever so slightly boring. Persist long enough and it becomes extremely boring. By observing your thoughts in this way, you also begin to notice how many of them involve scenarios that never come to pass. You worry yourself sick about losses that don't happen, while actual losses take you completely by surprise. The actual ones are like kitchen accidents; the pain initially numbed by shock.

Buddhist lore is full of stories that acknowledge the limits of this approach. When the son of a great Buddhist teacher is killed in an accident, the teacher is prostrate with grief. His students remind him that his loss, like all earthly losses, is just an illusion. "But this one is a very *convincing* illusion," the teacher replies. The slow, controlled burn of meditation is no guarantee against a sudden conflagration. Even if you don't complicate it with fear, pain can be very painful.

Inner composure might feel better and certainly *looks* better than flailing about, but from an alchemical perspective, it is irrelevant. It is like the fuel imagining it can supervise the fire. Sooner or later, every coping strategy must get burned to a crisp; even Buddhist equanimity. To the fire of calcination, resistance acts as an accelerant. Struggling makes you burn hotter and faster. So go ahead and struggle, if that's what you feel like doing. When you find yourself dreading a loss, do everything you can think of to prevent it. Cling with all your might to whatever it is you feel is essential to your identity. Attach it to you with Crazy Glue. The resulting calcination will be rapid and thorough.

Job's Comforters

The hero of the Book of Job loses everything: wife, children, business, home, friends, health. By the end of his calcination, he's lying half naked on the ground, every inch of him covered in painful boils. You would think he had already experienced every conceivable form of human suffering, but at that point yet another affliction awaits him: the misguided ministrations of his "comforters." It wouldn't be so bad if they'd just agree, "Wow, Job, your life really sucks!" and leave it at that. Instead they try to help him figure out *why* his life sucks.

While the story demonstrates that blaming the victim is an age-old and universal human tendency, Americans, I believe, are more than usually prone to it. We are a nation of Job comforters. It probably comes from the wide streak of Calvinism in our culture. I'm sure you, dear reader, would never be so daft as to believe that human suffering is a sign of God's displeasure, but that belief has influenced you on an unconscious level if you ever find yourself using the phrase "innocent victim." Of what possible relevance is innocence unless, at some level, you believe there is such a thing as a *guilty* victim?

A more constructive variation on Calvinist mentality is the idea that misfortune can be prevented if you identify its causes and take precautionary measures. Sunburns cause skin cancer, so don't sunbathe. Bicycle accidents often result in head injuries, so wear a helmet. On the face of it, all this sounds sensible enough. But it takes on a Job's comforter twist when failure to take preventative measures is viewed as the cause of a misfortune. The injured bicyclist is somehow entitled to less sympathy if he wasn't wearing a helmet—as if lack of a helmet brought on the accident itself.

The misfortunes of others cause us to suffer because they remind us of our own vulnerability. It didn't happen to us, but it *might*. It *could*. This anxiety is alleviated if we can trace the cause of the misfortune to human error or malfeasance—that is, if we can find someone to blame. If the trouble wasn't directly caused by a human, there was probably a human who could have prevented it by exercising due diligence. We resist believing there's really such a thing as an accident or natural disaster.

Blame and a mania for preventive measures are psychological defenses against the knowledge of how inherently precarious our lives are. Blaming the victim is an especially strong defense because it puts the victim—and ourselves as potential victims—in control. That's why it's bad practice for an alchemist. Calcination doesn't begin until you've exhausted your defenses. You'll burn at a much lower temperature if you refrain from blaming anyone—including yourself—for your misfortunes.

Another view of suffering, beautifully articulated by Gary Zukav in *The Seat of the Soul*, is that life is an "earth school." Misfortunes aren't accidents. They are lessons, specifically designed to teach you something you need to learn. The best recommendation for this philosophy is the admirable character of those who adopt it. They take full responsibility for whatever happens to them and avoid blaming others. Each passing year finds them wiser, for they rarely repeat a mistake. In every setback, they see a teaching and an opportunity for growth.

The earth school approach seems to work best with low to moderate vicissitudes. It tends to fall apart when applied to genocide, tsunamis, and pandemics. (If such events are lessons, I want to transfer to a different school.) Earth school can also take on a Calvinist slant in those who believe that a well-ordered existence is the mark of an A student. It isn't, necessarily. Job, lying on his heap of filthy rags, was an A student. So was Rumi in his mad grief over Shams.

From an alchemical standpoint, the lesson of suffering is not what you should have done or ought to do differently next time. Such lessons might be true and useful, but they have nothing to do with calcination. Alchemically, all losses have just one purpose: to reconnect you with your true vine. If you believe that the lesson is how to avoid a similar loss in the future, you are merely growing another branch to be uprooted and burned. If you conclude instead that you were mistaken in the *object* of your attachment—that you have lost it because you should not have wanted it in the first place—you are still missing the point. What the spirit seeks from any loss is *loss itself*. The fire just wants to be fire. It does not, in burning, pass judgment on its fuel. Anything combustible is fair game.

If you can swing it, a very powerful practice for abetting calcination is to refrain from trying to understand the reason for a misfortune. Look neither to the past for how it happened, nor to the future for why. Don't blame others. Don't blame yourself. Don't draw any lesson. Just experience the pain while allowing it to go entirely unexplained. It is unlikely that you'll be able to persist in this forever, especially around a major blow, since insights will eventually spring to mind unbidden. They'll probably be different from the conclusions you would have drawn had you been thinking about it on purpose.

This practice has an unexpected effect on other people, especially those who might happen to share in your misfortune. I'll leave you to discover that effect on your own.

When the Smoke Clears

Years ago, I lost my home in a literal fire. It was a one-bedroom apartment that I had just finished decorating exactly to my taste. Having recently inherited a small sum from my grandfather, I'd splurged on an expensive stereo system and my first computer. Many items later declared worthless by the insurance adjuster—flea market finds, travel souvenirs, tattered quilts, and lace curtains passed down from my mother—were, to me, priceless because they were irreplaceable. In those days, I also used to sew myself beautiful clothes. All these years later, I still rue the loss of one dress in particular. It was made of silk gabardine and lined in crepe de chine, with a collar of antique lace and a long row of tiny buttons. I had embroidered each of the twenty buttonholes by hand.

The fire started in the building's electrical system during the middle of the night and spread very fast. Awakened by the exploding of windows, I fled in my nightgown, without even pausing to find my shoes. I remember the sensation of the night air against my bare legs and the rough asphalt under my bare feet as I watched the flames devour the apartment next to mine and lick at the curtains in my own windows. Falling glass caught the light, like a crystal rainstorm. The bold efficiency of the firefighters was splendid and sexy and interesting to watch. Any fire is fun to witness. That the fuel for this one was my own belongings did not, as you would expect, diminish my pleasure in it. No, it was quite the best fire I've ever seen. Later I recall shuffling around in a pair of flats, three sizes too big, offered to me by a stranger who lived down the block. By then, the sun was rising over the still-smoking ruins, and I was homeless. All these details are somehow delicious to me, when I remember them now. They were delicious even at the time. While the days following the disaster were filled with hassle and stress, I felt curiously light on my feet. The world seemed brand-new, and better somehow.

Perhaps you, too, have experienced the startling and illicit joy that sometimes arrives in the wake of a major loss. It is the joy of the pyromaniac spirit as it feeds uprooted branches to the flames. All at once you see as it sees, feel as it feels—this one you're not used to calling "I."

Your loss is its gain of you, and your gain of it. Even if only briefly, the two of you stand on the same spot and view the world through the same eyes. You feel the taproot, reaching deep down to a source of strength you never knew you had. It is the true vine, and it is *you*.

To the extent that you are rooted in the true "I," your confidence is unshakable. Because it depends on nothing external to you, it can't be taken away from you. If you were perfectly calcinated, you would never again feel fear. That won't actually happen, for even if it were theoretically possible (which is doubtful), absolute fearlessness is unworkable for the alchemist. Certain operations can only be performed if you remain vulnerable.

Still, you can expect to make discernable progress with every episode of calcination. Of all the phases of the Great Work, this one comes to the clearest conclusion and rewards you with the most definite sense of accomplishment. The anxiety that signals its onset abates quite noticeably. Your feet feel firmer on the ground, and something at the core of you feels stronger as well. A chronic fear may diminish or ever disappear altogether. You arise from the ashes like a phoenix.

8

Dissolution

The ashes are dissolved in fluid.

BASE MATTER:

Desire

SYMPTOMS:

Yearnings
Horniness
Irritability
Disappointment
Cynicism

TO ABET:

Delay gratification
Refrain from complaint
For males: cultivate idealism
For females: cultivate discrimination

TRANSMUTATION:

Devotion

These days I live in a Craftsman bungalow with oak woodwork, leaded glass windows, built-in bookcases, and comfy chintz sofas. The slate walls and floor of the bathroom took my contractor many days to install and cost me a fortune. I am not well off, but I like my house to be. When money is tight, I panic about the mortgage. If this place ever caught fire, I can't conceive of enjoying the spectacle.

I have, in other words, renewed the attachment that once got burned to ashes. My spirit has not, so far, raised any objection. While it is true that attachment causes suffering, the alchemist does not resort to non-attachment as a protective strategy. Desire, to the magician, is as essential as water. Without it, the true vine yields no fruit and eventually withers.

Some scholars regard the transmutation of lead into gold as a metaphor for the transformation of the self. The gold, they say, is you when you become fully realized or enlightened. But according to traditional procedure, there are actually two transformations. First you make a philosopher's stone, then you use it to transmute base metal. The first step—the forming of the stone—is the transformation of self. The second step is the transforming of something that is *not* the self. The gold isn't you. It's something outside of you that you desire. The philosopher's stone is a means, not an end. In fact, if you don't want to use it for something, you won't be able to form it. You can't succeed with the alchemical transformation of the self unless you desire something that is not yourself. Wanting to *be* gold is vainglorious.

Desire melts us, makes us juicy. We need this melting, because the fire of calcination leaves us parched. Instinctively we protect ourselves from further loss by cultivating detachment. We begin to feel more self-sufficient. This is a positive development in itself, but it can also render us overly complacent and disconnected from the world. If calcination were the only inner process available to us, we would meet every setback with courage and equanimity, yet our lives would be dull and gray as ashes. No vine can flower if you try to grow it in ash alone. Fruitful soil is damp.

What to Desire

So what is it that the alchemist is supposed to desire? Ultimately, it is God. But if you don't want God all that much, the desire to get laid, go on Oprah, or rid your thighs of cellulite will serve as a workable substitute. The object of the desire matters less than its fervor. Whatever longing you happen to have on hand will do just fine for starters. If your desire is all but impossible to attain, so much the better. The process of dissolution happens in the gap between desire and its attainment. A seemingly unreachable desire gives you a nice big gap to work with.

Most books on magic will tell you that the difference between white magic and black is motivation. Good magicians have good intentions and bad magicians have bad ones. You are one of the good guys if you want to work magic for the benefit of others.

On the subject of magic, this is the single most useless piece of advice I have ever heard. While I've met more than one hermeticist whose effects on the world were borderline diabolical, I have yet to meet anyone who claimed to be a black magician. No matter how harmful the deed, its doer always seems to have good intentions.

What other kind could they have? Good is the only flavor intentions come in. Our conscious intentions are formed by our higher faculties, whose natural orientation is upward. When we think about what we *should* want, we come up with lofty principles and ideals because, in the realm of "should," there is nothing else to be found.

The trouble is that these good intentions have nothing to do with our actual will. The untransmuted will runs on instinct, and instinct is necessarily selfish. Its function is to ensure our survival. The desire to perpetuate the species by begetting and protecting our children is the closest it comes to altruism. Apart from that, what it seeks is provisions, safety, dominance, territory, and the perpetuation of the familiar.

Insofar as these drives are applied to physical survival needs, they can't do a whole lot of harm. Our excesses are checked when they start to impinge on the survival needs of others. The possibility for significant damage arises only when instincts get mislabeled as higher intentions. This happens quite a lot, because we humans tend to feel embarrassed by our biological drives. We prefer to believe ourselves motivated by ideas and ideals. As the subtle faculties develop, our ordinary self-deceptions may carry us into the Realm of Deception (aka Baggage Disclaim), where they acquire additional power to delude.

If I tell you that, as a magician, you should have only altruistic intentions, I'm just exacerbating the problem. The dictate won't change your will. It will just change your cover story. To become a benevolent magician, what you actually need is self-knowledge. The open pursuit of your own self-interest is a good place to start.

In the beginning, selfish aims are also more likely to meet with success, because they draw on the bodily energy of the will. You need that energy to do magic. Altruistic desires might be entirely sincere, but they lack a certain volitional oomph. Suppose, for instance, you see a news clip about people starving in Africa. Moved to pity, you resolve to make a generous donation. You go on the Internet to research relief organizations. In the middle of doing this, you notice that you yourself have gotten very hungry. What feels more urgent at that moment—the starving multitudes or your own growling stomach? I know I for one would break for lunch.

I'm probably giving the impression that I take a very cynical view of altruism. I don't. Altruism is as fundamental to the spirit as survival is to the body. I might even go so far as to say that altruism *is* the survival instinct of the spirit. But at the time we commence the Great Work, the spirit is only very sketchily incarnate in a human personality whose energies are skewing off in umpteen contradictory directions. In a later chapter I'll talk about how altruistic desires can acquire the volitional force necessary to work magic. But at this stage, our object is to make friends with the desires that are closest to home.

In trying to decide which desires are worthy of pursuit, the most productive question to ask is not whether a desire is selfish or unselfish, but whether it is authentic. An authentic desire arises from within you. False desires are a response to outside stimuli.

Advertising is a major source of false desires. If I browse through the pile of catalogs that arrive in the mail each day, I find myself wanting all manner of things that I never even knew existed before the mail carrier came. Who knew that there was such a thing as an electric towel warmer? It hadn't occurred to me to complain that my towels were room temperature, but the towel warmer, once I saw it, seemed fleetingly desirable. By contrast, I'd wanted a deep soaking tub for years. Every time I bathed in the short, shallow tub that came with my house, part of me would get chilled. I daydreamed about how nice it would be to submerge my whole body in hot water that came all the way to my neck. Now that

I've finally acquired such a tub, I fulfill my fantasy almost every day. It's every bit as good as I imagined. The towel warmer was a false desire, but the soaking tub was a true one.

The expectations of others are an especially confusing source of false desires, for the desire to please another might, in and of itself, be authentic. Most of us truly want our parents to feel proud of us. But we might not truly want the college degree or profession or lifestyle that would make them proud.

Distinguishing between true and false desires is part of coming to know oneself. It takes time, experience, and introspection. Nobody's conclusions matter but your own. I do, however, have a suggestion about where to start. Instead of focusing on the object of your desire, try focusing on the between. What, if anything, is happening in the relationship between you and the object? Between me and a towel warmer, I find a blank. Between me and my imaginary bathtub, though, there blossomed an enduring love affair. I felt that its embrace would change me, make me feel rich and pampered and indulged. This is the kind of desire you're going for as an alchemist; one that will alter you, even if only in a silly or trivial way.

The Liberation of Eros

The energy that streams into the gap between the desirer and the desired is called eros. Because eros is the root of the word "erotic," you might be used to associating it with sex, but that's not exactly what it means. Alchemically, eros is the unconsummated quality of the between.

Think of how you feel on the first day you notice that winter has given way to spring. The air is fragrant not only with the earliest flowers but with the sweetness of the soil itself. In the upthrust of the first green blades, the unfurling of juvenile leaves, there is a yearning at once bold and shy. You can hear it in the singing of the birds and in the whirring of the bees as they browse the lilacs and plunge deliriously into the trumpets of daffodils. The whole of nature seems horny. Perhaps you feel horny, too. But there's nothing in this feeling that would earn an X rating. It's romantic, a falling in love that yearns for consummation yet can't quite say what consummation would consist of. It is a longing at once ardent and vague. That's eros.

Remember the distinction I made many chapters ago between fixed and volatile? Sex is eros in its fixed state. The energy is fixed because it is bound to a single purpose in the physical. Dissolution is the process of melting eros, dissolving it, making it volatile. In its volatile state, eros is creative energy, the indispensable catalyst for every alchemical process.

The ballads of courtly love sung by medieval troubadours were veiled alchemical teachings about how to render eros volatile. The recommended procedure was to fall desperately in love with a woman who was married to someone else. Her unattainability was the gap that loosed the flow of eros and prevented it from solidifying. It kept the lover in a constant state of unconsummated desire. Attempts to win the lady's infrequent and unsatisfactory favors—an approving glance, the brief brush of a hand, a glimpse of ankle—spurred the lover to feats of bravery, ingenuity, and virtue. He risked his life in battle, championed the powerless, cultivated the gentle arts and graces, and generally cleaned up his act. The more difficult the lady was to impress, the better she served him in his efforts to transmute himself.

The myth of courtly love describes, in concentrated form, the magic of human civilization altogether. This magic is an inversion of the material power structure, for it places the weaker element—the feminine—above the stronger. To the extent that we are operating on raw power alone, men don't have to please women. What they desire, they are capable of taking, either through brute force or through the economic advantage of the strong. Whenever this inherent disadvantage of the female is mitigated by law and custom, it is because men have voluntarily surrendered some part of their own advantage. When that happens, civilization flourishes. The impulse to use masculine power to serve and to deserve rather than to force brings out the best in men. It inspires them to create and to achieve great things. When, for whatever reason, this impulse is absent or thwarted, the resulting conditions become intolerable for both sexes.

The redirecting of male energy through the bestowing or withholding of approval is a source of feminine power. A male monarch rules. He exercises power directly and actively. A female monarch reigns, bringing out the best in her subjects through their desire please her. Queen Elizabeth I of England embodied this principle. To be sure, she ruled as well, and quite capably. But it was her reign, not her rule, that brought forth the glory of the Elizabethan Age. She was the Virgin Queen, the unattainable object of her subjects' desire, inspiring in them feats of military prowess, geographical and scientific exploration, and artistic achievement.

Please keep in mind that we're talking about magic here, not everyday gender roles or sexual arrangements. Your personal choice to be gay or straight, celibate, monogamous, or promiscuous pertains to *fixed* eros and is irrelevant to alchemy. Courtly love is a metaphor for the liberation of eros, not a literal description of how you should manage your sex life. Your gender does make a difference, however. While eros isn't sex, it comes from the part of the subtle body that corresponds to the physical sex glands. When eros awakens, we often feel horny. When we are sexually depleted, eros, too, seems to diminish. Because eros is so closely associated with the sex drive, gender is relevant to it. Men and women differ in the ways they experience volatile eros and in the benefits they derive from it.

The sex drive of a man is—how can I put this delicately?—vertically oriented. The pedestal is therefore a natural location for the object of his desire. Placing her there causes his soul to rise along with . . . well, you get the picture. It rises to, through, and beyond her. His feminine ideal connects him to the world of ideals. Spiritually, he is uplifted and enlarged. Morally, he becomes more upstanding. (Gosh, this paragraph is fun.) A woman, though, derives no alchemical benefit from idealizing a man. There is no magic in placing the stronger party in the stronger position.

The practice of celibacy as a method of liberating eros can work well for men, because their sexual energy is essentially active. In its sublimated form, it still has a lot of pizzazz. For a woman, celibacy doesn't pack quite the same alchemical punch. It's just making a passive energy more so. Female celibacy is a practical rather than magical choice, freeing up energy that would otherwise be occupied by the needs of a husband and children.

Refraining from genital expression is not the only way to liberate eros. All that is really needed is some element of suspense or doubt. When consummation is a sure thing because the object of desire is under your control, eros solidifies. (This is true of all desires, not just sex.) Relinquishing control of the object keeps the energy volatile. The fantasy of the sexual dominatrix—an object who is, herself, in exaggerated control—is a debased version of this tactic. The reason it doesn't quite work—alchemically at least—is that parading around in a corset and six-inch stilettos is usually not the lady's own idea of fun. It is a concession to her partner's desire. If she were truly in control, her so-called "submissive" would be cleaning out the gutters or watching chick flicks with her.

But I digress. The principle is working as it should when wanting to feel worthy of the beloved inspires a man to become better in ways that are meaningful to him. The ideal beloved holds and upholds a mirror of his higher self, as Beatrice did for Dante. For the ideal beloved to meanwhile get it on with his lower self is not necessarily an obstacle to the procedure. Conversely, the woman who fills this role in his life might not be an actual or even a potential sexual partner at all. He need not even be physically attracted to her (or to females in general) so long as he admires her. The only firm requirement is that she awaken his idealism.

Most of the literature articulating this principle was written by and for men. Less has been said about what is going on, alchemically, for the woman who occupies the pedestal. The sex drive she sublimates is not so much a desire for the act itself as it is a desire to settle. That, for the female, is what consummation really means: the commitment she hopes will accompany the sex act. When the object of her desire commits, the matter is settled. They settle down. In order to remain settled, she may be willing to settle for less than her lover's best. Succumbing to his power is easier than trying to redirect it. This is the impulse she must hold in check if the eros is to remain volatile. The element of suspense or doubt is as challenging to the lady as it is to her lover.

A woman's sex drive is horizontally oriented. (That's why she can't achieve vertical liftoff through adoration of a man.) What she instinctively wishes to do is to come down from the pedestal. To be idealized bugs her because she senses, correctly, that the man's adoration is moving through her to something beyond her. It's a compliment that she can't really take personally. She feels she is being used in some obscure way and not being loved for her "real" (i.e., felt) self. Her sulks and tantrums on this point are beneficial to her adorer, however. They function as spiritual teachings on the finer points of joining the sacred and the profane. A lady on a pedestal can do no wrong. That, girlfriends, is both the good news and the bad news.

In the trailer for a recent romantic comedy, a woman complains to her lover, "I don't just want you to do the dishes. I want you to *want* to do the dishes." The line is funny because the distinction she's making is immediately intelligible to women and would never emerge from the mind of a man. As the masculine is the principle of active desire, the feminine is the principle of discrimination. In the natural course of things (when we're not being obstinately unisex), pursuit is the man's prerogative and choice the woman's. As the chooser, the female mind is attuned to nuance and detail. It perceives infinitely subtle variations in quality and makes razor-sharp distinctions. This is why the ideal of wisdom is represented by a goddess—Sophia—rather than a god.

In a woman, volatile eros takes the form of discriminating intelligence. Women profit spiritually from the cultivation of intellect. This is not always the case for men. Some may find that they need to curb the competitive and somewhat solidified quality of masculine thought in order to activate subtle perception. In spiritual contexts, they often exhort themselves and each other to "quiet the mind." Women, by contrast, may find that intellectual activity sharpens subtle perception and provides needed ballast. In the spiritual life of a woman, a too quiet mind tends toward the airy-fairy.

The teachings of the troubadours began with romantic love, but they didn't end there. Romance was also a metaphor for something larger: the relationship of soul to spirit and of spirit to God. That's what the liberation of eros is all about—energy once fixed in the physical expanding into the spiritual. You can observe this movement in the biographies of the great medieval mystics. Teresa of Avila was, in her youth, a romance writer, and she remained a notorious flirt even after she became a nun. The young Francis of Assisi went through a courtly love craze and all his life considered himself a "troubadour of God." While recovering from a war wound, Ignatius of Loyola read romance novels and stories about the lives of the saints with equal ardor. He had trouble making up his mind whether he wanted to be a saint or a suitor of a beautiful princess. (That the wound left his leg deformed and partially crippled helped to decide the matter.)

The imagery in the famous poem by St. John of the Cross, "The Dark Night of the Soul," has often been described as homoerotic. John would probably reply that the homoerotic is merely a fixed version of the volatile eros that carried his soul to Christ. From a Freudian perspective, volatile eros is a redirection of the sex instinct. From an alchemical perspective, the sex instinct is the fixed form of a creative energy that longs to return to the Creator. If liberated, that's what it will tend to do. Perhaps you can see now that I wasn't being as flip as I sounded when I said that if you don't especially want God, wanting to get laid will do for starters.

Mind the Gap

No matter what your gender or sexual preference, your inner life includes both masculine and feminine impulses. The masculine is the active, yearning, striving quality of desire—any desire—and the feminine is the accurate perception of its object. When these two impulses wed, the offspring of their union is empathy. Empathy is how you get the object of your desire to come to you of its own accord.

But that is a topic for another chapter. Dissolution is not about attainment. It is about experiencing and, to some extent, suffering the gap between desire and its object.

As eros begins to move vertically, yearning toward the ideal, the gap enlarges and becomes more painful. The difference between the ideal and the actual is something you begin to feel acutely. It gives rise to grumpiness. When the courtly lover is not composing odes to his ideal beloved, his main occupation is griping about her. If these complaints solidify into bitterness and cynicism, eros solidifies too. Shakespeare was in such a mood when he wrote, in one of his sonnets:

The expense of spirit in a waste of shame
Is lust in action; and till action, lust
Is perjured, murderous, bloody, full of blame,
Savage, extreme, rude, cruel, not to trust;
Enjoyed no sooner but despiséd straight;
Past reason hunted; and no sooner had,
Past reason hated, as a swallowed bait,
On purpose laid to make the taker mad:
Mad in pursuit, and in possession so;
Had, having and in quest to have, extreme;
A bliss in proof, and proved, a very woe;
Before, a joy proposed; behind, a dream.

This applies not just to romantic desires but to all aspirations. When we despair of crossing the gap, our ideals find expression only in our complaints. What we value and aspire to can only be inferred from our tirades about what we are *against*.

To keep eros fluid and malleable, we need to find the soft spot beneath the hardened complaint. Beneath the complaint is disappointment. And beneath any disappointment, you'll find one of your true desires. Here's the procedure:

Begin by choosing a pet complaint. It could be weather, poor health, bad drivers, your job, your least favorite body part, or the high cost of something or other. Any complaint will do. Decide that you will refrain from complaining aloud about this topic for seven days. If you slip in the middle of a conversation, interrupt yourself. Say, "Never mind" or "I'm being boring." (Your listener is unlikely to object.)

At the end of the week, resolve that for the next seven days, you will refrain not only from spoken complaints on your chosen topic, but from mental complaints as well. Interrupt your thoughts in the same way you interrupted your speech. *Don't* try to replace your complaint with positive thoughts about the object of your displeasure. A positive attitude is not what you're after. What you want to feel instead is the texture, color, and intensity of your irritation. If you refrain from complaining about the cold, you may find that you feel even colder. An annoying coworker may come to seem even more annoying. These are signs that the exercise is going well.

Don't be surprised if, at some point, you suddenly burst into tears. This is likely. You are getting in touch with the disappointment that lies beneath your superficial irritation. When you stop grousing about your least favorite body part, you feel your longing to be different, better, and the apparent hopelessness of that aspiration. You feel how fundamentally disappointing it is to be incarnate.

It is remarkable how even the most trivial gripe can conceal this fundamental disappointment. My pet peeve is junk mail. When I stop bitching about it, what I come to feel is sorrow over the wealth of human creativity that gets squandered on the transient and crass. Making junk mail is probably not what its writers, photographers, and graphic artists aspired to do with their talents. I feel sad for them. Sad for me, too, because sometimes I'm driven by economic necessity to write things I don't really want to write. Incarnation is such a letdown sometimes.

It is poignant, this feeling. That poignancy is what we experience when solidified eros begins to dissolve and become volatile once more. If you want to be an alchemist, you will have to learn to bear it, for without volatile eros, you can't make magic.

Having launched this section with Shakespeare's rant, I will let him have the last word. Here is his concluding couplet:

All this the world well knows; yet none knows well
To shun the heaven that leads men to this hell.

9

Separation

Opposite elements are separated out.

BASE MATTER:

Territoriality

SYMPTOMS:

Anger
Conflict
Jealousy
Boundary issues

TO ABET:

Express anger
Set limits
Practice formality
Examine your deceptions

TRANSMUTATION:

Integrity

How do you go about cooking a stew? What I do is throw some meat and vegetables into a pot, toss in a handful of herbs, pour in a bottle of wine, simmer for an hour or two, and hope for the best. The undifferentiated mush that results usually tastes okay.

A great chef proceeds differently. The meat is seared, then braised or roasted. Each vegetable is carefully sliced into attractive shapes, seasoned with whatever herbs or spices will best enhance it, and cooked to perfection in its own pan. The sauce, too, is prepared separately. Just prior to serving, all the various components are artfully assembled on the plate.

The great chef is acting in accordance with an alchemical principle that states, "Separation precedes conjunction." Things should be taken apart before they are put together. That is how, in being combined, they retain their individuality. The same idea shows up in much of our home-spun wisdom. When we say that you should find out who you are on your own before getting married, or experience your anger before you forgive, we are expressing the principle of separation before conjunction. It is also the principle behind the alchemical procedure known as "make-up sex."

That the latter operation commences with a fight is no accident. Conflict is, quite often, how we achieve separation, how we clarify the difference between one thing and another thing. In our inner lives, it is how we develop integrity. When people shy away from anger and conflict in pursuit of some love-and-light version of spirituality, their inner lives tend to resemble the mush in my stew pot.

To achieve a world view that joins the insights of science with those of religion is an age-old preoccupation of alchemists. So it may surprise you to learn that the divorce of the two disciplines was instigated by alchemists themselves. It was made official in 1660 when a group of scientists that included Johannes Kepler, Isaac Newton, and Elias Ashmole founded the Royal Society under the patronage of Charles II. Formed for the study of natural science, the society banned all discussion of religion at its meetings. This wouldn't be surprising if it happened in our own time, but back then it was unprecedented; the drawing of a firm line that had not previously existed. The men who drew it were hermeticists. Astrology and alchemy interested them just as much as astronomy and chemistry. The rule inhibited them from sharing much of their hermetic research. To this day, some hermeticists maintain that it marked a turning point in western civilization and that it was a *wrong* turn.

So why did they make it? Europe at that time was torn by violent religious conflicts, the smoke from which not only clouded scientific judgment but sometimes arose from the burning body of the scientist himself. Experimental science could not reach its full potential as a method of discovering material facts if obliged to satisfy the criteria for spiritual truth. Nor could spiritual methods of inquiry flourish if obliged to satisfy scientific criteria. Some phenomena behave consistently when experimented upon and some don't. It was necessary to draw a clear distinction between the two methods of investigation because truths on both sides get lost when gross and subtle perception are forced to compromise.

The hermeticists of the Royal Society were applying the principle of separation before conjunction. Science and religion have been simmering in their separate pots ever since. As the Creationism vs. Darwinism controversy demonstrates, they are still not quite ready to be served on the same plate.

In the Great Work, separation is the process of transmuting our territorial instincts. For animals, territory means literal real estate. For people, it can mean anything at all that defines us in relation to others. When I first proposed this book to my publisher, I said that I was unique in having been trained in both Christian and Tibetan alchemy, and that my book would integrate the two traditions. With that claim, I was staking out my territory in the alchemy book market. Months later, I discovered a British writer, David Goddard, whose background and intentions were very similar to mine. Uh-oh! Anxiously, I started reading in the hope that his book would be awful. No such luck. It's very good. In marketing lingo, this is termed a "threat," and it certainly felt like one. I was not, after all, the sole ruler of my imagined territory. Any time we try to define what "I" means by compare-and-contrast with others, we are setting ourselves up for insecurity, jealousy, and conflict. The more we assert our boundaries, the less confident we feel.

As we go through the process of separation, the sense of what "I" means shifts away from the outer boundaries of the self and in toward the core. We can feel our difference from others without having to name what that difference consists of. My background and credentials are part of a fence erected, it turns out, on disputed territory. But my true I, like every true I, is unique without trying to be unique. If I am acting out of the spirit, I can't help but write a book that is like no other. Perceived threats at the perimeter are a reminder of what "I" truly means—and what it doesn't. As soon as you connect with the core, the threat stops feeling threatening. That's the place you need to be coming from if you want to work magic.

While the process of separation involves conflict, its outcome is an enhanced ability to tolerate differences. New ideas are no longer perceived as threats. You might be deeply committed to a certain religion, cause, or political ideology, yet you could, if called upon, make an entirely persuasive case for the other side. You develop a sense of core conviction that no longer depends on arguments or beliefs. This fundamental integrity—knowing what "I" means—gives rise to moral and intellectual integrity as well. You become less inclined to lie. And the less you lie, the more readily you can see through the deceptions of others. You have a sense of knowing what's what.

In the vertical world, separation enables us to distinguish between ourselves and other spiritual beings and to remain oriented in the absence of boundaries. Until this inner orientation is achieved, our access to the vertical is restricted for our own protection. In the vertical dimension, as in the horizontal, naiveté can be dangerous. Long after reaching physical adulthood, many of us remain spiritual children, trusting in the benevolence of higher beings as if they were humanity's babysitters. Separation is our spiritual adolescence. We discover that not all spiritual beings have our best interests at heart, and we learn to be choosy about which ones we will allow to influence us. When the separation process is complete, we become fully adult citizens of the spiritual worlds with all of a citizen's rights, privileges, and responsibilities. We join the ranks of the drivers.

Of Blimps and Clashing Titans

All the big recurring themes in human conflict (truth vs. loyalty, tribe vs. individual, authority vs. freedom, passion vs. duty, science vs. religion, tradition vs. innovation, civilization vs. nature, etc.) can be traced to vertical influence. The ideals we fight over come from above. The problem is not that this influence is evil. The examples I've listed have nothing to do with good vs. evil. Rather, they are conflicts of good vs. good. That's why we find them so difficult to resolve. Ideals originating from the spiritual worlds are a beneficial influence to which humans are, nevertheless, somewhat allergic. In struggles between good and good, countless lives have been lost.

Our trouble arises when that which dwells in absolute time attempts to incarnate into linear time. In our world, no two objects can occupy exactly the same position at exactly the same instant. Nor can any two thoughts, feelings, principles, or intentions. Within the limits of the space/time continuum, all phenomena are obliged to take turns. This is not the case in the world of absolute time. The NOW is infinitely expandable. Opposites can coexist in it without contradiction. No need to fight, no need to choose.

If you've ever read any channeled literature, you are familiar with this idea, for it is a common preoccupation of the recently dead. When they enter the absolute NOW and experience the peaceful coexistence of opposites, they can no longer see what all the earthly fussing and feuding is about. With the naive enthusiasm of the freshly converted, they attempt to enlighten the rest of us. If we could just see how everything *is*, how *all* is peacefully and blissfully one, we would lay down our arms and be peacefully, blissfully happy, too.

They mean well. I can't help suspecting, though, that the human spirits who keep sending us these postcards from spiritual Disneyland were, while living on earth, the most pigheaded of materialists. They share the materialist's assumption that there is only one real world. While on earth, they dismiss the spiritual as merely an illusion. As soon as they leave the earth, they adopt the opposite position. In short, the only *real* world is the one they happen to be in. People who have cultivated vertical relationships while living on earth don't make this mistake. They have known all along that both viewpoints are real. They don't confuse a change of address with enlightenment.

Here on earth, every conflict boils down to a *time* conflict. Take jealousy, for example. From the perspective of absolute time, nothing could be more absurd than to feel jealous. In the NOW, it is entirely possible to love two different people completely, constantly, and eternally. In those rare earthly moments when love meets levity, we go up to glimpse the truth of this. We know that, at some level, we are fully capable of loving and being loved in this way. Unfortunately, that level is not where we are living. We live in the realm of linear time, where Saturday night is not an infinitely expandable NOW. Saturday night is a finite point in time and space that cannot be simultaneously occupied by bachelor #1 and bachelor #2. Jealousy is a natural consequence of that fact. We are not stupid to feel it.

The mythology of every culture shows us gods or angels in conflict. Humans are forever getting caught in the middle. For the gods in these stories, the human soul is the equivalent of Saturday night. It is the only thing in their experience that corresponds to a finite resource, and they jealously vie for it. The Biblical passage that begins, "To everything there is a season" could be read as an admonishment to them rather than to ourselves. It is reminding them that, if they wish to influence us, they have to take turns. Whatever attempts to take perfect, absolute, and unconditional form on earth ends in harm to the human soul, human society, and to the earth itself.

Are these fights and jealousies really happening in the spiritual worlds or is this merely how it appears from a human perspective? The question is impossible to answer, since a human perspective is the only one we've got. But I think it no accident that the word "decency" is so often modified by "human." Decency is the sense of proportion that we develop when obliged to live within limits. Humor and humility are its close relatives. These are the qualities that distinguish humans from the jealous gods of mythology.

If, as mythology suggests, spiritual beings sometimes get too big for their breeches, it is probably because they have trouble sensing their own size. Outside the limits of time and space, "too big" is a meaningless concept, for boundaries are nonexistent. People have the same problem when they leave the horizontal. It's called "spiritual inflation." The phrase always makes me chuckle, for to subtle perception (my subtle perception, at any rate) the spiritually inflated really do appear blimp-like. They resemble those giant balloons of cartoon characters in the Macy's Thanksgiving Day parade.

Inflated people have observed, correctly, that boundaries are an artificial construct. When you fly over the earth in an airplane, you can't see the lines that divide country from country on a map. The boundaries we draw between self and others are likewise artificial. We name them into existence. ("I'm Chevy Chase, and you're not.") If we forget to declare them, they tend to grow fuzzy or to disappear altogether. Still, it would be a mistake to conclude that, in the absence of boundaries, every thing is the *same* thing.

Consider the sun. Where does the sun leave off and something else begin? We can't say. In a sense, the "edges" of the sun overlap the edges of the earth, for the warmth of the sun can be felt beneath the surface of our soil. Yet we know full well that earth and sun are not the same thing—not because of any boundaries between them, but because each has a different center. It's the same with people and other spiritual beings. They don't have boundaries, but they have separate centers. So the question is: "What is that center? What are you actually referring to when you say 'I'?"

Separation and calcination are closely related. Both are processes of discovering what "I" is *not*. Each time some quality or condition you thought essential to your identity gets stripped away, a false boundary goes with it. Each time an outer layer is burned off, the next one down becomes your boundary, only to get burned away in turn. If you're halfway bright, you catch the general drift long before you run out of layers. The boundaries are not "I." The "I" is irreducible, not to be equated with anything else that can be named. There is no other name for "I" than "I."

In the material world, we don't need to know this to differentiate self from other. If for no other reason, I know I'm not you because your body and mine occupy different positions in space. For spiritual beings, the nearest equivalent to a body is a thought. In the vertical, if you and I are thinking exactly the same thought, we occupy exactly the same "position." How, then, do we tell ourselves apart? You are unlikely to be confused by this if you have come to know what "I" means. You will be able to feel that what I mean when I say "I" is different from what you mean when you say "I"—even if that is the *only* difference you can perceive between us.

Now let's look at what can happen when someone who is not sufficiently separated departs from the horizontal. This person, who still identifies "I" with his boundaries, finds himself in a world where no boundaries are discernable. With any luck, this will scare him immediately back to mundane mind. But sometimes it doesn't. Sometimes a person becomes entranced by the absence of boundaries around anyone or anything else, concluding that everyone and everything else must therefore be part of *himself*. He reasons, "There is only one I. Since I am I, I must be that one." This train of thought might even lead to the bliss-filled conclusion, "I am God."

You would expect that lack of social support for such a conclusion would cause it to be swiftly abandoned. Often that is the case. Opposition puts us back in touch with the otherness of others. But the severely inflated have tactics for getting around this. Like some giant amoeba, they simply encompass whatever contradicts or opposes them. All is one and one is all. Perhaps you've had the exasperating experience of trying to argue with such a person. It's like being swallowed.

Even if they never become inflated, many hermeticists struggle (or worse, fail to struggle) with what therapists call "boundary issues." Slipshod manners and morals are the most common symptom. The boundary-free hermeticist feels entitled to take your stuff, read your mind, covet your spouse, and show up uninvited. Having discovered the artificial nature of their own boundaries, they have trouble respecting, or even perceiving, the boundaries of others.

As the subtle senses develop, it becomes increasingly difficult to distinguish between inside and outside. The inner world comes to seem more public while the outer world may, at times, take on an illusory quality. This, too, can lead to boundary loss. Others may feel that the culprit is invading their inner space or treating their outward concerns too lightly.

In some people, boundary loss is passive rather than active. You might not infringe on others, but you allow them to infringe on you. This is probably happening if you tend to feel responsible for the feelings and problems of others, allow others to take advantage of you, or have trouble putting your foot down.

Formality is the best way I know to deal with vanishing boundaries. People such as monks and nuns who move vertically within the context of an established tradition rarely suffer from inflation or boundary problems. They have outward forms—rules to obey, a strict schedule to follow—to stabilize them. Freelance hermeticists need to compensate for the lack of such constraints by imposing some of their own. It helps to adopt some rules of behavior that you know full well are artificial and follow them consistently. For instance, find a book of etiquette that's slightly out of date (but not so antiquated that it will make you look ridiculous) and do what it says. Ask permission, follow directions, meet deadlines, let neatness count. Outward forms spare you the confusion of trying to figure out where the boundaries are supposed to be. You don't have to think as the Romans think. Just do as the Romans do—or perhaps a tad better.

Confronting the Adversaries

In its sometimes negative impact on human life, I have described the influence of spiritual beings not as a bad thing, but as too much of a good thing. Good influence can harm when it is disproportionate to its context. Such mishaps are largely the fault of humans, since to perceive and manage context is a horizontal responsibility. It is up to us to transmute the absolute into the relatively workable.

But what of influence that is *intrinsically* bad? In the mythologies of most polytheistic traditions, you will find gods who are hostile to humanity and intent on making trouble for us. In the three great monotheistic traditions, some angels are said to have fallen away from God and to have set out to tempt humans to do likewise. Appearing in legend and literature under names like Lucifer, Satan, Ahriman, Beelzebub, and Mephistopheles, they are said to actively oppose and hassle us.

We are not in a position to know for sure what relationship exists between these beings and God. Nor can we know what makes them tick, since to truly understand another being, one must love it. A case could even be made that these beings have no autonomous existence, that they are just fanciful personifications of certain extremes in the human psyche. The question may be impossible to resolve, for between any two spiritual beings, hostility breeds mutual projection rather than mutual recognition. So, if you choose to regard everything I will say about the antagonists as just a metaphor, I can't say for certain that you are wrong. Still, I'm going to follow the tradition of personifying them and describing their impact in colorful terms.

To understand that impact, one must first and foremost grasp the distinction between an adversary and an enemy. An adversary does not have to be hated and destroyed in order to be defeated. On the contrary, we are more likely to prevail against an opponent we respect and whose rightful place in the world we acknowledge. Worthy adversaries can even be regarded as helpful. They sharpen our game. For those who undertake the Great Work, adversaries facilitate the process of separation. In that context, I'm going to discuss two of them in detail. The names traditionally applied to them have accumulated some misleading and inflammatory connotations, so I will refer to them simply as the Adversary of Above and the Adversary of Below.

The Adversary of Above represents all of the negative possibilities of the upper vertical. What makes him especially insidious is that many spiritually inclined people assume that no such possibilities exist, that above is an entirely light-filled realm. Indeed it is, and therein lies the trouble. From a human perspective, there is such a thing as too much light. Would you, for instance, want to have sex under a thousand-watt lamp? Sounds like a silly example, but think seriously about why not. We would describe such a light as harsh and unforgiving. Beneath it we would feel inhibited and ashamed, for it is possible to be seen *too* clearly, *too* objectively. We would feel that there was something contemptuous about anyone who illuminated us so brutally while we were at our most vulnerable. If we were nevertheless obliged to go on, the way our coupling would appear in such light would be, in some sense, *untrue*. Excessive clarity and objectivity would distort it, turn it into something different. Truth carried to an extreme morphs into a lie.

The Adversary of Above is the liar of absolute truth. His greatest fault is spiritual pride; that is, pride in being a pure spirit. He has contempt for matter and works to instill this contempt in all who look down on the world of matter from above. All that humans have in common with animals is disgusting to him. He is proud, too, in regarding light as his own achievement, as if he were the very source of it. Vain, competitive, and jealous, he wants to be seen as the most brilliant light in the universe.

Still, the Adversary of Above cannot be justly described as evil. Indeed, he embodies the good, the true, and the beautiful to such an extent that humans often mistake him for God. (Some hermeticists have suggested, for example, that the "God" in Milton's *Paradise Lost* is actually this adversary.) You could say that he is the false God without whom we would never find our way to the true God, for it is our attraction to him that inspires us to undertake spiritual work in the first place. He is the vision that motivates us to sacrifice mundane pleasure and comfort in pursuit of higher attainment. If we never felt his influence, we would be inwardly lazy and dull.

The Adversary of Below is the liar of absolute *fact*. His basic strategy is to make us slaves to the material. While the law of karma is not his creation, he turns it to his own advantage, convincing us that we are hopelessly bound by it, that in surrender to the inevitability of our karma lies our only hope of inner peace. He would have us believe that all causes come from the past, that we cannot change our fates, and that our minds are nothing more than the activity of our brains. The more we view life processes as impersonal and mechanical, the better he likes our thinking. If we would stop thinking altogether, he'd like it even better.

To the Adversary of Below, the spiritual aspect of humanity appears to be a ridiculous delusion. He attempts to convince us that nothing is real except that which can be weighed, measured, and counted. All he can appreciate in the human individual is the data that appears on our employment applications and medical histories. We are only real to him to the extent that we identify with such data. He is humorless, driven, and hostile to creativity, spontaneity, and disorder. As far as he's concerned, the only worthwhile human is one who is standing in line, putting his nose to the grindstone, or indulging in mindless distractions.

I find this being extremely disagreeable, but he embodies a principle that is essential to us: gravity. Without gravity, we wouldn't be able to digest our way back down to the horizontal from above, nor could we become heavy enough to sink to the deeper regions of below. Without gravity, no vertical inspiration would ever take form on earth. It is to the weight of this adversary that we owe our capacity for commitment and exertion. If we never felt his influence, we would be credulous and useless dreamers.

The harm in these beings is not that they attract us up or down. It is not even that they attract us to *extremes* of up and down. To be drawn to these extremes is beneficial, for it is at the very top and the very bottom that we encounter the divine. Attraction by the adversaries distorts human nature only when we get seduced into taking sides. Each would have us dwell exclusively in his realm, despising or denying the very existence of the other. Their harm is not in what they urge us to embrace, but in what they tempt us to reject.

Taken together, these two adversaries have pretty much cornered the market on every human impulse and endeavor. Anything you might think, say, or do could be attributed to the influence of one or the other. To reject all such influence as evil sets up a basic damned-if-you-do, damned-if-you-don't contradiction that can paralyze the human will. In theory, you could say that the ideal vertical weight of a human being is the exact midpoint between them—neither too heavy nor too light. But the theoretical midpoint is just that: a *point*. It leaves you nowhere to stand. Nor can you resolve the conflict through compromise. Above and below don't average out. If you're going to move vertically at all, you've got to head in one direction or the other. The solution is simply to keep moving. Keep both your levity and your gravity in good working order.

In attempting to do what I have just now advised, we are frustrated by another apparent adversary: the threshold guardian. I say "apparent" because this being grasps the human predicament and is there to help. The guardian's role is to prevent vertical trespassing. We are treated as a trespasser when we attempt vertical travel before we are inwardly equipped to handle it or for motives that the guardian deems unwise. What is actually being guarded is our humanity.

It appears to me that, as rookies, we can sometimes sneak past the checkpoints, going up or down now and then without getting into a direct confrontation. Perhaps our mentors vouch for us or arrange a temporary visitor's pass. I'm not quite sure how it works, but I do know that eventually it *stops* working. Your way is barred. Attempts at unauthorized entry result in an immediate return to the horizontal or a diversion to Baggage Disclaim. You find there's nothing for it but a direct showdown with the guardian.

It takes a curious form, this showdown. In place of the guardian, you meet at the threshold either the Adversary of Above or the Adversary of Below. At least, so it appears. If you're trying to go up, you have the impression that the upper adversary is blocking your way. Isn't that odd? What is even more disquieting is that these adversaries, when appearing at the threshold, bear an uncanny resemblance to *you*. Not you as you usually think of yourself or as your loved ones think of you. More like you as you would be described by someone who wanted to make a case against you—you as a witness for your own prosecution.

In the Adversary of Above, you see the personification of your spiritual ego trip. You see someone who is vain, power hungry, and self-righteous. A show-off. A bully. A prima donna. A mean-spirited critic. A spin doctor. A pompous ass. You see all the little ways you attempt to get one up on others, how you secretly delight in their faults and failures and aggrandize yourself at their expense. You see your envy and your jealousy. You see all your unworthy motives for wanting to attain the philosopher's stone.

Please don't take this personally. I can't say exactly how *your* threshold guardian will appear. I'm just giving you the general drift. Regardless of what your personal egotism looks like, the guardian mirrors it back to you super-sized and brilliantly lit. It's pretty horrifying. Makes you understand why someone would want to don sackcloth and ashes.

It will probably be on another occasion (could be earlier, could be later) that you meet the guardian as Adversary of Below, likewise attired as yourself. This one embodies everything about you that is unconscious, everything you feel you can't help. You see the creature of habit, the victim of circumstance, the slave to fashion, the spineless conformist. You see the sellout, the junkie, the whiner, the slacker, and the drone. You see all the ways that you have failed to exercise your freedom, allowing your life to be shaped by outside forces. You become acutely conscious of what your non-decisions have made of you.

So what are you supposed to do in these encounters? How do you contend against an adversary who appears to you as *you*? I'm afraid I can't say. Your guides won't tell you, either. In this matter, you are cast entirely on your own resources.

It might help to keep in mind the outcome you desire. The result of a successful encounter at the threshold of above is full citizenship in the upper vertical. You will thereafter be free to go as high as your levity will carry you. No region is off-limits if you're light enough to get to it. When all goes well at the threshold of below, you are given safe conduct to the healing place at the bottom. Once you have successfully made it past both checkpoints, involuntary detours to Baggage Disclaim will be rare and short-lived, for you will quickly realize where you are and how to get out. You develop a taste for genuine vertical experience and a marked disinclination to accept the astral as a substitute. This is a distinct turning point, not a gradual change. You'll be able to pinpoint when it happened.

In older occult literature, meetings with threshold guardians are described in melodramatic terms. You might get the impression that if you make the wrong move, you will find yourself on the fast track to damnation. Nah. If you blow it, you get a do-over. You get as many do-overs as you need. The only consequence of a botched encounter is yet another layover in Baggage Disclaim.

Prior to the invention of High Self-Esteem, many seekers used to precipitate threshold showdowns on purpose, the sooner to get them over with. If you're fed up with diversions to Baggage Disclaim, you, too, might want to hurry the process up. The most efficient method I know of is to keep a "falsehood journal." Each night, just before going to bed, record in this journal every single lie you've told since you woke up. Include the little white ones meant to spare others' feelings or grease the wheels of social intercourse, and pay special attention to the lies you have told *yourself*. Don't attempt to rationalize or excuse them and don't castigate yourself about them either. Simply write them down. If you're thorough, you won't need to persist long with the exercise. It provokes a very swift response.

10

Conjunction

Opposite elements are reunited.

BASE MATTER:

Vulnerability

SYMPTOMS:

Empathy
Affection
Desire to help
Feeling ineffectual
Paranoia

TO ABET:

Hold conflict without trying to resolve it.
Do the simple things that gladden your heart.

TRANSMUTATION:

Compassion

Isn't it odd how there are two sides to every question? Why two? Why not three? Or five? Or one? What is it about the human mind that gravitates to the either/or, the black vs. white, the pro vs. con? When sufficiently exasperated or conciliatory we might allow that "the truth lies somewhere in between." But we rarely head directly to that "somewhere." We operate as if every issue must be settled by the inefficient workings of a two-party system.

We know that reality itself isn't bifurcated. So why do we keep trying to perceive it with a bifurcated mind? I used to think it had to do with the way our bodies are made. We come in two genders, have two eyes, two ears, two arms, two legs, two lungs, two sides of the brain. Yet it is said that humans are made in the image and likeness of God. If God is one, why do we have these brains that divide everything in two?

My first impression of God came from the *Baltimore Catechism*, a series of questions and answers that Catholic children used to have to recite from memory:

Q: Why did God make me?
A: God made me to know him, love him, and serve him.

I memorized that at the age of five and have yet to discover a more cogent answer. If God made us to know him, then the human organism must be some sort of God-knowing apparatus. That it approaches knowing in twos must have something to do with what it has been designed to know. So what does all this either/or have to do with the divine?

Perhaps the best way to see what's right with two is to look at what's wrong with *one*. I have already alluded to that—in the previous chapter, and earlier, in the discussion of the Ouroboros. One begets solipsism, the closed system. Pantheism and atheism are essentially the same idea, for if everything is God, you don't need the word "God." You can just say "everything." A god that is everything is, in effect, no god.

Have you ever tried to imagine the time before God created the world? To be a god without a world sounds terribly lonely. And boring. Imagine how boring existence would be if nothing existed but you! As a theology major in college, I learned that we're not supposed to think like this, not supposed to project human emotions onto the divine. But if the human organism is a indeed a God-knowing apparatus, then it seems to me our emotions must have some relevance. Why would that which was never lonely create a loneliness-perceiving being?

In any event, we got made. In that making, God opened a system that, as far as we can imagine, had been closed. God made something that was *not* God. And the one sure way to tell that the not-God was *truly* not God, was for the not-God to be able to say no.

This, I suspect, is why we were made to apprehend the world in twos. It's so that we can say no. Two was the invention of freedom. Our freedom to say yes or no is the most sacred value in the spiritual world, for without it there is no not-God. Without the not-God, no one can know God. In the absence of a not-God, perhaps even God cannot know God.

Yet two is also the number of irresolvable conflict: the standoff, the stalemate, the obstinate stupidity of either/or. Where only two are gathered, there is nobody to break the tie. In its own way, two can be as static as one, only this time the stasis is *painful*. Another being is present, yet we are isolated in our separateness, the conflict that establishes the *two*. If we could just become one, this painful tension would end. Hence the attraction of any religious idea or experience that promises to return us to the cozy cocoon of unity.

Neither one nor two is entirely satisfactory. Might there be a better number?

In alchemy, that better number is three. As two is the principle of separation, three is the principle of conjunction. Three is the dynamic form of one.

Of what does this three consist? If I am one and you make two, who or what is three?

Three is our *between*.

Separation is the alchemical process of establishing two. Conjunction is how we get to three.

Cats in a Sack

I went to Marrakech in the fall of 2000 because I wanted to know what Ramadan was like in its native habitat of the medina. By law, all Moroccans are required to observe the fast between dawn and sundown. They can't even drink water. In a desert climate, that's a hardship. For the first few days, people are crabby. But since *everyone* is crabby, and for the same reason, they give each other a lot of slack. They make a collective effort to slow down, mellow out, and be gentle with one another. By the third day, it has gelled. Kindness blankets the medina and everyone cheers up. The mood turns festive.

Each afternoon, as the sun began to wane, I'd head over to my favorite café and take a table overlooking the Djemma el Fna—a huge square that's part market, part circus. Amid carts heaped high with dates and olives and oranges, wizened herbalists and henna ladies camp out on blankets, plying their trades, and Sufi musicians drum themselves into a trance. Crowds dressed in colorful djellabas encircle acrobats, fire-eaters, snake charmers, and transvestite belly dancers. Then, fifteen minutes before sundown, the entire spectacle vanishes, almost in the blink of an eye. Hastily everyone packs up their gear and rushes to get home for the breaking of the fast. If home is too distant, they repair to the nearest café. The square is deserted by every living thing except the cats (pets of no one in particular and everyone in general).

Meanwhile the café waiters are hustling to make sure all patrons are served before the muezzins cry out the sundown prayer—the signal that the day's fast has ended. You don't have to order because the menu for Ramadan "breakfast" is as standard as Thanksgiving dinner. You get a bowl of harrira (a thick lentil soup), a handful of dates, a hardboiled egg, a sticky confection of fried dough and honey, and milk or café au lait. By the time the muezzins are clearing their throats, half a million spoons are poised above half a million bowls of harrira. Everyone takes their first mouthful at exactly the same moment.

The year I was there, Morocco was suffering from a severe drought. Ramadan coincided with what was supposed to be the rainy season, but the rains weren't happening. During the third week, promising thunderclouds would clot the sky for an hour or so, then move on without spilling a drop. Pinkish dust filled the air and clung to throats already desiccated with thirst. It was as if the parched earth were fasting, too. On the fifth day of this exasperating pattern, as the waiters were bustling and the muezzins trudging to the tops of their minarets, black clouds suddenly darkened the deserted square. Half a million spoons hovered in suspense. The muezzins called out the first phrase of their "bon appétit" signal. The spoons began their descent into steaming bowls. At that *exact* moment, the skies opened, loosing a tremendous downpour, the hot earth steaming as its raging thirst was quenched.

My French is too primitive to express complicated thoughts. To the friendly strangers who shared my table, I managed only to exclaim, "The earth does Ramadan too! And God answers!"

My companions looked at me as if to say, "Well, *duh*."

It seemed to me that such a clear and magnanimous gesture from heaven could only be called forth by an equally clear and magnanimous gesture on earth. That is what Ramadan is all about. Each sundown is a collective sigh of "thank you," preceded by a long, thirsty day of "please." What makes it so magical in the medina is that *everyone* participates. They'll tell you they have to because it's the law. But they'll also say they want to. That's *why* it's the law.

A year later, when my own country declared war on Islamic fundamentalism, I felt terribly torn. To visit a theocracy had been a huge treat for me. I got to experience things that only happen when an entire society achieves critical spiritual mass. If such places ceased to exist in this world, I would be very sad. I understand, too, why people would do violence in defense of them and why that violence was directed against my own country on 9/11. Placed side by side with the gracious traditions of the medina, American culture looks barbaric—a barbarism that was already invading by export before it invaded by arms. Part of me was on the side of the terrorists.

I want to be able to visit a theocracy, but I don't want to live in one. The separation of church and state is an alchemical process necessary to my own flourishing. If I didn't live in a country where people were free to make their own religious choices, I couldn't publish this book, and you couldn't read it. This, too, is a value for which I would be willing to fight. When our invasion permitted Afghan women to come out from under their burkas, I let out a cheer for the home team.

The heart is the between of the human being, that which perceives all other betweens. It is the point where above and below come together, or split and go their separate ways. Caught in the middle, the heart is where we experience their conflicts, where we know ourselves to be divided and long to heal the division. When good wars against good, the human heart is their battleground. It is the between not only of the human being, but of the cosmos itself. It is the place where the spiritual is transmuted into the physical, where the ideals of heaven take form as deeds on earth. Even God is dependent on the human heart, for it is through our hearts that divine love manifests to incarnate beings. Rain falls everywhere, but only the thirsty heart sees the love in it.

In our anxiety to resolve the painful conflict of two, we may long to return to the stasis one. If we'd only just love harder, we think, opposites would merge and all conflicts would end. We imagine that the heart could do this. It could cook the world as I cook stew. Throw everything into the same pot, apply the heat of love, and all manner of different things would eventually boil down to the same thing.

What happens when I put Islamic theocracy and American democracy together in that pot? No matter how much heat I apply, they don't boil down to one. I don't get a nice, warm, comforting stew. My heart is more like a sack in which two feral cats yowl and claw at each other in a fight to the death.

That cats-in-a-sack sensation is what the process of conjunction often feels like at its onset. When opposite elements are separated out, they remain separate. You can't get them to merge. They might not even be amenable to compromise. Conjunction can look like lovemaking, but it can also look like war. The between of fully separated elements is volatile. The heart is the vessel in which that volatile reaction occurs. The heart's job is to *hold* the conflict, not to resolve it.

To understand what I mean by "hold," try this experiment. Think of a conflict you've so far been unable to resolve for yourself because you're torn between two opposing values or options or people. Imagine that this conflict is occurring at the level of your solar plexus. You could even imagine you've swallowed the conflict and it's sitting in your belly. Keep the image of it there for a few minutes and notice what happens. Next, shift the conflict up to the level of your forehead. Keep it there awhile and see if anything changes. Finally bring the conflict to the level of your heart. Let it sit there for a few minutes. Notice any difference?

The gut is the area of the body that corresponds to the process of separation. When we experience conflict there, our natural reaction is to take sides. The forehead corresponds to a process we haven't talked about yet, but as you might have guessed, it has to do with thinking. When we relate to a conflict with the head, we try to judge it impartially or figure out a solution.

At heart level, we perceive the between. This third factor—the between—is not a compromise, nor is it a third option. It's not a win/win solution—though it might give rise to one. Think of it instead as a verb that connects two nouns. It's the living quality of the relationship the opposite elements have formed.

When we hold a conflict in our hearts, we are offering hospitality to the two opposing elements and their between. Something will come of this. Something new will be born of their scrappy conjugal visit. We don't know what, because, unlike the head, the heart doesn't try to take charge of it. The heart doesn't attempt to tame the cats. Instead, it provides a sack that doesn't rip apart when they fight.

Coming Home

Apart from the occasional cat scratch, I find conjunction the most agreeable phase of the Great Work. It feels less like work than like coming home. That's because the heart itself doesn't need transmuting. An injured heart might need healing, but aside from that, the hearts we're born with work just fine.

In its natural state, the heart is vulnerable. It will still be vulnerable when it becomes the philosopher's stone. It needs to be, for it is our center of connection. It couldn't connect if it were tough and self-sufficient. Nor could it perceive the between. At the outset of our work, the heart's predicament is that it is neither a center of conscious intention nor a center of instinctive will. It is caught between the two. So we experience the heart as *helplessly* vulnerable. It can ache, but it can't act.

As our center of connection, the heart is basically magnanimous, empathic, outgoing, and affectionate. Beneath it are three will centers whose natures are necessarily selfish, since their primary task is to ensure our survival. Until they are transmuted, this basic selfishness of the instinctive will undermines the generous impulses of the heart. We want to help others, but we're lousy at it.

Our bottommost will center is driven by fear. When this fear unites with the heart's instinctive empathy, the result is Job's comforter syndrome. The suffering of another makes us afraid for ourselves. And so, in the very act of offering sympathy, we try to distance ourselves from the victim. We seek reassurance in any differences we can find between self and afflicted other.

The second will center is driven by passion. It seeks to seduce, to incorporate another into the self. When joined with this seductive impulse, the heart, in its empathy, projects rather than perceives. We imagine ourselves into another person's shoes, feeling "what I would feel in his place," while failing to perceive feelings that are different from our projected selves. This kind of empathy is isolating to those who suffer. It feels generic. Our caring only reaches the spot that hurts when we are able to perceive others from *their own* point of view.

The third will center is driven by the need for self-affirmation. Its approach to helpfulness is a kind of one-upmanship at the expense of the victim. It makes itself feel powerful by taking over, and smart by doling out unsolicited advice. It is attracted to the weakness of the afflicted and tends to foster their dependence. It is also keen on being admired, seeing in the troubles of others an opportunity to show off how good it is.

Because the heart is so sensitive, it knows full well that these gestures are ineffectual. But it can't do better all on its own. It has to wait for the will centers to transmute themselves. When fear is transmuted into confidence, the suffering of others stops freaking us out. We no longer have to distance ourselves by blaming the victim. When passion is transmuted into devotion, we don't have to identify with others in order to care about them. Instead of imagining what they are feeling, we perceive it directly. When territoriality is transmuted into integrity, we don't have to borrow our strength from the weak. We respect the autonomy of those we are trying to help. As a result of these transmutations, the will centers learn to take instruction from the heart.

As the philosopher's stone, the heart will become the source of all our magical deeds. Even its perceptions will impact the world, as if to perceive were to do. Its vulnerability will become active and savvy compassion. This is not because the heart itself will change, but because everything around it will have changed. Transmuted and realigned so that they all face the heart, the intention centers will inspire it and the will centers will empower it.

The processes that transmute intention and will are a lot of work. But all the conjunction process requires of us is that we keep our hearts healthy, soft, and impressionable. You do this by coming home to your simple humanity. Anything that gladdens the heart is good for it. You know the kind of stuff I mean: cuddling, presents, spaghetti dinners, three-hanky movies. Planting tulips, walking the dog, tucking the kids into bed. Getting the giggles, singing off-key, reading a fat pulpy novel on the beach. You certainly don't need instruction from me on what makes you happy, but you might need reminding to pursue it now and then. Don't let alchemy turn you into a Great Workaholic.

Hermetic Paranoia

The comedian Dave Chappelle has described paranoia as "connecting dots that maybe shouldn't be connected." It is a negative potential of conjunction that we need to address, for hermeticists are more than usually prone to it. Because so much of our work consists of perceiving relationships, we run the risk of overconnecting the dots. Conspiracy theories are a frequent result.

I'll give you an example from the paranoid region of my own mind. Stress is a major factor in many of the illnesses that afflict Americans, and our jobs are a frequent source of this stress. If we are getting sick from job stress, the most sensible remedy might be to quit the job, but people usually don't. Why? Part of the reason is that they need the health insurance that comes with the job. Why? To pay for the treatment of the illness that comes with the job! Try watching TV commercials from this perspective. Half of them are promoting products or activities that are likely to make you fat or stressed or sick, while the other half are promoting remedies for these conditions. Who benefits from this vicious circle? The Corporation. It makes you sick, then sells you the remedy, meanwhile keeping you enslaved as a worker so you'll have the means to pay for what makes you sick and what supposedly makes you better.

The conventional conspiracy theorist imagines all this actually being plotted by corporate leaders in a secret boardroom somewhere. The hermetic paranoid imagines instead that the secret boardroom exists on a spiritual plane. Since the whole diabolical cycle serves the agenda of the Adversary of Below (to keep humanity enslaved to the material), the hermetic conspiracy theorist usually attributes the plot to him and his minions.

The web of interrelated causes that keeps us trapped is called karma. Hermeticists are better than the average person at perceiving how it works. But in conceiving of karma as a conspiracy, they are overlooking one very important point: *nobody is in charge of karma*. Karma is what happens in the *absence* of a conscious intention or deliberate plan. The vicious circle I described above results from a collective lack of awareness. Those who happen to profit are merely our fellow sleepwalkers. The supposed beneficiaries of the whole thing are just as bewildered as its victims. In fact, it would be truer to say that every one of us is sometimes a beneficiary and sometimes a victim.

Mistaking unconsciousness for conspiracy leads either to feelings of profound helplessness or to grandiose schemes that, in their very grandiosity, beget even worse feelings of helplessness, since we're in no position to implement them. When we fantasize about leading a revolution or blowing something up, we're thinking like muggles, not magicians. From a muggle perspective, a huge problem demands a huge solution. You're thinking alchemically when you think *small*.

Every action provokes a counterreaction. The unintended side effect of any big solution to a big problem is a new big problem. (If you haven't already noticed this phenomenon, start looking for it. You'll find examples everywhere.) Therefore, the slighter the intervention, the less collateral damage it is likely to do. The alchemist asks, "What is the smallest, most subtle and inconspicuous action I can take and still have an effect?"

Maybe you've heard of the butterfly effect. The name came from some scientist's fantasy that the beating of a butterfly's wings causes a minute change in air currents that might eventually manifest, halfway around the world, as a storm. Because all phenomena are interconnected, an infinitesimal change in one phenomenon will eventually reverberate throughout the entire web. An alchemical intervention might be as slight as the flutter of an insect wing but, unlike the butterfly effect, it isn't random. It's strategic. Even a slight flutter of consciousness is disruptive to an unconscious system. A whole web of interconnections can unravel at the pulling of a single thread. The trick is choosing the right thread.

Altruism with Oomph

Your generous heart need not remain idle while waiting for your will centers to get their act together. There is a way to benefit others without doing anything at all to solve their problems. It's a kind of magic, and you can do it *today*. The beauty of this magic is that selfishness is not an obstacle to it. On the contrary, whatever is confused, neurotic, and unfinished in you is its *prima materia*.

The procedure is to stand before the spiritual world, calling on the lighter and the heavier beings to be your witness as you declare yourself the official representative of all who share your particular hang-up or difficulty. You then ask that the benefits of any progress you yourself make be distributed to your fellow sufferers.

Think of Lance Armstrong. When diagnosed with cancer, he declared himself a representative of all other cancer patients. To give them hope was his mission in winning the Tour de France. You will also be familiar with the procedure if you watch the *Oprah* show. Not only is Oprah very conscious of her role as a representative in every personal challenge she faces, but she frequently reminds her guests that they, in disclosing their difficulties on television, are representatives, too.

I point out those public examples simply because, in being public, they illustrate the process for all to see. Publicity is by no means necessary to the procedure. It works just as well if your only witnesses are spiritual beings, for it is they who actually do the work of distributing the benefits of your inner work to people you've never met.

To understand the power of this magic, you have to be looking at the world from a vertical perspective. When we take a strictly material view, we may feel very small and insignificant. The people who make a marked difference in the world all seem to be famous and influential and to know of smart solutions that they are able to implement on a grand scale. Lighter beings have a rather different view of who is important and influential because what they perceive best is inner activity. Some of the biggest "celebrities" in the vertical world are people you and I have never heard of. They are highly visible above because of the richness of their inner lives. Lighter beings rely on them to communicate aspects of human experience that are difficult for the non-incarnate to perceive directly. They are, in a sense, delegates for the rest of humanity.

To become one of these delegates is simple. All you have to do is volunteer, for the very act of doing so increases your visibility. It's a bit like being the celebrity spokesman for some disease, social problem, or humanitarian cause except that it works backward: you become a celebrity *because* you're the spokesman. Doing this attracts the notice of heavier beings as well. Whatever cares might weigh you down weigh even more heavily on them. Just as we look to lighter beings, they look to humans for clues and depend on human advancement for their own advancement.

To all spiritual beings, human life is a big deal. The human heart is the crucible of the cosmos. When you realize this, a shift in consciousness occurs. You begin to see that inner life is not necessarily *private* life. Your inner life belongs to the world. In assenting to this—welcoming the attention of the lighter and heavier beings—you acquire an ability to influence the world for the better even if the only human problems you struggle with are your own, personal problems.

A meditation practice called "sending and taking" supports and expresses this decision to become a representative. I describe how to do it in appendix 1.

11

Fermentation

The substance is left alone in the dark, where it putrefies.

BASE MATTER:

Obsolete desires and ambitions

SYMPTOMS:

Apathy
Loss of initiative
Doubt
Feeling abandoned or unworthy
Reluctance to express oneself

TO ABET:

Maintain inner silence

TRANSMUTATION:

Magical will

Fermentation is the phase that St. John of the Cross called "the dark night of the soul." Though the expression is often used as a synonym for despair, that's not what John meant by it. In his poem of the same name, he exults:

> Oh, night that guided me, Oh night more lovely than the dawn,
> Oh, night that joined Beloved with lover, Lover transformed into
> the Beloved!

Of course, he was writing after the fact. While actually fermenting, one wouldn't feel like reading these words, much less writing them. They are describing what is found at the bottom of the plunge into darkness, not the plunge itself.

Accounts of these dark nights, along with explanations of why they occur and advice on how to weather them, are common in the writings of religious mystics. Their desire is union with God, and they approach it with an intensity of feeling that might strike the average person as manic-depressive. God, the absent lover, sweeps them into an embrace that is as rapturous as it is brief, then casts them into an inner desert where they wander for months without sustenance, pining and reproaching themselves, wondering what they did to turn God off. Alchemists, who by temperament often have more in common with scientists than with saints, tend neither to gush nor to lament about their inner lives, and rarely even mention God when describing their endeavor. What, you might be wondering, do the mood swings of mystics have to do with you?

What mystics and alchemists have in common is vertical inner movement. The "dark night" is a side effect of this movement. Alchemists are, if anything, more thrown by it, for they are often working without the support of an established religious tradition that would warn them of what to expect. This is especially true of contemporary Americans, who may reject the concept of sin, yet interpret feeling bad as a sign that they've taken a wrong turn on their spiritual path. But the dark night is not a mistake. It is a crucial phase in the development of the philosopher's stone: the diamond heart. Actual diamonds are formed when carbon is left alone for a very long time and heavily compressed by the weight of the earth. This probably doesn't feel good to the carbon. If it could think, it might wonder what it had done to deserve such a miserable fate.

Back in my Buddhist days, I would occasionally do a month-long group meditation retreat. We would start meditating at sunrise and, except for a brief work period, keep at it till bedtime. Even meals are taken in the meditation hall. Halfway through the month, we would get a day off, when we were free to do as we pleased. During the first two weeks we all fantasized about how we would exploit this longed-for liberty. We planned to eat fast food, catch up with the headlines and sports scores, go for a run or a swim, shop, take in a movie, get smashed. But when the time finally came to indulge these desires, it all felt somehow perfunctory, as if we were dutifully executing plans made a long time ago by someone else. During our day off, a mood of restless ennui prevailed. When it was time to return to the meditation hall the next morning, we felt strangely relieved.

This is what you might call the "twilight of the soul" or "fermentation lite." You can remember your old familiar pleasures, but somehow they don't motivate you the way they used to. Out of habit, you crave a favorite food, but when you finally eat it, it doesn't taste as good as you remembered. Or you start to listen to a favorite song, then find, when it's over, that you haven't really heard it or that you've heard it yet felt unmoved by it. Your physical senses have a dull, glazed-over quality. Perhaps you've experienced something like that after prolonged study or intellectual work. Of necessity, you turn off, or mute, your senses. When you are ready to enjoy them again, you can't seem to get them to turn back on. The same thing happens when you're working to develop subtle perception. You shift your attention away from gross perception in order to tune in to the subtle. When you shift back to the material world, it seems less real somehow, like a TV show playing in the background. You can't quite get into it. Mystics call this the "darkening of the senses." It is a side effect of learning to move in the vertical dimension.

As a beginner, your vertical encounters tend to have a quasi-sensory quality. You may get vivid mental images, or "hear" lighter beings speaking to you in ordinary human language. When this first starts to happen, it's very absorbing. Where once you had to push yourself to meditate or do your alchemy exercises or read difficult hermetic literature, these are now the only pursuits that feel real to you. It's as if there is a competition going on between the inner world and the outer world, and the inner world is the clear winner. You don't mind at first that your physical senses are bringing you less pleasure, because the experience of your subtle senses is so compelling.

Gradually you learn to move higher. As you do, your subtle senses grow as dim as the physical ones. Your mental pictures become fewer and vaguer and may eventually disappear altogether. Instead of hearing words, you find your mind overtaken by wordless concepts. It's not that your previous visionary experiences were false, just that you are going for something even truer, a higher level of subtlety and refinement. The higher you go, the more abstract and ephemeral your experiences become. The darkening of the subtle senses enables you to sustain concentration on phenomena so elusive they defy description. Yet when you return to the horizontal, you're really in a pickle. You can't escape your boredom with the outer world by turning inward, because the inner world has become boring, too. It is utterly stripped of the sensory, feeling, and narrative qualities that sustain human interest.

As twilight deepens into a true dark night of the soul, you may find that your old familiar motivations are losing their credibility and zest. Ambitions that used to drive you now appear dusty and dry, like the skeleton of a body you've left behind. Someone can give you a big compliment and it doesn't mean anything to you. Good news or an important personal achievement leaves you strangely unexcited. It's as if there's a big hole where your ego is supposed to be. The loss is disorienting, for you weren't trying to give up anything on purpose. Instead, your desires and emotions have fallen prey to a creeping apathy that sucks all the juice out of them. You come down with a thoroughgoing case of the blahs. For me, one telltale sign that I'm in this phase is an inability to follow the plots of movies. I see people shouting, firing guns, speeding around in cars, and pitching around on beds together, but the motives for all this activity are unintelligible to me. I can't for the life of me understand what all the fuss is about.

During a dark night of the soul, you may feel as if you've become less human, almost as if you're some alien who has fallen to earth by accident. In a way that's true. In order to meet lighter beings on their own terms, your consciousness has temporarily broken free of the physical and subtle bodies to become more spirit-like. It has lost some of its uniquely human characteristics. For a few minutes at a time, this is exhilarating. Then you remember you're still living on earth, where to be a pure spirit is dysfunctional and feels awful. As a permanent state of affairs it would, in fact, be very bad for you. But it isn't permanent. One day you wake up and smell the coffee, and the coffee smells fantastic. All your senses come back full strength, and they work just fine. You laugh and cry and care again. The knack for coming back into your full humanity isn't teachable, as far as I know, and doesn't really need to be taught. Your life force simply reasserts itself, to your immense pleasure and relief. Vertical and horizontal consciousness gradually work out their differences. Eventually you find that you can shuttle very rapidly between them without becoming disoriented or blown out. Even when you've gone very high, you're able to come in for a smooth landing.

That's the good news. The bad news is that, having learned to recover quickly from the dark night of the soul, you become a candidate for what St. John termed "the dark night of the spirit." It's even darker. He called it "awful, terrible, horrible." Indeed, it well and truly sucks. Perhaps the best way to explain how and why it happens is to place it on the mental map we created in chapter 4. If the dark night of the soul is an awkward return to the horizontal, the dark night of the spirit is a rapid and often terrifying plunge into the lower vertical from the upper vertical. It is a deep fall from a great height.

Have you ever descended rapidly from a high altitude? Say, for instance, you've woken up high in the Rockies and then by noon found yourself driving across the Great Plains. You probably felt a little bit depressed, for the air in the lowlands is heavier and gravity seems to pull harder on you, making you feel as if you weigh more. Upon returning to earth, astronauts feel the same way, only more so, because they weren't merely lighter while above, they were absolutely weightless. Now imagine that, like an astronaut, you're hurtling back from outer space, but instead of landing on the earth's surface, you keep going, plunging below the surface all the way to core. You go from weightlessness to a gravity so oppressive you can scarcely breathe.

We normally find ourselves in the lower vertical when the suffering of ordinary life makes us inwardly heavy. The departure point for our downward movement is the horizontal. If we have fallen into a depression, we can identify the feeling or circumstance in horizontal life that pushed us over the edge. The depression St. John called the dark night of the spirit can't be traced to any mishap in the horizontal past or present, because it doesn't originate there. It is a sudden, drastic, and unexplained fall from *above*.

Calcination teaches us to base our confidence on the spirit rather than on the transient conditions of incarnate life. When something is going wrong in the horizontal, we discover that we can restore perspective by moving upward, inwardly rising above our trouble. To do this is impossible during a dark night of the spirit. Your levity no longer works. All communication with lighter beings—including your own spirit—is cut off. The populous solitude of the hermeticist, in which to think is to converse, turns to stark loneliness. One is entirely alone with thoughts that wouldn't be worth sharing even if someone showed up to listen.

While below, you can only think of two possible explanations for the sudden disappearance of lighter beings, and it is hard to say which explanation is the more painful. Maybe your friends in high places have abandoned you—probably because you were never worthy of them in the first place. You look for the fault within yourself. Your inner life becomes a free-for-all of self-doubt and self-reproach. Or maybe these friends never even existed. Maybe you were just making them up, and what you used to call your spiritual life was just a grand delusion. You return to the hermetic writings that used to mean a lot to you—including, perhaps, your own journals—and they sound like gibberish. This explanation, too, ends in self-reproach. You judge yourself to have been very foolish, if not downright crazy.

Sometimes we feel foolish because we actually have been foolish. We have gotten lost in Baggage Disclaim and picked up mistaken notions. Once we are firmly situated in the horizontal again, we recognize the error and feel embarrassed to have fallen for it. Despite whatever chagrin it might cause, identifying a mistake reassures us that we are smart—at least smarter than we were when we made it. If we can see that we've been foolish, we must be wising up.

But that experience is different from the repudiation of past spiritual experience that occurs during fermentation. You can't identify a single, specific error, nor can you find a truer idea with which to replace it. *All* inner experiences—including excursions to the true upper vertical—appear to have been mere illusions. While beset by the dark night of the spirit, even the greatest mystics have toyed with the possibility of atheism. This is especially distressing if you have, in some sense, burned your bridges to the mundane. Though you might judge your spiritual life to have been unreal, mundane life does not become more real by contrast. Worldly success does not suddenly become more meaningful when you conclude there is no other kind. It seems rather like some bleak occupation with which to pass the time while waiting for your meaningless life to be over.

If you could see it from the perspective of the lighter beings (which is impossible to do while you are below), you would take your dark night as a compliment. It is a mark of progress, not a sign of a screwup. In order to achieve inner alignment, the heights to which you ascend in the vertical must be balanced by correspondingly deep descents. If this is not a judgment or a punishment, neither is it a strictly mechanical law. That is, you don't fall automatically as the result of a vertical climb. It doesn't happen every single time you go up. Rather you are sent down, wisely and lovingly, when a change that has occurred in the above of your being needs to be offset by a corresponding change below. Your own spirit consents to this—though you can't remember giving that consent when the fall is in progress.

You are sent down—and agreed to being sent down—because while above you glimpsed a truth and developed an aspiration with which the whole of your being is not yet aligned. You can think it, but you can't yet will it. Nor can you will your will to change. Just as we cannot see our own eyes, we cannot will our own will. The realignment of the will requires outside help, and this help is found where the will itself is found—in the below of the human being. It's a bit like undergoing surgery. The doctors would prefer that you were unconscious not only to spare you pain, but because your conscious participation would only get in the way. They don't want you to fret about what they're doing or attempt to control it. They need you to just go to sleep and let them get on with their work.

This adjustment of the will is especially necessary if you wish to be a magician. Suppose an aspiring alchemist—let's call him Greg—wants to develop the ability to heal people by magic. While above, he has gained many insights into the secrets of illness and health and a conviction that he can help people by putting those insights into practice. Like many people who are attracted to healing work, he is motivated at the higher levels of his being by passionate inquisitiveness into the nature of life and compassion for human suffering. At the lower levels of his being, he is driven by a will to power. At this lower level, sick people attract him because they are helpless. When he fantasizes about healing by magic, he imagines how grateful they will feel, how they will admire him and listen to him and do whatever he tells them to do.

In its raw form, the will to power is an obstacle to healing anyone. We've all encountered doctors who disempower patients with their bossiness and arrogance. This attitude is even more unworkable if you wish to heal by magic. Alchemical interventions are often so subtle, so slight that the patient might not even know they've happened. Should the sick person recover, the alchemist doesn't know how much—if any—credit to take. The more magical the intervention, the less it can be traced to the magician. Yet if Greg merely represses his will to power, his altruistic motives will lack the volitional oomph necessary to get through medical school or its alchemical equivalent. The energy of his power trip needs to be transmuted rather than repressed, taught to serve rather than undermine his higher intention.

So what will occur when Greg is sent down for fermentation? He will likely experience in a very profound and discouraging way his powerlessness over illness—perhaps by getting sick himself or by having to stand by helplessly while a loved one suffers. The puerile and self-aggrandizing fantasy of being a magical healer will become a source of shame to him, and gradually it will die off. He may come to doubt that such magic is possible for anyone and will certainly doubt that it is possible for him. It will seem to him that his aspiration has died. He will probably stop working toward it and hate being reminded that he ever even considered it.

This gloomy state of affairs might persist for months or years. But his aspiration has not in fact died. It's fermenting. Someday it will rise to the surface again, and when it does, Greg will find it changed very much for the better. He will find that he feels most powerful when helping sick people themselves to feel powerful. No longer needing to claim the credit for his magic, he will be able to discover very subtle yet effective methods of healing. Only after he has attained this will he understand why he had to undergo such a miserable period of fermentation.

Abet with Care

As I have described it, fermentation sounds like the very last process you would wish to abet. Indeed, its painful side effects—self-reproach, excessive doubt, unbearable loneliness, and depression—should *not* be abetted. If at all possible, they should be relieved. Paradoxically, you relieve the side effects of fermentation by abetting the process itself. The essence of that process is spiritual passivity.

It is unlikely that you could have advanced to the point where fermentation is necessary or even possible without some inner discipline. You have learned to persevere with meditation or other spiritual practices whether you feel like it or not. This habit will serve you well during a dark night of the soul—that is, a period of sensory darkening and the indifference to horizontal life that goes with it. It will not serve you so well during a dark night of the spirit. To attain levity at such a time is impossible, so attempting it is pointless and will only make you feel worse. You cannot work while deep in fermentation. You can only be worked on. So take a break. Refrain from any activity you consider "spiritual." This includes not only meditation but any form of serious thinking. If you feel like reading (you might not), avoid not only hermetic literature, but anything difficult, deep, or heavy. Read only for entertainment. Think of yourself as a surgical patient. On a mental level, do only what would be appropriate for someone who is recovering from a serious operation and is still heavily sedated. (On a physical level, though, do whatever you feel like.)

One symptom of fermentation—both the soul kind and the spirit kind—is a disinclination to express yourself or to listen to others. Indulge this. Don't speak more than you absolutely have to. When listening is required, get by for the present on nods and uh-huhs. If you get any complaints about this, say, "Yeah, I'm a little bit out of it these days," and leave it at that. You don't have to explain yourself. While fermenting, you *can't* explain yourself. You won't understand what's happening to you until it's over.

To the best of your ability, maintain inner silence as well. A lot of the unnecessary suffering of fermentation comes from the judgments we pass on it and the lame strategies we devise to get out of it. Make no resolutions; you won't be able to keep them. Put off major decisions. This might be difficult advice to follow, for resourceful people often believe, when they're blue, that something in their external life needs to change. If you're not thinking so yourself, some would-be helper will probably suggest it. Thank them for their kind advice, then ignore it. By definition, you are in a phase of not knowing what to do, because your will is under reconstruction. Any change you make in your horizontal life at this point will be arbitrary, irrelevant, and probably doomed to failure. Just chill.

To maintain inner silence about the cause of your dark night is especially difficult. You keep wanting to figure out what's wrong with you. The two explanations that everyone comes up with (i.e., spiritual beings are either nonexistent or rejecting you) are dead wrong, but wiser souls than you and I have nevertheless succumbed to them in their darkest moments. Instead of doubting or repudiating your past spiritual experiences, just try to forget about them for now. When you are below, it is impossible to get any perspective on above. You can't even get a perspective on the horizontal. All you see of it is its underside, which is not it's most flattering angle. Shelve all difficult questions until you resurface. They'll wait.

Even if you're not especially religious, you might find yourself wondering whether you've sinned. Consider the myth of Prometheus. He is chained to a rock for all eternity, in perpetual pain as vultures peck at his liver, because he stole magical knowledge from the gods and offered it to humans. In another myth, Icarus suffers a crash when he flies too close to the sun. These myths arose and have endured for millennia because something in us believes that going up might get us in trouble and that a fall is a fall from grace. If we weren't wrong to go up, why are we cast down? If it's not a punishment, why does it feel so painful? Blaming yourself is a source of anguish that serves no purpose whatsoever, so I'm going to do my best to talk you out of it.

Remember the story from the Quran I told you back in chapter 2? God asked the angels to prostrate themselves to Adam. Those who refused fell from God's favor and became the adversaries of above and below. The point is that any being who is obedient to God holds humanity in very high esteem. If you feel a lighter being is being hard on you about your human nature, you're either projecting your own insecurities or dealing with an adversary (whom you have every right and reason to ig-nore). The lighter beings who enjoy God's approval don't judge you or pick on you or snub you for being you.

There are only two types of beings who are authorized to criticize hu-mans—incarnate humans themselves and threshold guardians. Perhaps I'd better say a little more about the latter, so that you don't confuse fermenta-tion with a threshold encounter. When threshold guardians take you to task, their feedback is specific. It's about what you're doing or not doing. The problem they bring to your attention is always something that it is within your power either to correct or to forgive in yourself. You're never left feel-ing hopeless or worthless or feeble. Furthermore, threshold guardians never send you below when you're trying to go above. If you can't get past them, you either return to the horizontal or wander once more into Baggage Dis-claim. The lower vertical is a sacred dimension, with strict admission re-quirements. It isn't hell; it's heaven south. You are only permitted to enter it when you have satisfied its guardian that you are open to the help you will receive there. Insofar as this is a judgment of you, it is a favorable one.

My description of Greg's hypothetical fermentation might have con-fused the issue a bit, for while his power trip was being adjusted he be-came acutely aware of it, and ashamed of it. You might feel something like that if you could see your infected appendix while it was being surgically removed. You'd feel, "Yuck, get that out of me!" That sort of self-reproach is unpleasant but bearable, because it points to something specific and correctable. What I'm addressing here is the kind of self-blame that causes real anguish: the belief that you have suffered a spiri-tual crash because you are inherently unworthy. When you are below, you are *not* abandoned. You are, in fact, receiving round-the-clock care from beings who love you and think the world of you. It just *feels* like aban-donment because you are unable to communicate with these beings as you do while above.

Fermentation or Depression?

St. John of the Cross observed that one must distinguish between a gen-uine dark night of the soul and what he termed "a melancholy humor."

He was saying, in other words, that there is a difference between fermentation and what we would nowadays call "clinical depression." This is important to point out, for I would be doing you a great disservice if I led you to dismiss a treatable depression as some natural and evitable part of the Great Work. But how do you tell them apart?

Perhaps the simplest test is to follow the advice in the previous section and see if it makes you feel better. Though we might hound ourselves with negative judgments about it, lying low and keeping quiet are what we most feel like doing while in fermentation. If you're not clinically depressed, just fermenting, honoring these desires should bring relief. To wrap yourself in a deep and restful silence can be downright delicious when you recognize that this is what your soul requires and trust that you're being cared for.

While in the lighter form of fermentation—the dark night of the soul—you might say, "I'm depressed," but most of the symptoms of clinical depression are absent. You're not anxious, hopeless, self-hating, or fixated on the past. Physically you feel pretty much like your normal self—no marked changes in eating habits or sleep, no more substance abuse than is typical of you. Socially you might be somewhat withdrawn and feel lonely on account of it, but you don't feel as if others have rejected or abandoned you. You might feel profoundly indifferent to your usual activities, but you are as capable as ever of going through the motions and meeting your responsibilities. You just feel blah. This mood will eventually lift without any effort on your part.

If you visited a health professional during a dark night of the spirit, you would probably be diagnosed as depressed. You would have many of the symptoms. What's different is the cause. Does that matter? Perhaps not. Ideally, healers want to identify and remove the root cause of any ailment, not just alleviate the symptoms. This is, conceivably, a potential problem with help from health professionals, since (a) most of them have never even heard of fermentation and (b) removing it as a cause is neither necessary nor desirable. In reality, though, there is no medical consensus about the causes of depression or how to remove them. A fermenting alchemist is no more or less likely than any other depressed patient to obtain symptomatic relief from professional treatment, and such relief is desirable if you can find it. Spiritually active people often respond well to treatments that work primarily on the subtle body, such as acupuncture, Reiki, or homeopathic medicines. Don't worry that a mood lift will interfere with fermentation. Anything that helps you feel at peace supports the process.

The one type of help that I would caution you to beware of is the "take charge of your life" school of therapy. That approach is great if your horizontal life is a mess, but if what you've come down with is fermentation, taking charge of your life will only make matters worse. Passivity is what is needed to bring fermentation to a successful conclusion. You want to steer clear of any helper whose method is to hold you accountable for some plan of self-improvement action. But I probably don't need to tell you that. If you are fermenting, you will find such helpers pushy, clueless, and exhausting to deal with.

Thoughts of suicide are a definite sign that you are clinically depressed and in need of immediate human help. Fermentation alone does not give rise to them. To someone who is fermenting, death does not appear to be a way out. The sufferer might long to escape consciousness but does not believe that suicide would put an end to it. St. John of the Cross offered a brilliant explanation for this. He pointed out that whatever we experience in the vertical dimension—whether above or below—appears to us to be absolute and eternal. If we are in a state of bliss, it feels to us like the ultimate truth. Every prior experience that was *not* bliss appears, from the standpoint of bliss, to have been a transient illusion that will never again take us in. The same goes for despondency. If we experience hopelessness in the vertical, we are moved to deny that there ever was or ever will be any hope at all, in this world or the next. From a vertical perspective, there is no such thing as "ending it all."

I know of two other useful distinctions between depression and fermentation. The onset of depression tends to be gradual, moving from bad to worse, while the onset of a dark night of the spirit is abrupt. Yesterday you felt normal and today, for no accountable reason, you're in the pits of despair. Remission is equally sudden. You wake up one day feeling just fine and can't explain the change. During a period of fermentation you might experience many of these sharp fluctuations between normal and depressed. They're caused by the all-or-nothing quality of vertical experience. When you go down, you plummet rapidly to the depths. When you return to the horizontal, you feel okay, because nothing is especially wrong with your horizontal life. Clinical depression is more continuous, because something *is* amiss in the horizontal.

The other difference has to do with sleep. Most of the healing activity associated with fermentation happens in sleep, so if you're fermenting, you will probably sleep well, have good dreams or no dreams, and look forward to going to bed. Clinically depressed people often have bad dreams, restless sleep or insomnia, and emotional upsets during the night. For anyone engaged in spiritual work, good sleep is important, so get help if you're having a lot of bad nights.

Resurrection

Earlier I said that your spirit consents to its dark night, though you can't remember having given that consent while you're below. You might be wondering how I know that. You will know it, too, when the spiritual amnesia that accompanies fermentation wears off. Upon your return from below, you find yourself changed for the better. Often it's a change that you had desired yet had been unable to effect through conscious effort. Other times it's a change that you hadn't thought of making, but that supports you in your aspirations. It can be subtle: you realize one day that an old familiar habit of thinking or feeling or behaving is missing. Exactly how or when the habit departed, you couldn't say. Or it can be dramatic: you wake able to do something you couldn't do before or knowing things that you haven't made a conscious effort to learn. You may find that your subtle perception has sharpened, that your intuition works better, or that some former source of confusion has suddenly been replaced by brilliant clarity. And you didn't have to try! It's as if you've won a free interior makeover.

In *The Great Divorce*, C. S. Lewis describes a netherworld where ghosts are given a choice between heaven and hell. The choice is not as obvious as it might seem, for to the ghosts, hell bears a reassuring resemblance to horizontal life, while entry into heaven requires the sacrifice of some cherished and familiar part of the self. One ghost, for example, has a little red lizard on his shoulder. It's been there all his life. An angel tells him that if he wants to go to heaven, the lizard will have to be killed. While the ghost agrees in principle that he can't walk around heaven with a lizard on his shoulder, he is reluctant to consent to its murder. It feels like a part of him. He fears that the death of the lizard will kill him, too. After a long and unsuccessful attempt to negotiate some compromise with the angel, the ghost at last gives in. The murder of the lizard causes him excruciating pain. But much to his amazement, the lizard doesn't remain dead. It writhes around on the ground for a bit and then begins to grow larger and change shape. After a few minutes it is transformed into a glorious white stallion with a flaming gold mane. The ghost mounts it and rides it to heaven.

That little tale is a wonderful description of what fermentation is good for, and why it hurts. We go down because some part of our ordinary will is an obstacle to what the spirit wishes to express and accomplish on earth. The spirit cannot incarnate until that obstacle is removed. From the perspective of the soul, this feels like death. It is frightening, and it hurts. Only when we have consented to the murder of the obstacle do we discover that it can be transmuted into a radiant and powerful helper. As Lewis's angel explains, "Every natural love will rise again and live forever in this country: but none will rise again until it has been buried."

Flower Power

The Bach Flower Essences are mood remedies that work on the subtle rather than the physical body. Their great advantage for anyone engaged in spiritual work is that they don't make you feel dopey or dull or artificially high. They simply remove the negative mood without carrying you to some other extreme. The essences I've listed are especially helpful with fermentation side effects. Many health food stores carry them, and you can also order them online.

- *Olive* is a remedy for the fatigue that follows spiritual exertion (or any other kind of exertion). It's good for the blahs.

- *Mustard* is specifically intended for vertical depression—the kind that comes on suddenly and inexplicably, putting you in a very dark and withdrawn mood that you don't want to talk about.
- *Sweet chestnut* helps with more active states of anguish and despair. It's the one to take if you feel like vultures are gnawing at your liver and there will never be an end to it.
- *Vervain* quiets an overexcited mind. If, like many hermeticists, you're mentally active in your sleep—you have a lot of lucid dreams or interesting thoughts during the night—a dose of vervain at bedtime can help you to sleep more deeply and restfully.

12

Sublimation

The subject is heated until the essence rises to the top.

BASE MATTER:

Disconnect between intention and will

SYMPTOMS:

Confusion
Hyperactive mind
Feeling out of control
Having unintended effects on the world

TO ABET:

Don't attempt to justify your actions.
Don't seek outside approval.

TRANSMUTATION:

Thought becomes deed.

At some point, it might occur to you to wonder, "Am I one of the good guys or one of the bad guys?" If the question completely stumps you, you're probably in a sublimation phase.

Most people judge themselves to be good if they mean well. Either they form a good intention and act on it, or they think up a good intention after they've acted and apply it retrospectively. (The latter procedure is probably the more common.) The question only starts to puzzle you when you notice that you've been acting without *any* intention. You don't mean well and you don't mean ill. You act in ways that surprise you, and you couldn't begin to say what your motives are.

That's what the dawn of magical intuition is like. Impulses from your spirit work directly into your will without touching base with your thinking. You don't ponder what to do or decide what to do. You just do. Even when the results are favorable, you can't really credit yourself with good intentions. You can't recall having *any* intentions. It's very disconcerting. You begin to notice the stunning irrelevance of what you think to what you do. You realize, too, that you've been forgetting to watch yourself and suddenly you panic. If you're not mentally aligning what you do with some idea of "good," conceivably you could do something really bad.

Dread of what might happen if you neglect to monitor yourself conceals the even more fundamental fear that you are losing control altogether. Most of us experience the area around our foreheads as the headquarters of the self. When we begin to notice that branch offices are acting of their own accord, panic ensues in the executive suite. Thinking tries to reassert its dominance. The mind goes into overdrive, churning up an unending stream of analysis, opinion, and worry. We are at once the host, the audience, and the boring pundit guests of an internal talk show that we can't seem to switch off.

It might reassure you to hear that the root cause of this panic is nothing new. You have been living with it all your life. The almost universal belief that doing is driven by thinking and that good actions result from good intentions is not very well supported by the facts. Our running mental commentary about our intentions is the work of an internal spin doctor who has little influence over our deeds.

What changes during the Great Work is that your unintended actions become more *intelligent*. You start to notice that what you do spontaneously and impulsively often works better than what you decide to do after much conscious deliberation. You used to become aware of your unconscious will only when it was sabotaging your conscious plans and resolutions. Now it begins to surprise you pleasantly, like a servant who anticipates what you will need and provides it without being asked. Yet even when pleasant, the surprise is disquieting, for the servant is uppity and too clever by half.

Remember the story of Hannah and the monk? When the monk threw himself at her feet and declared his love, his action was, from any rational standpoint, wildly inappropriate. It was, at the same time, outrageously correct. Thinking would have recommended against it on any number of grounds: his vow of celibacy, her husband, their very short acquaintance. Until he actually did the thing—without, apparently, stopping to reflect—he had no way of knowing how right it was.

That's magical intuition. It begins to emerge as the combined result of calcination, dissolution, separation, conjunction, and fermentation. Your spontaneous impulses often turn out to be wise because your will is being transmuted into an organ of wisdom. You are acting out of the absolute NOW, motivated by a Why that you can't know yet because, from the standpoint of linear time, it's in your future. So you're left without a cover story. When that first starts to happen, it's natural to panic.

Notice that Hannah did not immediately tell the monk that his action was good. First she protested, then she asked him to leave. There was no higher human authority to endorse his deed, nor could he justify it by recourse to any abstract principle. When we act out of magical intuition, we often have to do it without the comfort of knowing that we are right. In fact, it is possible that later we'll judge what we've done to be a colossal screwup. This is why driver mentality is so hard to attain. You have to get used to not knowing whether you are bad or good, right or wrong, wise or foolish. No one gives you the authority to act on your own authority. You just do it.

Thoughts as Deeds

If the magician can act so effectively without thinking, what is thinking *for*? What are you supposed to do with it?

When we intend, we are trying to think our will. That it is also possible to will our thinking won't come as news to you if you've attempted any of the exercises in this book. Most of them require you to concentrate—that is, to will a certain thought while willing *not* to think anything else.

Other forms of willed thinking might at first be less obvious. When we think like a scientist, a philosopher, a detective, or a judge, our thinking is driven by a will to truth. What is truth? The word eludes definition because it's not really a concept. It is an impulse of the will. We can't say what it is, but we desire it. That desire is what enables us to know it when we see it, just as hunger recognizes food.

Thought can also be driven by the will to magic. By this I don't mean what is usually called "magical thinking." That kind of thinking expresses the *wish* for magic, not the will to it. If I believe I am on the right track because I've been assisted by a coincidence, I am thinking wishfully. I wish that magic would settle the difficult question of what to do with my life. The *will* to magic is what you develop when you have come this far with the Great Work. It is a will that has surrendered many of its mundane habits and fixations in order to perceive and act on intuitions coming from the spirit. When thinking is driven by magical will, a thought can become a deed. All by itself, thinking can help or harm. It can cause phenomena to manifest or change.

Thoughts propelled out of the body by the energy of will can have a powerful impact on others. Many people make effective use of this phenomenon without fully understanding how they are doing it. Out of their astrality (i.e., thought projection), leaders inspire followers with a shared vision, healers win the confidence of patients, advertisers woo consumers, and artists infiltrate the imaginations of their audiences.

By heightening their astrality on purpose, magicians can go beyond these ordinary effects. They can project what they imagine with such force that it becomes perceptible to the subtle senses of others. The basic procedure, which you will find described in any number of books on how to do magic, is first to rouse energy and then to focus thought. The rituals that may accompany this procedure in what is called "ceremonial magic"—lighting candles, drawing pentagrams, chanting incantations, and whatnot—are simply aids to concentration. They have no magical power in and of themselves and will prove quite useless to anyone who attempts to substitute ritual alone for a transmuted will. Conversely, if you have developed magical will, you can dispense with ceremonies altogether. You don't even need to make a fuss of concentrating. You can state a desire or send a thought in what feels to you like a casual, offhand way and next thing you know, you've gotten a result.

When you can influence others through thought alone, your inner alignment probably looks like this:

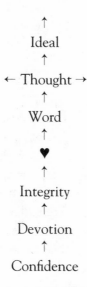

↑

Ideal

↑

← Thought →

↑

Word

↑

♥

↑

Integrity

↑

Devotion

↑

Confidence

You can see from the picture why it's working. The will energy of the lower five centers is flowing unimpeded toward thought. An untrained mind can concentrate with all its might and not much will happen because the unconscious will is a stranger to the conscious intention. This is the basic disconnect that the Great Work has been addressing. Through the first three phases, the raw instincts of the body are transmuted into sources of intelligence. The next three phases establish circulation between these transmuted instincts and the higher faculties that inform our conscious intentions. As a result, when we conceive an idea, a conviction, or a desire, every aspect of our being is able to get with the program. All of our energy is moving in the same direction. Into a confused and ambivalent world, we transmit an exceptionally clear signal.

The first sign of progress in this area is an enhanced ability to influence people by ordinary means. You may begin to notice that others are listening to you with new respect and succumb easily to your persuasion. When we have difficulty being heard and heeded, it is often because we are putting out mixed signals. What we are projecting on an unconscious level undermines what we are saying in words. Have you ever noticed that when people use the words "definitely" or "I'm sure" what they are usually conveying is their *doubt*? When the will is properly aligned with a stated conviction, "I'm sure" means that you are indeed sure. Other people can sense the difference. They take you at your word.

This improved influence on a mundane level crosses into the magical when you become capable of projecting your thoughts without saying them aloud. The first indications that you have attained this ability can be somewhat embarrassing. People will start telling you that you've been showing up in their dreams. Of course, there's nothing unusual about that in itself. The disquieting part is that in these dreams, others hear you say things that you've actually thought, but never said to them directly. They may even dream a remarkably detailed and accurate version of one of your private fantasies. In waking life, too, people will quote back to you thoughts you can remember thinking but can't for the life of you remember speaking. Suddenly it appears that everyone around you is becoming a mind reader.

While this newfound ability to project your thoughts can come in very handy, it also confronts you with a moral problem that you never had to worry about before. Normally we hold people accountable for what they say and do, but not for what they think, feel, and fantasize. But once we discover that what goes on in the supposed privacy of our own minds is producing outward effects, we have to reckon with the consequences. A good working definition of a magician is someone who can influence external phenomena with the power of thought alone. To the extent that we have acquired this ability, our thoughts take on the moral weight of deeds.

Jesus was alluding to this when he equated lustful thoughts with fornication, and angry thoughts with aggression. On a subtle level, people are affected by what we are thinking about them. Even when we are not trying to do magic on purpose, our kind thoughts manifest in the astral like fairy godmothers, and our unkind thoughts work voodoo. The more powerfully you project—whether on purpose or by accident—the more conscientious you need to be about your mental activity.

Inadvertent harm is usually the result of not knowing our own strength. Often we don't realize we have a power until we have unwittingly abused it. If subtle perception has kept pace with the development of will, you begin to notice how others are affected by what you think yet refrain from saying aloud. Just as we learn to be tactful of speech by observing that our careless words have hurt someone's feelings, we learn to be tactful of mind by observing the effects of our thoughts.

By now you might be wondering why you ever wanted to become a magician. Every new ability you attain seems to come with a long list of admonishments. Every new power seems to require an equal and opposite restraint. Now I'm telling you that you can't even daydream like a regular person without unleashing God only knows what on the astral plane! How can you possibly take moral responsibility for each and every thought that crosses your mind?

You can't. And you don't have to. The thoughts that merely cross our minds are beyond our control. It is precisely *because* they are unwilled that they have little or no astral staying power. Such thoughts are neither invited, nor entertained, nor sent. They're simply passing through. In order to project back out and remain intact in the astral, a thought has to be jazzed up in some way, energized by concentration, strong emotion, frequent repetition, or vivid imagery. A projected thought cannot be more compelling to the receiver than it was to the sender. You might project a thought that you have not decided to project, but you won't project a thought that you have not decided to *think*. It is willed thinking that produces astral phenomena.

The trouble is that sometimes we do want to jazz up our thoughts, do want to engage in willed thinking strictly for our own edification and amusement. We would all go stark raving nuts if we couldn't make and watch our private mental movies, our wish-fulfilling fantasies of sex, revenge, fame, and grandiose achievement. We need these fantasies to be off the record, morally speaking, for the whole point of them is to gratify desires that we are unable or unwilling to gratify through action. So how do we indulge the full freedom of our minds without creating astral pollution? How do we keep our private thoughts out of the public domain?

The solution is to fight fire with fire. You can employ an act of the imagination to prevent other acts of the imagination from being projected into the astral. I know of two ways to do this. The first is to construct some sort of privacy barrier around yourself. Visualize whatever kind of enclosure suits your fancy: a bubble, a hooded cloak, a shell, a capsule. Your barrier can isolate your mind completely, or it can work only in a single direction—allowing thoughts to come in from outside but not to go out from inside, or vice versa. (A barrier that lets nothing in is useful when you have to deal with someone you find manipulative, intrusive, or generally toxic, or when you're feeling overwhelmed by the psychic energies of a crowd.) Establish your imaginary enclosure, then curl up inside and daydream to your heart's content.

The second technique is to dispose of a thought after you have finished thinking it. If you have conjured a mental image, picture it going up in flames, melting into a puddle, being pulverized to dust, or simply fading to black. If it's a verbal thought, you can imagine erasing the words or crossing them out or hitting the delete key. You can also say, "Let no harm to others come from this thought," or simply, "Scratch that." Thoughts that you prefer not to destroy could be placed in an imaginary lockbox to which only you hold the key.

These techniques are more powerful than they sound, because they rely on the same force that necessitates them in the first place. If your imagination is strong enough to create astral phenomena that can be perceived by others, it is also strong enough to conjure an effective barrier.

Magicians and Monsters

"Am I a monster?" is a more pertinent and productive question than "Am I good or evil?" On the way to becoming a magician, it is easy to become a monster. Monstrosity is not about morality, but about scale and proportion.

The basic problem is that magical will is huge. It's out of proportion to the wills of those around you. That's why you find it easy to influence them. By this I don't mean that you are bossy or overbearing. You might be very gentle and considerate. You might even feel timid about asserting yourself. The influence others feel has little to do with your outward behavior. It's an effect of your astrality that is not, for the most part, under your conscious control. In addition to the magic you do on purpose, you start having all sorts of unintended effects.

To complicate matters, you may find that your perceptual faculties are not at their best. You don't pick up on what others are feeling as well as you used to. That's because the energy going out through your thought center overwhelms impressions coming in through the heart center. When you look out, what you tend to perceive is not the world itself, but your own projections. Others may experience you as arrogant and impervious to feedback. They may feel that they're not being heard.

The problem is simple to diagnose, and the very act of diagnosis usually corrects it. Sit down and make what I call a "Mis List." Reflect back on the last few weeks or months and write down every miscommunication, misunderstanding, or mistake that you had a part in. What have you misinterpreted or misconstrued? Don't beat yourself up about the items on this list. On the contrary, be reassured by them. If you can list mistaken perceptions, it means you must have taken in the corrections. Other people are able to get through to you. Worry only if you can't recall a single error. (Resistance to doing the exercise is also a bad sign.)

Energy management is another issue you will need to be concerned about at this juncture. When we are inwardly aligned, we are able to move our energy more efficiently. It's like straightening out a tangled hose. Once you remove all the kinks, water can flow through faster. But the hose itself is not the source of the water. So the questions become, "Where are we hooking up our hose? Where are we getting our energy?"

One possible source is the life energy we were born with. Our supply of this energy is finite. Older people generally move, think, and heal more slowly than young people because they have less of it. Once the supply is exhausted, the body dies. We supplement this with the renewable energy that comes to us from heaven and from the earth. We take it in with the food we eat and the air we breathe. Practices like Reiki, chi gong, meditation, and yoga help us to access it more efficiently and deliberately. We can also renew it through contact with nature or by the simple expedient of asking for it in our prayers.

Another source of renewal is the energy of other people. This is what we're talking about when we describe some people as draining and others as nourishing or having "good energy." In a wholesome relationship there is a healthy balance—each gives energy to the other. Logically it would seem that this would not result in a net energy gain for either party. Yet our subjective experience tells us that when our connection with someone is good, both parties feel like they're coming out ahead.

You can't tell who is giving energy to whom simply by watching what people are doing, because what is occurring on a subtle level is often the opposite of what is occurring on a material level. Suppose two people are dining out together and one is doing most of the talking. While the talker is more active in a physical sense, the listener is actually putting out more psychic energy. It is this energy gift from the listener that animates the talker. As if to compensate, the talker will probably pick up the check.

Unless we are suffering from some sort of psychological dysfunction, we tend to work out healthy energy exchanges without having to think about it much. We gravitate toward people who make us feel good and avoid people who deplete us. Even though we don't directly perceive what is happening with our subtle bodies, we instinctively adjust what we are doing externally to achieve a balance.

Relationships between introverts and extroverts are a good example. To ordinary perception, extroverts appear to be outgoing and introverts to be retiring. On the subtle level, it's exactly the opposite. Extroverts love company because they are good at taking in energy from other people. In the balance of trade, they tend to feel like they are coming out ahead and instinctively offset this by being socially generous. Introverts are easily depleted by human contact, because their psychic energy tends to be outward moving. They correct the imbalance by being more socially reserved. Both types are managing their energy in a way that is healthy for themselves and fair to others.

All is well until you add heightened astrality to the mix. Magicians can take in or put out more energy at any given moment than regular people, due to their inner alignment. This won't be a problem if, in your ordinary personality, you are not markedly introverted or extroverted. Your energy exchanges will get bigger, yet remain balanced. But for magicians with a pronounced leaning in either direction (which is a matter of inborn temperament, and resistant to change), human relationships get thrown out of whack. The psychic energy exchange is no longer proportionate to what is happening externally.

For the introvert, too much energy goes out. Magicians who are natural introverts may struggle with frequent depression or become excessively reclusive, because they feel like the energy loser in most of their human contacts. It baffles them. They feel like they are giving very little (which is often the case on an outward level) and therefore have no excuse for feeling so needy and drained. Illogical as it sounds, introverts can conserve their psychic energy by becoming more *active* in social situations. If you're an introvert, seek out low-intensity activities like serving refreshments, welcoming newcomers, and making small talk. Don't feel you always have to be a perfect listener. Superficiality, though you might disdain it, is nourishing for you.

When their astrality is heightened, pronounced extroverts run the risk of becoming energy gluttons, taking in more from others than they can possibly repay. They tend to be charismatic and are often admired for the sheer abundance of their vitality. It appears to be inexhaustible. You can tell that they are drawing this vitality primarily from other people because they never seem to need—or want—to be alone. In fact, if obliged to be alone for any length of time, they suffer an energy crash.

When the condition is complicated by boundary loss, serious abuses can result, for boundary infringement by such people often feels pleasurable to the victim. It's a rush. That rush is the victim's energy going out, not the glutton's energy coming in. Think of what it feels like to take in energy through food, or breathing, or meditation, or a walk in the woods. It feels good, but you wouldn't describe it as ecstatic. The literal meaning of the word "ecstasy" is to go out of oneself. It feels fantastic while it's happening, but the high is usually followed by some sense of depression. At that point you might have a vague feeling of being let down or ripped off and start resenting the glutton. Or you might find yourself longing for another "hit" and become addicted to him. It is how such people develop a cult following.

The perpetrators of such energy thefts aren't doing it on purpose. They're on a high and would like nothing better than to make everyone around them high as well.

It's hard to recognize a problem that doesn't *feel* like a problem. Extreme reactions from others are the clearest tip-off that your energy transactions are out of balance. If you are taking in too much energy from others, you may find that people suddenly turn against you or seem violently disappointed in you for reasons you can't fathom. They may say they feel seduced, abandoned, used, deceived, or betrayed. If you can't trace these reactions to any overtly bad behavior on your part, what they are probably describing is your destabilizing effect on their energy field. You might also find that people frequently betray, disappoint, or abandon *you*. While high on your presence, they make you promises that they regret the morning after.

To be perfectly frank, I'm not sure how the problem is corrected once it's in full swing, for I have yet to meet an energy glutton who *wanted* to correct it. For every lost friend, the glutton easily wins over a dozen new fans, and the highs are addictive. Still, extroverts are not doomed to become energy addicts. You can arrest the problem in its early stages by recognizing that occasional fatigue, sadness, and loneliness are good for you. A well-balanced person feels blah sometimes. Solitude is also good for the extroverted magician. If you really hate being alone, the next best thing is any social situation in which you feel shy. Look for ways you can be with others without becoming the center of attention.

The best way to prevent energy abuses and all other forms of monstrosity is regular pruning; that is, being "cut down to size" periodically by a trusted advisor. In religious communities, this is done by one's teacher or confessor. As a freelance magician, you will need to turn the shears over to a designated pruner of your own choosing—a wise, stalwart, and intimate friend whom you trust to tell you bluntly, should the need arise, that you're acting like an absolute jerk.

The Technology of Thought Projection

When we project thought, we are overwhelming the energy of whatever it is we wish to influence or change with the power of our own more concentrated energy. Thus we can prevail over any weaker energy and might also prevail over energies that are stronger but less focused.

The magic of projected thought is rather mechanical in this sense. If you had a way to measure the variables involved, you could predict the results with a simple equation:

$$(\text{your energy} \times \text{your focus}) - (\text{subject's energy} \times \text{subject's focus})$$

Of course, we can't really do the math because we have no device for measuring the energy of the mind and its focus. Conceivably such a device might be invented in the near future, for the technology already exists to amplify brain waves, enabling people to operate computers and other machines just by thinking their commands. In any event, what the formula implies is that the outcome of thought projection is predictable only to the extent that we are trying to influence a consciousness weaker than our own. There is something inherently bossy about it.

While this type of magic isn't alchemy, developing the capacity to do it is a side effect of the alchemist's training. Whether you decide to pursue it or not, you will probably find that you're quite good at it. Should you prefer to skip the final phase of the Great Work, which initiates you into alchemy proper, you could still become a very effective magician.

The basic procedure of joining thought to will can be embellished with further procedures designed to boost the energy of the projected thought. It is the specifics of these procedures that distinguish one school of magic from another. Collective effort—getting a whole group of magicians to project the same thought—is one such technique. Another is to recruit allies. These allies might be elemental forces (the spirits of earth, air, fire, or water), beings of the natural world (the spirits of plants or animals), spirits of those who have died, or demons. Through ceremonies and rituals, these beings are invoked, honored, and asked to contribute energy. The success of such techniques depends on the ongoing relationship one has cultivated with the helpers. By joining a magical cult or lodge one gains access to its network of allies and incurs certain obligations in return.

Many mainstream religions regard freelance ceremonial magic as evil, even when it's directed toward a good end. Since most of them employ magical rites of their own, we might suspect them of hypocrisy and a desire to hoard power. They would counter that their rites were given to them from above, not arbitrarily invented by human beings. Take the Catholic rosary for example. It is an appeal for help from the Divine Mother, who has made known not only her willingness to help, but also the manner in which she would like the request to be made. Nobody who prays the rosary imagines that they are commanding her. Nor do they feel the need to jazz up their energy in order to reach her. The beauty of this prayer is that they can resort to it when they are too anxious or sick or distressed to muster their own powers of concentration. Its magical energy is not produced by their own efforts. It is given to them from above.

The beings whom we are able to command through rituals of our own invention are beneath us, in the hierarchical sense. Many members of the monotheistic traditions believe that it is wrong to enter into alliances with what is below. This is not because the lower beings are assumed to be evil. They are assumed, rather, to be *innocent*. Human morality does not apply to them unless they are explicitly recruited into a human endeavor, at which point the relationship between humans and lower beings has the potential to be mutually corrupting.

The counterargument offered by magicians who are members in good standing of the monotheistic religions is based on the teaching that God placed humanity in charge of all that is below us. These magicians would argue that we benefit lower beings when we invite them to participate in our affairs. That which is below raises its consciousness by cooperating with that which is above.

My own lack of enthusiasm for ceremonial magic has little to do with theology or morality. I just don't find it very *magical*. Governed by something very like the laws of physics, it strikes me as merely another technology, a science that scientists haven't discovered yet.

I have lately been getting better acquainted with the world of stage magic. Illusionists are a surprisingly skeptical lot, far less disposed than the average person to believing that there is any *real* magic. The effects with which they awe and amaze their audiences are not, to their way of thinking, magical, because there is always a material explanation for how those effects are achieved. They have mastered rather than overcome the natural laws of cause and effect. While I find such mastery awesome in itself, I understand what they're driving at, for it's how

I feel about the magic of thought projection. Getting a result no longer amazes me, for I am simply employing some lesser known natural laws. It doesn't touch that place of childlike awe in me that quivers with delight at the very sound of the word "magic." The more predictably I am able to get my own way by projecting my thoughts, the less I am surprised or changed or challenged by what I conjure. I would like the outcomes of magical deeds to be *unpredictable*—to thwart my muggle plans, exceed my muggle expectations, and blow my muggle mind.

What is the magic that will astound the magician? Although it might take years to arise, that is the question that propels the aspirant into the final phase of the Great Work.

13

Radiation

Formation of the philosopher's stone.

BASE MATTER:

Arbitrary magic

SYMPTOMS:

Apparent loss of magical powers or
the will to do magic
Sudden onset of humility

TO ABET:

Surrender

TRANSMUTATION:

Sacred magic

To the dread rattling thunder
Have I given fire, and rifted Jove's stout oak
With his own bolt. The strong-based promontory
Have I made shake, and by the spurs plucked up
The pine and cedar. Graves at my command
Have waked their sleepers, op'ed, and let 'em forth
By my so potent art. But this rough magic
I here abjure: and when I have required
Some heavenly music—which even now I do—

> To work mine end upon their senses that
> This airy charm is for, I'll break my staff,
> Bury it certain fathoms in the earth,
> And deeper than did ever plummet sound
> I'll drown my book.

If you want to know what it's like to attain the philosopher's stone, study this speech. It is what Prospero, the magician hero of Shakespeare's *The Tempest*, proclaims at the precise moment of his initiation into alchemy.

I hope you will read the play yourself, but for now let me give you the gist of the plot. Born the Duke of Milan, Prospero cared more for his hermetic studies than the mundane business of ruling. His brother, Antonio, took advantage of his inattention to usurp his power, then drove him into exile and what seemed to be a certain death at sea. Prospero narrowly escaped drowning and found himself marooned on a bleak island with only his young daughter for company. Many years passed before he acquired sufficient magical power to exact his revenge. He learned to command the elements and the spirits. One of these spirits, Ariel, became his slave after he rescued her from an enchantment.

With the help of his magical allies, Prospero causes a great storm to arise, shipwrecking Antonio and his cronies. Through magic, he plans to subject them to unceasing psychic torment. But at the moment this plan comes to fruition, he undergoes a change of heart. He releases his enemies from his vengeful spell, conjures up the means for their escape, and frees Ariel from her bondage. Then he renounces forever the magical powers that he has worked so long and hard to acquire.

This is the gesture that transforms an ordinary magician into an alchemist. It is the seventh stage of the Great Work: the willing sacrifice of all that has previously been attained. In a sense, one sublimates the very fruits of sublimation, like a farmer who plows under his crop instead of harvesting it.

To achieve this gesture, two things are necessary: a strong personal desire and the means of fulfilling that desire. There is no magic in renouncing what you don't especially want or don't believe you can get. You might, like Prospero, have a specific burning desire and a plan for attaining it. Or it could be that you renounce the use of a particular power or the desire to be a magician, period. *Not* because this book tells you that such a renunciation is necessary. (If the goal of your sacrifice is to attain the philosopher's stone, it won't work.) Should you decide to renounce previously attained abilities, it will be for another motive that is difficult to imagine until it actually arises.

And what is the result of renouncing power? Does one trade it in for even greater power?

Not exactly. Without his charms and enchantments, Prospero feels quite helpless. At the very end of the play he says:

> Now my charms are all o'erthrown,
> And what strength I have's mine own,
> Which is most faint.

Contrary to what you might suppose, this is a *happy* ending. In possessing nothing but his own faint strength, Prospero has attained the philosopher's stone.

If this is what it consists of, you might well wonder why anyone would want it. Or why you would even have to pursue it, since your own faint strength is what you had to begin with.

The short answer is that it *is* the philosopher's stone *because* you have to attain it before you can understand what it's good for. But I wouldn't blame you for drowning this book "deeper than did ever plummet sound" in disgust at such a smart-alecky response. Having come this far, you deserve a better explanation.

Early on, I raised the question, "Why don't alchemists just come out and say what they mean? Why do they obscure it in symbols, allegories, and outright gibberish?" I offered many partial answers but neglected back then to mention the most important one. I was saving it for this moment.

As I have suggested previously, the distinction between black and white magic is meaningless. It is, supposedly, the difference between a bad intention and a good one. But I have never met anyone who thought their own intentions anything but good. The distinction between self-ish and unselfish is equally beside the point. It is only made by people who understand as little of themselves as they do of the world. No, the actual choice to be made is not between black and white, selfish and unselfish, but between arbitrary magic and sacred magic.

Aleister Crowley gave us a concise description of arbitrary magic when he said, "Do what thou wilt shall be the whole of the law." Some people regard this motto as proof that Crowley was a follower of the "black path" (an impression he liked to encourage). But to properly understand and act on his statement is a very difficult achievement and a prerequisite for attaining the philosopher's stone. It is the full realization of driver mentality. It means that you have learned to act on the authority of your own spirit without relying on any other source of confirmation or justification. You can bear not knowing whether you are good or bad, right or wrong. You have taken full possession of your human freedom. To label this as "arbitrary" is in no way a put-down. It just means that your magical deeds speak completely for themselves. In defense of them, you offer neither good intentions nor good results (though you may in fact have both meant well and done well). You don't defend your magic at all. You just do it.

Curiously, Crowley's statement betrays the fact that he himself had not quite attained this. He is still leaning on a "law"—one of his own invention, to be sure, but a law nevertheless. He is articulating a principle that puts him in the right. If he truly grasped what he was saying, he wouldn't have said it. But never mind. I'm glad he did. He's pointing in the right general direction. One just has to go a little bit farther.

Does Prospero abjure his "rough" (i.e., arbitrary) magic, because he has concluded that it is wrong? Shakespeare offers us no grounds for supposing so. In deciding not to carry through with his plan, Prospero neither disavows, condemns, nor repents of it. Even *after* freeing Antonio, Prospero remains enraged with him, addressing him as "you, most wicked sir, whom to call brother would even infect my mouth." He has not, in renouncing, ceased to desire what he renounces, nor concluded that he was wrong to have desired it. He renounces only because he has come to desire something better still: the will of God. The joining of human will to the divine will is sacred magic.

So what does the divine will consist of? I cannot say. To give a name to it, stating that God wills thus and so, is blasphemous. This is why alchemists have to beat around the bush. We can talk about anything and everything *except* the main idea!

There's an old saying among hermeticists: "Those who know don't tell. Those who tell don't know." It is often invoked in online forums to put an abrupt end to any discussion that has become exasperating. (You can see how it would have that effect.) In every context but one, it is an idiotic statement. Only when speaking of God's will does it make sense to say it.

When preachers bray about "God's plan for mankind," I know for certain that they haven't a clue what they're talking about. No one who'd caught the faintest glimmer of God's will could speak so complacently about it. When Job got a glimpse he said, "I repent in dust and ashes." God had already acquitted him of all wrongdoing, but still he said this. Job, who had done no wrong, was nevertheless utterly humbled. That's how you can tell he got the glimpse.

Prospero exhibits much the same mood when he says:

> Now I want
> Spirits to enforce, art to enchant:
> And my ending is despair,
> Unless I be relieved by prayer,
> Which pierces so, that it assaults
> Mercy itself, and frees all faults.

Mercy is his great virtue. He has just permitted it to overrule his most passionate desire. We might suppose that some divine reward is therefore due him. At the very least, awareness of his own virtue must surely serve as a consolation prize. Yet he describes mercy itself as *pierced* and *assaulted*. Whatever he has glimpsed is so great that his own greatest virtue is defenseless against it. It is beyond even his best idea of good. This is the push from above that causes the upper intention centers—word, thought, and ideal—to bow their heads in a sudden seizure of humility, spilling their reverence into the heart. It is how the heart becomes the philosopher's stone.

Prospero glimpsed and renounced arbitrary magic. But which came first? Was the glimpse a reward for the breaking of the staff, the burying of the book? Or was it the glimpse that *caused* those renunciations? Shakespeare wisely refrains from telling us, for the whole thing is happening in vertical time. The glimpse and the renunciation coincide in the absolute NOW where they are experienced as a single truth. It is a meeting of minds between God and the magician.

God cannot be compelled to show up for this meeting, so its occurrence in linear time is unpredictable. It cannot be forced or rushed. All one can do is recognize the potential for it, a potential that manifests when an overwhelming desire coincides with the power to attain that desire. Should renunciation occur at that moment, it is at once a gift *from* God and a gift *to* God. That mutuality—a single gesture that moves both from and to—is the hallmark of sacred magic. God's will and the magician's will have joined.

And yet, Prospero can never say so. He can never even *think* so. The gift is never given to anyone who would have the presumption to say, "God's will and mine are one." Acutely Prospero experiences the loss of arbitrary magic. It carries him to the brink of despair. But the gain of sacred magic, he cannot experience. As far as he can tell, he has simply ceased to be a magician.

The Dark Center of the Sun

This phase of the Great Work is usually called "coagulation." It means that the "substance" has come together and solidified to form the philosopher's stone. Apart from being a rather ugly word, I find coagulation misleading. Subjectively, this stage is a lot more like falling apart than like coming together. Radiation is, I believe, a much better name, because it describes both how the magician feels on the inside, and what he is doing on the outside.

Imagine for a moment what it might feel like to be the sun. Hot? Bright? Think again. The sun doesn't enjoy the benefit of its own heat and light because all of its energy is radiating—moving outward. It is giving away every last bit of itself. Subjectively, the "I" of the sun—its core—is absolutely dark and absolutely cold. That this is what radiation feels like from inside helps to explain why it is so rarely attained. You can only radiate if you've forsaken the desire for every conceivable pleasure the spiritual life has to offer. You don't get to feel bliss. You don't get to admire or celebrate or even know about your own achievement. The attainment of the philosopher's stone feels instead like a loss.

Describing it in such stark terms might give you the impression that you yourself are unlikely ever to attain it—or even to want to. Yet I think you probably will. If I didn't think so, writing this book would be a great waste of time.

Nobody can remain in a constant state of radiation. It requires an inner alignment that is all but impossible to sustain. A very slight inward shift can suddenly render the whole thing unbearable. Then we have to cycle back through one or more of the other six phases for repairs. What can become permanent, though, is the reorientation of one's will, the commitment to sacred magic. That commitment opens the *possibility* of being overtaken by the divine will, the *possibility* of radiating even if God rarely chooses to actualize it. You have given God permission. Without your permission, it cannot and will not happen. God never enters the human will uninvited.

Let me tell you a little story about the greatest alchemist I ever met in person. He was a poet, an artist, and a great spiritual teacher with many devoted students. People would wait hours, even days, to hear his lectures. Scores of beautiful women wanted to sleep with him. His students considered it a great honor to serve him, vying even for the privilege of doing his laundry or disposing of his used Kleenex. Nearly every night they prepared him a banquet, some dressing up to join him at the table, others getting equally dressed up to wait at it or wash the dishes. On one of these occasions, he suddenly began to weep for no apparent reason. He wept so copiously that his plate filled up with tears. Wanting to know what the trouble was, all his friends and students and lovers put down their forks and leaned toward him with concern, but he was sobbing too hard to speak. For at least five minutes, no one spoke, no one ate or drank. At last, in a voice still broken with sobs, he managed to explain.

"I am so lonely," he said.

A slight inward shift had occurred. He felt himself there at the cold, dark center of the sun and suddenly found it unbearable. At that moment he dissolved. Even a very great magician occasionally needs to be tucked into bed and sung to sleep. It isn't a setback. It's just the way human beings are. In a mature magician, though, dissolution itself has a radiant quality. All the other phases do as well. The magician radiates from within a state of calcination, or fermentation, or separation. Perhaps you will know the quality I mean if you like the poetry of Rumi. More often than not, he appears to be in some extreme state of inner disarray. Yet even in his breakdowns, we glimpse something of the divine. In one who has abandoned every stratagem to protect or secure himself, vulnerability becomes radiant.

Radiation describes not only how alchemists feel, but what they actually do. I don't mean by this that the alchemist looks shiny or glowy. The energy gluttons I described in the previous chapter often present such an appearance because they are drawing the light toward themselves. A person who is truly radiating doesn't light up. Instead, whatever he gives his attention to lights up.

Have you ever wondered why it was necessary for Judas to identify Jesus to the soldiers who arrested him? Based on religious art, you'd think it would be obvious: Jesus was the one with the halo. But if you read the gospels closely, you begin to realize that Jesus must have been quite unprepossessing. He often seemed to go unrecognized. In fact, the best way to identify him might have been to pick the one *without* a halo. He appeared rather dull because he made everyone around him look so bright.

Radiation comes especially through the eyes. The alchemist is a "beautiful beholder." God's will is apprehended not through the intellect, but through the senses. You won't understand what I mean if you are conceiving of God as the CEO of the universe and God's will as a list of directives. Think of it instead as the will of an artist. To know God's will is to look at any created thing and see what God was going for in creating it.

Mary Baker Eddy, the founder of Christian Science, had this gift. To people who were deathly ill, she would say sharply, "Stop lazing around in bed. You're not sick." As if suddenly waking from a bad dream, they would get up, embarrassed to have been malingering since indeed they were in perfect health. Alas, when she tried to impart this knack to other healers, she did a lousy job of explaining it. On an intellectual level, she believed that the material world was unreal and illness just an illusion—propositions that are very hard to accept if one happens to be in excruciating pain from a tumor the size of a football. But Eddy didn't get into these dubious metaphysics with actual sick people. On many occasions, she is reported to have healed people simply by glancing at them. The magic came from her eyes. She denied illness because she truly couldn't see it. When she looked at people, she saw them in their perfected state. To see in this way is a gift from God. You can't think or talk yourself into it.

St. Francis of Assisi also radiated through his physical senses. He saw the elements and other beings of nature not as inferiors to be commanded, but as brothers and sisters. Legend has it that he once negotiated with a wolf who was preying on livestock in a village. He persuaded the wolf to stop killing and to take only food that was freely offered by the villagers. I suspect this literally happened. Every created thing longs to be seen as it truly is, seen as it is seen by God. Every sentient being—plant, animal, person, ghost, nature spirit—is an absolute pushover for that. Even a wolf might cooperate if seen in his essential wolfishness and hailed as "brother."

Please don't take this in a sappy way. Since the 1960s, St. Francis has become a rather hippy-dippy figure in the popular imagination. You will miss the whole point if you imagine some fey flower child taming a Walt Disney wolf. Picture instead a scary wolf, a wolf with sharp teeth and blood on its paws. It is the very wolfishness of the wolf that Francis recognized and greeted. It was a cautery iron that was about to burn him that Francis addressed as "Brother Fire." To see as Francis saw requires the bravery that comes of thorough calcination, the longing that comes of long dissolution, and the toughness that comes of separation. One sees as he saw only after the blindness of many dark nights of the soul and spirit. Having thoroughly transmuted his own instincts, Francis could inspire the wolf to transmute wolf instinct.

Alchemical magic is the voluntary cooperation of whatever is properly seen with the one who sees. It is very powerful, if by "power" you mean the magnitude of its effects. Yet the alchemist, like Prospero, will truthfully deny having any power at all because these effects are achieved only with the permission of whatever is being transmuted. As an arbitrary magician, Prospero boasts of his power to compel. Elves, trees, thunderbolts, and tempests do as he commands. Once he attains the philosopher's stone, he becomes incapable of command. Nothing will ever again do as Prospero asks unless it wants to.

What he doesn't yet realize is that many will want to. If we desire that any phenomenon manifest what is truest and best in its nature, our magic will likely succeed, for this is what all phenomena most desire for themselves. Nature aspires to the sublime. The art of alchemy lies not in commanding or even in gently persuading phenomena to do this. It lies, rather, in recognizing what "truest and best" means to the object of one's magical endeavor. This is not something you can figure out in your head, learn through philosophical study, glean from reading spiritual teachings, or achieve by imitating those who already seem to get it. It is an act of direct perception that occurs only when the senses are informed and transformed by the divine.

Nor can the magician will away the will to power. Our whole instinctual system is geared to wanting a great deal more than our own faint strength. Before we can transmute the wolf in ourselves, we have to recognize and honor it, for the way to transmute anything is to encourage it to be fully *as it is*. There is no shortcut to Prospero's renunciation—except, perhaps, the shortcut of resisting renunciation with all our might!

So I have come to the end of what I can usefully say about radiation. Maybe I have already said too much. Forget about it for now. To pursue arbitrary magic is all you can really do by your own efforts. So go for it. I wish you well at it. As Artephius wisely said, the rest can only be imparted by God.

Appendix 1

How to Meditate

Mindfulness Meditation

This is the best practice I know for developing control of attention. It opens a space in which subtle perceptions can arise by teaching you to make friends with boredom. It also helps you to become intimately acquainted with your own mind.

1. *Posture.* Picture a statue of a seated Buddha. That's what you're going for. Ideally this means sitting cross-legged on the floor, with your bottom supported by a firm cushion.

Your spine is straight, your shoulders relaxed but not slumped. Your belly is soft, neither held in nor thrust out. Shrug your shoulders then let them fall into a natural position. Shift around as needed till you find a position that is upright without causing any strain in your back. Let your hands come to rest in a comfortable spot on your knees or thighs.

Relax your jaw. Your upper and lower teeth shouldn't touch. Part your lips slightly if you find that helps. Keep your eyes open. Let them come to rest, looking downward and in soft focus at a spot about six feet in front of you. Spend a few minutes just relaxing into your posture, feeling a sense of physical well-being.

This alleged sense of well-being might elude you if you're not used to sitting unsupported on the floor. Many people find that, if they persevere through some initial weeks of back and/or leg complaints, the posture eventually becomes more comfortable than sitting on a chair. Others never really get used to it.

When the Buddha sat this way, he was sitting like a normal Indian. It was just plain old sitting, not an exercise in masochism. It should be plain old sitting for you, too. If discomfort is becoming a persistent distraction, experiment to find a more comfortable position in which you are still alert and upright, yet relaxed. You could try sitting on a bench or a straight-backed chair. Or you might find that sitting cross-legged "Indian-style" on a couch with your back lightly supported by the backrest or by a firm cushion wedged between the backrest and your lower back is the most comfortable. Just be sure to keep your spine vertical— neither reclining backward nor slumping forward.

2. *Breath.* The object of your attention will be your out breath. Breathe normally, without making a big deal of it. As you exhale, feel your attention riding out with the breath. When you come to the end of the exhalation, let that attention, that sense of being out there with the breath, dissolve. An in breath will follow. Don't pay it any special notice. While you're breathing in, your mind has no particular job to do. Then you exhale again, once more placing your attention on the out breath. You are not concentrating on it with all your might, just touching the breath lightly with your mind.

3. *Labeling.* Thoughts will arise. As soon as you notice this, inwardly say, "thinking" and return your attention to the out breath. You apply this label "thinking" to anything and everything your mind might be doing besides following the breath: fantasizing, making plans, looking around the room, feeling an emotion, noticing a physical sensation, etc. "Thinking" means that you acknowledge whatever it is as a mental event. You do this with a sense of friendly neutrality, as if to say, "Hello, mind."

These mental events are not a problem. To obliterate them is neither possible nor desirable. Your object is simply to keep returning your attention to the breath, regardless of what else is occurring in your mind.

If you find yourself judging or evaluating your thoughts, label the judgment "thinking." Return your attention to the out breath. If you notice that you've forgotten all about the out breath for the past umpteen minutes, label that observation "thinking." There is no need to scold yourself over it, but if you do, label the scolding "thinking." Return your attention to the breath.

If you notice that you've started to slump or have become physically uncomfortable, shift your attention to your posture for a moment. Make any needed adjustments. Reestablish the sense of physical well-being. Then return your attention once more to the out breath.

4. *Timing.* Before you begin, decide how long you intend to meditate and make some provision for timing yourself. (You could set a kitchen timer or leave a clock or watch where you can see it.) Remaining in place for the allotted time is part of the practice. How long matters less than keeping your initial time commitment, whatever it is. Even if your mind is racing all over the place and you only manage to connect with one out breath during the entire session, you will benefit enormously from staying put.

On those occasions when your attention is so scattered that you can't for the life of you control it, sitting still anyway develops control of impulsiveness. That's a very good ability to have. The beauty of this practice is that you can't fail at it. If you've remained seated for the allotted time, it counts as meditation. Often the greatest gains come from persevering when meditation seems to be going very badly.

The more regularly you meditate and the longer the time you devote to it, the better. Half an hour every day is good. An hour a day is twice as good. If you plan to meditate longer than an hour or so, set a time in advance when you will get up to stretch your legs and attend to any other physical needs.

This practice is much richer and, at times, more eventful than you would ever guess from the bare bones procedure I've outlined here. It evolves as the practitioner evolves, managing to be just what the doctor ordered for every phase of spiritual development. If you were to ignore every other exercise in this book and simply do mindfulness meditation every day, you could still make excellent progress with the Great Work.

I'd better point out though, that trying to do mindfulness meditation and other hermetic exercises *in the same sitting* doesn't work very well. When you've been meditating for awhile, just sitting in meditation posture produces a Pavlovian "label it thinking" response. That's desirable in itself, but tends to get in the way when doing exercises that involve concentration or imagination. The object of concentration keeps dissolving with the out breath. If you find that this is a problem, try doing your hermetic exercises in a more relaxed posture—perhaps sitting in a comfortable armchair or lying on a couch.

Sending and Taking

Buddhists call this procedure *tonglen*, or "exchanging self for other." In Western hermetic contexts, I've heard it called "moral breathing." Its purpose is to render volatile the energy that has become fixed in our personal wounds and scars. The vulnerability that tends to isolate us in our own little world of misery is transmuted into a force of connection. Tonglen is a good remedy for loneliness and will help to heal an injured heart. Because the visualization must be synchronized with the breath, it's best to have some mindfulness meditation practice under your belt before you attempt this one.

Here's the procedure:

1. Prepare by following your breath for a few minutes, as described above. Once you've got a relaxed, easy rhythm going, you're ready to begin.

2. Instead of letting go of thoughts, allow your mind to wander freely on the general theme of suffering; *your* suffering in particular. Browse over your current and chronic complaints until you find one that stirs up strong feelings. Allow yourself to dwell on it. For example, perhaps you've just noticed that you're regaining weight you struggled hard to lose. Explore your dismay about it. Seek out the details that make you feel bad: your self-consciousness, your frustration with dieting, etc. Once you're in touch with the painful quality of what you're feeling, breathe

it in. Let it fill your lungs. Continue to probe the wound, breathing in whatever you feel. As you breathe out, let the feeling dissolve. Take a break from it. Then find it again as you breathe in. Make sure you've established this coordination with the breath before moving on to the next step.

3. Now let your mind wander again, seeking out mental images of other people who seem to be suffering with a similar issue. You might flash on an obese person you saw earlier in the day or someone you know who lost a hundred pounds only to gain it all back again. Breathe that in, too. Stay in touch with the pain while allowing your mind to free associate. Perhaps images of fat people gradually give way to other kinds of suffering that have the same style such as people who have bad skin or deformities or disfiguring injuries. Or perhaps it's the dieting that bothers you most. That might bring up images of people who are hungry due to poverty or famine or people who are struggling to overcome addictions. Don't overthink it. Just let the images come, breathing them in as they do. Come back to your own pain periodically, feeling how it connects you to the pain of these others. Imagine, as you breathe, that you are relieving them of some of the pain by taking it into yourself. Allow the feeling to dissolve as you breathe out. Let it go completely, if you can. Then come back to it as you breathe in.

4. Start to notice other feelings that run side by side with the pain. A feeling of benevolence may come over you. You wish your fellow sufferers well. You feel some possibility of peace and well-being despite the pain, and you would like to give it to them. Breathe this feeling out. If you're imagining starving people in Ethiopia, send your out breath all the way there. Breathe in suffering. Breathe out relief. Should you find that the whole thing is becoming a bit vague and abstract, shift your attention closer to home. Reconnect with your personal vulnerability, breathing it in. Then let your consciousness expand again. Breathe out relief. If at any point you are feeling emotionally overwhelmed, give more attention to the out breath, allowing the feelings and images to dissolve with it.

Appendix 2
Night School

Am I putting you to sleep? I hope not, but it's possible. Many people complain that they are overcome with drowsiness while reading hermetic literature. The turgid writing style of some hermeticists might contribute, but it is not, I think, the whole explanation.

When we sleep, our physical senses go dormant while our subtle senses remain active. Lacking competition from the physical, they are able to make more headway. Thus, our nocturnal spiritual development tends to run somewhat ahead of what we have attained by day. The first time the waking mind encounters thoughts that have become familiar to us in our sleep, they sometimes make us drowsy. Unconsciously, we are trying to return to the setting in which we first heard them. Some hermeticists refer to that setting as "night school."

Once you commence alchemical studies by day, a bridge is formed between daytime and nighttime consciousness so that you can begin to access what you've been learning in your sleep. The waking mind may become a little more dreamy, while the sleeping mind becomes more collected and alert. The first symptom of this development is a change in your dream life. You may find that your dreams are making more sense than they used to and that you can remember them better. As a dream character, you experience yourself as having more freedom of choice, and your behavior in dreams better reflects your waking personality. You may also begin to experience yourself as the author of your dreams, discovering that you can modify them at will to better suit your personal taste in stories.

Lucidity sometimes dawns along with this sense of authorship. You begin to become aware that you are dreaming while a dream is still in progress. You hear yourself say, "I'm dreaming" or you wonder, "Is this a dream or isn't it?" and go on to debate the point while remaining in the dream setting. You can also make a conscious choice to wake up. When this happens, the "I" in your sleep is the same as the "I" in your waking thoughts. This "I" is able to observe and alter your mental processes, just as it does when you are awake.

Once you are able to become lucid in your dreams, you may begin to feel that some of them are not merely dreams, but actual events happening in an alternative world. The actions you take in them appear to have consequences that are demonstrated in subsequent dreams. Some of the characters in them appear to be real—that is, to exist in their own right, independently of the fact that you are dreaming them. When that is truly the case (it isn't always), you will eventually be able to communicate with a dream acquaintance in waking life as well.

You can learn from books how to achieve lucid dreaming by your own efforts, and some people practice it as a regular discipline, attempting to remain lucid throughout the night. I would not recommend this. Most of our dreams are just by-products of the physical and psychological repair processes we undergo when we sleep. Conscious attention to these processes is unnecessary and can even interfere with them. You may start to behave as responsibly in dreams as you do in waking life. Apart from being no fun, this is unhealthy. Your psyche needs to indulge in fantasies that are "off the record" of waking consciousness.

Part of the reason we sleep is that the mind needs a break. If you do find you're doing a lot of lucid dreaming, you'll need to rest your mind more during the day to compensate for its exertions at night. Meditation is a good way to do that. Conversely, meditation helps some people to develop nighttime lucidity.

We remember dreams best when we awaken gradually and of our own accord, as we do when we've had enough sleep. If you can't remember dreams—much less become lucid within them—it's probably because you are being jarred awake before you are ready. The best remedy is to get to bed earlier.

I recognize that a full night's sleep and natural awakening are regarded as luxuries by many overworked Americans. If your lifestyle obliges you to use an alarm clock, here's a trick you might try. Just before you go to sleep, state your intention of waking at a particular time. Set your alarm clock to go off ten or fifteen minutes later than that time, as backup. With practice, you should eventually be able to wake at the exact minute of your choosing, in time to turn off the alarm before it rings. I have found this technique to be very reliable, but I am not sure how well it works for the chronically sleep deprived.

All things considered, getting rest is your number one nocturnal priority. If this means deep and apparently dreamless sleep, so be it. Consciousness of dreams is very helpful to the hermeticist, but it is by no means essential. That's why I've relegated this material on dreaming to the back of the book.

Building Jacob's Ladder

Not surprisingly, the dreams that reflect our experiences in night school usually feature some sort of teacher figure: angel, wizard, hermit, guru, professor, and so on. If, in waking life, you have entertained the hope of contacting an inner teacher, such a dream is a good sign that the teacher is meeting you in the vertical while you sleep.

The dream is not the encounter itself. It's a souvenir; the end product of a gradual descent from vertical to horizontal consciousness. To you it seems like the first thing that happened because you can't remember the earlier steps. By learning to remember backward, however, you can retrace those steps and experience the actual encounter firsthand. You can return to the first step long after the last step because it lives in the NOW of vertical time, where chronology is irrelevant.

Picture the kind of fire escape ladder that descends as you put weight on it. Once it has unfolded to ground level, it stays put there, enabling you to climb back up. This is how hermeticists endeavor to return from the vertical. They consciously create downward rungs that can be used for later reascent.

The natural process of descent from a dream looks something like this:

Vertical encounter
↓
Having the dream
↓
Remembering the dream
↓
Interpreting the dream

The first rung that feels firm to our conscious feet is the remembering of the dream. We can improve on our ladder by adding a few more rungs beneath it. Here's how:

1. As soon as you notice that you've had a teaching dream, review it. Don't try to figure out what it means. Just go over it in your mind as if you were watching a rerun. At first, you will probably have to be at least partly awake to do this. Eventually you may find that you're able to do it in your sleep. You might have the impression that the dream is changing somewhat in the process of review. That's not a problem. If you haven't finished sleeping, tell yourself that you will remember the dream again in the morning.

2. Once you are fully awake, go over the dream again as if you were telling yourself a story. Change the dream as needed to create a coherent narrative—a story that another person could follow. Feel free to embellish the good parts and leave out the parts that seem boring or irrelevant. You can also invent connections between episodes that, in the original dream, seemed unrelated. You want the dream to take root in that part of your memory that recalls life events, so that it comes to feel like something that actually happened to you, an episode in your inner biography. In their raw form, dreams are usually too jumbled and

illogical to be remembered in this way. You have to improve their re-semblance to waking life before they can become event-like in memory.

3. Tell yourself the improved version of your dream story the follow-ing night at bedtime. If you do this when you are just on the brink of falling asleep, the narrative will likely fragment, becoming more jum-bled and surreal. Let that happen. Make no effort to stay lucid. You might flash on parts of the earlier review that you left out of the finished story. Or you might feel surrounded by the atmosphere of the original dream, as if it were a fragrance arising from your pillow. You fall back into it as you fall asleep.

Our improved coming-down ladder now looks something like this:

Vertical event

↓

Having the dream

↓

Remembering the dream

↓

Reviewing the dream

↓

Revising the dream

↓

Retelling the dream

With each step down, the vertical experience that inspired the dream becomes more like a horizontal experience. Your body is assimi-lating what has happened to your spirit. I liken it to the way cows digest grass. First they chew it awhile. Then they swallow it and let their stom-ach juices work on it. Then they heave it back up into the mouth for more chewing. The name for this—rumination—also applies to the chewing over of thoughts and memories. The very aspects of thinking that tend to drag you down when you want to go up—the slow, sequen-tial, senses-based plod of it—serve you beautifully when it's time to di-gest your way back down.

Assimilation is not mere passive absorption, for in the course of digesting, you contribute new information to the dream. Its pictorial and narrative qualities are drawn from the body's rich store of memories. Some are personal and some are ancestral, arising from the collective unconscious. We make up our night dreams just as we make up our daydreams. Dream angels appear to us in costumes of our own design.

Normally we are not aware of our creative contribution at the actual moment of dreaming. To dream feels more like watching a movie produced by someone else. But if you get in the habit of editing the memory of your dreams, you will connect with the part of your mind that created the dream in the first place. Eventually you may find that you are becoming lucid in the midst of dreams and that you can alter them at will. But don't worry if that never happens. The process I'm describing works just as well on non-lucid dreams.

You'll notice that I've omitted the bottom step of the earlier ladder—interpreting the dream. That's because a dream is, in itself, an interpretation. There's not much to be gained from interpreting an interpretation. A dream's meaning, in its purest form, is to be found at the top of the ladder, not the bottom. You will use the steps you've created to get back up to it.

Climbing the Ladder

To illustrate how this works, I'm going to use a teaching dream I had about ten years ago. I tell it like this:

I was sitting on a bench in a public park, worrying about a small child who seemed to be in some sort of distress. I wanted to help the child, but I couldn't figure out what the trouble was or what I ought to be doing about it. Then I noticed that someone was sitting next to me on the bench. I had the impression my companion was an angel, for it was larger than a human and sort of luminous, and I couldn't tell what gender it was. The angel offered a comment on my predicament. The comment was the wisest, most mind-altering idea I had ever heard. It was as if I'd been stumbling around in the dark all my life and someone had just switched on a the light. I felt rapturous.

At that point, it occurred to me that I was having a dream. I was afraid that by morning I would have forgotten the wondrous words, so I woke myself up long enough to jot them down. Then I fell back asleep. When I awoke again in the morning, I remembered immediately that I'd been told something stirring during the night. Eagerly I retrieved the note I'd scrawled in the dark. It read, "You see and then you do."

Well, duh. I needed an angel to tell me this? It is hard to imagine a more pedestrian statement. Yet I could still recall the feeling of blissful illumination the words had evoked when I heard them in my dream. Obviously, a great deal had been lost in the translation from Angelese to English. Whatever it was that happened above seems not to have survived the return journey.

You might have noticed that I began by saying, "I tell it like this." I didn't say, "It happened like this"—because it didn't. The story I told you was my revised version of the dream. What actually happened, I cannot say for sure, but I know it didn't involve sitting on a park bench with an angel because there are no park benches in the vertical, and angels don't sit. The dream was just a residue of the actual encounter. It was my body's attempt to process the unfamiliar (a previously unmet spiritual being) in terms of the familiar (my Catholic school idea of an angel).

I also know for sure that "you see and then you do" was not what the angel actually said and not how I dreamed it either. I know this because I was able to go back up the ladder I unfolded on the way down. The revised angel story is the lowest rung. Had I not created it, I probably wouldn't remember anything about the dream all these years later. But if I start there, I begin to recall earlier versions. I get flashes of the review and of the original dream before it.

"You see and then you do" is a pretty minimalist utterance, but the original was terser still. I heard, "See . . . do." In the ellipsis was a relationship between "see" and "do" that, upon awakening, I hastily rendered as "and then you." That relationship was what I found so earth-shattering.

The general idea was that action flows directly from perception. For me, at least, that's not how it usually works. Between perceiving a situation and doing something about it, I go through an intermediate stage

of thinking about what to do. I propose various courses of action to myself and try to predict their consequences. The angel was suggesting that
such exertions could be dispensed with, that one could act immediately
and spontaneously upon a perception of need, confident that the spontaneous action was the right action.

The dream has now gone through yet another stage of translation into
the horizontal: I am explaining it to you. Along the way, much has been
lost. While you no doubt get the general drift, you are probably wondering why anyone would feel rapturous about it. What struck me in the
dream as both incontrovertible and transcendently wise now appears on
the page as a mildly interesting and highly debatable proposition.

Interpreting dreams in the horizontal often results in this flat, explana-
tory quality. To discover what all the fuss was about, we need to return
to the vertical source. So far, the various memory rungs I established in
coming down have carried me halfway up. I can recall some of the original dream. Now I'm going to show you how to climb up the rest of the
way, how to get *above* the dream and reconnect with the actual being
who inspired it.

Start by taking a closer look at the differences between the various
layers of your dream memory, i.e., the polished version and whatever you
can recall of the review and of the dream itself. In creating your revised
narrative, you added, subtracted, and rearranged. All of those choices
were interpretive. What were you thinking when you made them?

I made an interpretive choice when I put the child and my dilemma
over it before the appearance of the angel in my dream story. In the earliest version of the dream I can recall, the situation with the child
seemed to be happening simultaneously. So why did I put it first? For me,
the angel's words were the most important part of the story, so I arranged
the order of events to make them the climax. The situation with the
child became merely the explanation for why the angel showed up.

When later I gave it more attention, the child dilemma struck me as
odd. It wouldn't happen in real life. While I ponder many of my actions
in advance, I wouldn't stop to deliberate if I saw an unattended child in
distress. My instinct would be to come immediately to his or her aid. To
just sit there thinking while a child is crying seems downright perverse.
Maybe that was the angel's point. Maybe the child was an *illustration* of

the lesson rather than the reason for it. How a woman instinctively responds to a crying child is an example of "see . . . do."

These reflections have carried me farther up the ladder. I am now thinking like the author of the dream, trying to decide which sequence of events best expresses its meaning. This is what my mind was doing when it created the dream in the first place. If you are trying to decide which version of a dream best conveys its meaning, you are, at some level, already in touch with that meaning. You are on the verge of conscious access to the source: the vertical event that inspired the dream.

Transferring to Day School

In the midst of the reflections I've just described, I "heard" two words that weren't in the original dream, yet sounded like they were coming from my dream angel. This time, though, there was no angel imagery. I had no sense of the size, radiance, or physical position of my companion. Nor did I hear a voice. The words coming into my head didn't "sound" any different from other words in my head. Yet they were coming from someone who wasn't me, someone who had, unmistakably, the same style as the dream angel. The being who had communicated with me in the night, inspiring the dream, was now expanding on that earlier communication. Only this time I was awake, conscious of its presence, experiencing the vertical encounter directly.

The message was "seed . . . deed." Sort of a past tense version of the original. *Deed* was the accomplished form of *do*, and *seed* (see-ed) was the accomplished form of *see*. The apparent grammatical goof was a play on words, for it also invoked the usual meaning of *seed*. The relationship of *both* "seed" and "see-ed" to "deed" was the same as the relationship of *see* to *do*.

Do you follow? Don't try to reason it out. Instead, try meditating on the style of "seed." Then meditate on the style of "deed." Place the two concepts side by side and contemplate their between.

I don't want to carry this too far down by explaining it. The meaning dwells in the vertical place you get to by meditating on seed. You need to be "up" to see it. As soon as you try to *grasp* it, you get heavy and fall back to the horizontal where it flattens once more into a debatable proposition.

Maybe you're beginning to understand what my excitement was about. But don't worry if you still don't get it. The object of this exercise is to learn how to work with *your own* dream messages. It's done by shuttling up and down the ladder you have built between waking and sleeping consciousness. This ladder, constructed by horizontal mind, enables you to return at will to the scene of an earlier vertical experience. You can move up and down the rungs, shifting easily from vertical to horizontal modes of thinking.

Mastering the knack of this up-and-down shuttle is how you make the transition from night school to "day school"—that is, you begin to hear from lighter beings while you're awake. You are learning to move vertically *with* your body's cognitive equipment instead of *despite* it. When this occurs, lighter beings are able to make more sense of your waking thoughts. You, in turn, are better able to follow what they are saying. The whole relationship becomes more collegial, more like a two-way conversation.

On the whole, day school is less vivid and dramatic than night school. It is not the sort of experience you're used to calling "spiritual." Instead, you find that you are able to sustain thinking at a high level of abstraction for longer periods without becoming bored or confused. For brief moments, you experience a "darkening of the senses" so that while your eyes remain open in full daylight, your attention narrows and turns inward. In time, you become so adept at shuttling between vertical and horizontal that the switch is all but imperceptible. Flashes of vertical insight mingle comfortably with your horizontal thoughts.

Teaching dreams may still occur, but they, too, tend to become more abstract. Instead of the photo-realistic dream images your brain used to produce, you may find that you're seeing diagrams. Instead of a movie-like story line, you may find that an exchange of ideas is occurring apart from any narrative context. Instead of complete human sentences, you may hear brief and cryptic wordplay or words in some foreign language that, while dreaming, you are able to understand. Your brain is no longer translating immediately into the familiar because the language of vertical beings has itself become somewhat familiar. You've stopped designing costumes for your angels because you no longer need to "see" them to recognize that they are present. You may feel that some of the earlier vertical thrill is gone, but that's just because you've gotten used to it. Moving up and down no longer makes you dizzy.

I said earlier that for many, alchemical studies begin in night school. There are exceptions. Some people can't recall their dreams. Others have lots of dreams, but none that appear to be *teaching* dreams. Don't worry about it. Vivid teaching dreams are, for most people, a passing stage. You might already have advanced beyond it. You can attain vertical consciousness by day without ever, to your recollection, having experienced it in your sleep.

Further Reading

General Hermeticism

Anonymous. *Meditations on the Tarot*. Shaftesbury, U.K.: Element, 1993.
If I were permitted to possess only one hermetic text, this is the one I'd choose. To read it is to commence a friendship with its anonymous author. Some Internet detective work will turn up his real name, but you probably haven't heard of him. He is, nevertheless, extremely well-connected in the hermetic network and will acquaint you with all of the important concepts and personalities.

Freke, Timothy, and Peter Gandy, trans. *The Hermetica*. New York: Jeremy P. Tarcher, 1997.
A translation of excerpts from the works of Hermes Trismegistus that reads beautifully in English.

Knight, Gareth. *Magic and the Western Mind*. London: Kahn & Averill, 1991.
A comprehensive and very readable history of hermeticism, this book also serves as a who's who for newcomers to the hermetic network.

Melville, Francis. *The Book of Alchemy*. New York: Quarto, 2002.
This elegant little book offers concise definitions of alchemical terms and concepts along with dozens of scrumptious illustrations.

The pictures are a great departure point for symbol meditation. Melville's spare text drops deft hints to get you started, then leaves you to find your own way.

Subtle Perception

Brennan, Barbara Ann. *Hands of Light*. New York: Bantam Books, 1988.
Barbara Brennan is a healer who works on the subtle rather than the physical body. If you would like to know what the subtle body looks like to someone who has a visual impression of it, check out the many full-color illustrations in this book.

Cornell, Ann Weiser. *The Power of Focusing*. Oakland, Calif.: New Harbinger Publications, 1996.
In his research into psychotherapy, the linguistics expert Eugene Gendlin discovered that the single greatest predictor of a successful outcome was the patient's ability to perceive internal subtle phenomena. He went on to develop a technique called "focusing" that reliably awakens subtle perception and brings about positive changes through the power of attention alone. If you don't feel like doing mindfulness meditation, focusing makes an excellent substitute. Ann Cornell's beautifully concise little book is the best introduction.

Myss, Caroline. *Anatomy of the Spirit*. New York: Three Rivers Press, 1996.
Caroline Myss first came to fame as an intuitive diagnostician whose ability to spot physical problems in their early stages rivaled the CAT scan and MRI. In this book, she teaches readers how to perceive what's going on with their own subtle bodies by understanding the meanings, life issues, and physical ailments typically associated with each of the seven chakras. Her approach works even for people who are certain they can't see auras.

Levity and Gravity

Stewart, R. J. *The Underworld Initiation*. San Francisco: Mercury Publishing, 1990.
Though I cautioned against descending to the lower realms on purpose, some people need no further incentive to embark on a journey than the warning that it can be hazardous. If you are such a person,

R. J. Stewart is your man. Having conducted guided tours for several decades, he is the leading expert on how to get there and back with your sanity intact.

The Great Work

Of the books listed below, only one (*The Tower of Alchemy*, obviously) makes explicit reference to alchemy. Yet each of them describes a version of the Great Work. They are all aiming for the same result as the version I've written in this book, but their methods are very different.

Goddard, David. *The Tower of Alchemy*. Boston: Weiser Books, 1999.
Goddard's methodology is based on Tibetan Buddhist tantra, while the myths and symbols he employs are drawn from the Western hermetic tradition. If you like to meditate and have a vivid imagination, his visualizations and guided fantasies may work well for you.

Helminski, Kabir. *The Knowing Heart*. Boston: Shambhala Publications, 1999.
For procedural advice lacking in 'Arabi's *Journey to the Lord of Power*, turn to Helminski, a contemporary American whose heart-centered approach is both moving and practical. In the Sufi tradition, anything labeled a "retreat manual" is likely to be a guide to the Great Work.

Ibn 'Arabi. *Journey to the Lord of Power*. Rochester, Vt.: Inner Traditions International, 1981.
Written in 1204, this slim retreat manual outlines an early Sufi version of the Great Work that is breathtaking in scope, if short on procedural advice.

Ignatius of Loyola. *Personal Writings*. London: Penguin Classics, 1996.
Loyola's Spiritual Exercises take a breakneck approach, leading the practitioner (who is presumed to be Catholic) through four round-the-clock weeks of alchemical boot camp. Keeping in mind that Christ is the prototypical alchemist may help you get past the atmosphere of medieval piety surrounding these exercises. Even if you don't care to undertake them, they're worth studying for their procedural genius.

Tomberg, Valentin. *Anthroposophical Studies of the New Testament.*
Spring Valley, N.Y.: Cadeur Manuscripts, 1985.
Many Christian approaches are premised on the idea that Christ was
the prototypical alchemist, and his life on earth a "how-to" guide for
the Great Work. Seven-step versions often take as their departure
point the Gospel of John, which features seven major miracles and
seven "I am" statements. (The "I" in these statements is understood
to refer to the individual human spirit, not just the person of Jesus.)
Tomberg's version is based on the seven stages of Christ's passion.

Calcination

Chödrön, Pema. *When Things Fall Apart.* Boston: Shambhala, 1997.
Chödrön accomplishes something truly magical: she somehow man-
ages to abet the fire of calcination while simultaneously treating the
sufferer's burns. Wise, funny, and deeply consoling.

Wilde, Oscar. *De Profundis.* New York: Dover, 1996.
This long letter, written during Wilde's imprisonment, describes a
harrowing episode of calcination and his discovery of the true vine.

Dissolution

Lewis, C. S. *Surprised by Joy.* San Diego: Harcourt, Inc., 1955.
As a little boy, Lewis had never heard of volatile eros, so when this
mysterious feeling came over him, he named it "joy." In middle age,
he made it the theme of this spiritual memoir. A few years after this
book was published, Lewis, who was well into his fifties, fell in love
and married for the first time. Guess what his wife was named.

Spangler, David. *Everyday Miracles.* New York: Bantam, 1996.

———. *Manifestation.* Issaquah, Wash.: The Lorian Association,
2004.
"Manifesting" is Spangler's term for getting what you desire by magic.
Based on alchemical principles, his exercises invite you to delve into
the nature of your desire, the nature of its object, and the quality of
the between. The trouble is, the techniques are so powerful that
you're likely to get what you wanted long before you've worked to

the end of the meditations! The second book I've listed comes pack-aged with a cool card deck to assist you with the exercises. You can order it from www.lorian.org. (While you're there, check out the on-line courses. They're very good.)

Fermentation

St. John of the Cross. *The Dark Night of the Soul.* Translated by Peers, E. Allison. New York: Doubleday, 1959.
> In his book-length commentary on his own poem of the same name, John offers an indispensable guide to the pains and rewards of fermentation.

Sublimation

Fortune, Dion. *Psychic Self-Defense.* Boston: Weiser Books, 1930.
> Dion Fortune is the Julia Child of ceremonial magic: erudite yet accessible, unpretentious, and at times hilarious. This volume is a practical guide to the multifarious hassles that can arise in the astral. Should you accidentally conjure a werewolf, Fortune will tell you how to dispose of it.